THE MEN AROUND CHURCHILL

BOOKS BY RENÉ KRAUS

THE MEN AROUND CHURCHILL

WINSTON CHURCHILL

THE PRIVATE AND PUBLIC LIFE OF SOCRATES

THEODORA, THE CIRCUS EMPRESS

The Men Around Churchill

by *René* **Kraus**
Author of *"Winston Churchill"*

14 Illustrations

J. B. LIPPINCOTT COMPANY
Philadelphia   New York

Again to Audrey, the inspiration,
whose help was invaluable

PREFACE

THIS IS A WAR BETWEEN MACHINE POWER AND STRENGTH of character—so far an inconclusive war. The British will not win this war on the strength of their character alone. But they have definitely and gloriously proved that no machine power can break their morale.

British morale is the miracle of this war. Even Hitler admits it. His mouthpiece, "Voelkischer Beobachter," speaks about the "strain of Nordic blood in the Englishmen which enables them to hold out." For Hitlerites this might be a sufficient explanation. Human beings will seek for deeper reasons.

The search for deeper reasons caused me to write this book. It is not a book on the war. Its theme is rather the origin of the war, and its prospective outcome. Both are conditioned by the British character. A wave of suicidal weakness brought disaster on them. A moral rebirth, without parallel in modern history, copes with the disaster and inspires confidence of survival and victory.

In the midst of the gravest peril the English changed their leader. Winston Churchill had to follow Neville Chamberlain as inevitably as the sun breaks through the clouds. But more remarkable than this spectacular change at the helm seems the fact that the team that pulls Great Britain through the war has remained, on the whole, unchanged. The fighters

7

of today are the petty politicians of yesterday. Eccentrics have become constructive. Revolutionaries are now pillars of state and society. Tories forget to wear the old school tie.

The English hate war. There is no English translation for "Stahlbad"—steel bath, to put it approximately—as the Teutons like to call the frolic of bloodshed. Yet the war brought about a great transformation in the British. I venture to show this transformation in a few test-cases. Three dates stand out on the road from appeasement to belligerency. The first was September, 1939, when war was declared; the second, and more important, May, 1940, when Churchill replaced Chamberlain; the third, September, 1940, when the aerial all-out assault on England was at its height. In most cases the men around Churchill, as this book will show, demonstrated their transformation no later than May, 1940. The men I describe are not necessarily great men, but they seem to be great examples.

Standing up against darkness and tyranny, the British might well set the example for all freedom-loving peoples. Only in the sense of personal and national sacrifice is this an "English war." It is not the first time that they are the first to hearken to the call. Remember Milton's dictum: "When God has some difficult task on hand, he sends for his Englishmen."

R. K.

CONTENTS

PART I—OLD SCHOOL TIE

PART II—LABOUR

PART III—SOLDIERS

PART IV—ECCENTRICS

PART V—SYMBOL

INDEX

PART ONE

Old School Tie

Enigma

LORD HALIFAX

BEWARE OF VISCOUNT HALIFAX! HE IS THE "HOLY FOX" TO those who combine the inside dope with a taste for puns. He is both religious—and Master of the Foxhounds. True, President Roosevelt accorded him a royal welcome at Annapolis when he landed on these shores. But in the wake of the Presidential welcome the wave of gossip rolled along. Isn't Lord Halifax an appeaser? And a war-monger into the bargain? He is a British Imperialist, an unrepentant old-school-tie Tory, representing an outworn feudal system. Or he was so, to many Americans, when he disembarked to assume what Winston Churchill termed "the most important post at this time which any British subject can occupy outside the United Kingdom." Since then a few months have gone by, and the Viscount—a quiet, unassuming man, full of the noblest home-grown inhibitions—is well on the way to becoming the most popular ambassador His Britannic Majesty has ever sent to this country.

Certainly he is the most courageous. He by no means limited his personal contacts to the upper set. Very much to the contrary he criss-crossed this country, singling out some of the allegedly hottest centers of Midwestern Isolationism,

13

to explain the British cause in a series of speeches which sometimes may have sounded unimaginative, but were always utterly convincing in their honesty. Everywhere the applause that bade him farewell sounded some degrees warmer than the welcome he had received.

One of his paramount achievements in the service of truth is to have cut through the muddle and confusion of wartime information from the battle-front. After a few months in his Washington office he established an entirely new and well co-ordinated news service that, now, gives Americans access to uncensored and undiluted facts. He trusts in America's sound judgment.

Moreover, he trusts in God. This faith in God, he reiterates, does not interfere with his matter-of-fact realism. To him, as to Americans, this faith is both soil and ceiling, out of and into which a practical approach to the problems grows. Those who have watched Halifax's development in later years are not astonished to observe how he has eased up in the American atmosphere. More freely than any of his predecessors he mingles with the people who speak the same language, if another slang. He is omnipresent at church services and club dinners, at benefits, parades, celebrations, in colleges and at the conference table. Differing slightly in manners and accent, the Yorkshireman fits perfectly into the social picture of Milwaukee and Kansas City.

Milwaukee and Kansas City, for their part, and Lord Halifax, for his, have recognized that, after all, neither is quite as bad as outworn prejudices may have made them seem.

This country is in good company, if it takes to him surprisingly quickly. His most embittered opponents have always fallen for Halifax. During his term as Viceroy of India, General Haushofer in his magnum opus *World Politics Today* wrote of him: "He is the one white man carrying the

LORD HALIFAX

burden of the heaviest responsibilities in our days." The joke is that the author of this sentence is Hitler's brain truster number one, the founder of the theory of German world domination, and a vitriolic foe of the British Empire. Another gentleman of the same persuasion, the Nazi-fed Indian revolutionary, Taraknath Das, in his book *India in World Politics*—which, of course, was first published in Germany—paid Viscount Halifax this compliment: "He always met the Indian leaders in an entirely different way than did the Viceroys before him. He always treated them with respect for their convictions." Midget-sized great Gandhi went to jail, where the Viceroy, much to his regret, was obliged to send him, with a declaration of brotherly sympathy for his vice-regal jailer. One of Halifax's latest personal conquests was, of all people, our own Joe Kennedy, who said: "Halifax is the noblest figure in public life I have encountered, almost a saint. Everybody becomes enamoured of him." Whereupon Mr. Kennedy returned home, where his speeches have served further to confuse English-American relations.

No doubt, Viscount Halifax is a mysterious figure. Mystery permeates his family. His father was a widely known collector of demoniacal masks which startled his visitors. Besides, he kept a large number of human skulls, acquired from London doctors, in his home. Finally, he wrote ghost-stories, which, incidentally, were published in Hearst's *American Weekly*, colorfully illustrated, after the old gentleman's death. Lady Halifax, the ambassador's wife, it is reported, had her forthcoming marriage to the then Mr. Edward Wood, predicted by a palmist. And the ambassador himself, famous as a religious mystic, reads the Bible every morning and mystery thrillers every night. Small wonder that there appears to be something enigmatic about him.

Perfect purity, alas, is an enigma in our times.

In spite of his high-sounding name and titles, Edward
Frederick Lindley Wood, third Viscount Halifax of Monk
Bretton, first Baron Irwin of Kirby Underdale, Knight of
the Garter, Privy Councillor, Knight Grand Commander of
the Star of India and Knight Grand Commander of the Indian Empire, is the average Englishman. Indeed, he is the
quintessence of the Englishman. To him applies the passage
that George Savile, first Marquess of Halifax, wrote with a
quill on old parchment: "Our Trimmer is far from idolatry
in other things, in one thing alone he cometh near it, his
country is in some degree his idol; he doth not worship the
sun, because 'tis not peculiar to us, it rambles about the
world, and it is less kind to us than to others; but for the
earth of England, though perhaps inferior to many places
abroad, to him there is divinity in it, and he would rather
die than see a spire of English grass trampled down by a foreign trespasser; he thinketh there are a great many things of
his mind, for all plants are apt to taste of the soil in which
they grow, and we that have grown here have a root that pro-
duceth in us a stalk of English juice, which is not to be
changed by grafting or foreign infusion."

There is, of course, no "foreign infusion" among the
Woods of Yorkshire. They have settled all over the county,
all of them distantly related to each other and to the Halifax
branch, which attained a baronetcy in 1784. Sir Charles
Wood, the grandfather of the present ambassador, was a
famous statesman in the second half of the last century.
From 1859 to 1866, he served as Secretary of State for India,
thus establishing the family's "Indian tradition" which his
grandson so successfully carried on. It is said that Sir Charles
inherited the Indian Empire for the Crown upon the disso-
lution of the East India Company. In 1866, Queen Victoria created him a Viscount. His son, the second Viscount

Halifax, although an important figure in domestic affairs, devoted his long life to Church matters, primarily to an effort to reunite the Church of England with the Roman Catholic Church. He interested Pope Leo XIII, the Archbishop of Canterbury, several Roman Cardinals and High Church Bishops in his project, which he zealously regarded as his sacred mission, without, however, realizing his dream. Nevertheless, it is important to note this devotion, since it is the most precious heritage the elder Halifax has passed on to his son, the present Viscount. The entire life of the man who now represents Great Britain in Washington unfolds against the background of his deep religious convictions. As a scholar and a reformer, a statesman, diplomat, member of more cabinets than any other man in England— with the single exception of Winston Churchill—as a politician, officer, Viceroy, he was, and he remains, first and foremost a devout Christian. Religious devotion is his strength and, some critics add, his weakness. Did his unwavering Christian love not lead Halifax down the way of appeasement? Does Christianity soften the believer? Perhaps. But there are numerous examples, from the Christians in the catacombs to Halifax's determined struggle for victory in the present war, to prove that religious conviction also makes tough fighters.

Like many devout institutionalists, Halifax's father was a strict disciplinarian at home. Like many strict disciplinarians he was a severely tested man. His three elder sons were afflicted with tuberculosis and died in their early childhood. The father bowed to the Almighty's will. He buried his sons in the churchyard of Hickleton Hall, near Doncaster, one of the two family seats acquired by the first Viscount in the year 1882. The other one, which the present

Viscount regards as his home, is the estate of Garrowby in the East Riding of Yorkshire, a red brick structure around a cobbled courtyard, standing in a green, hilly park in the woods. Amazingly, the old man is said to have decorated the three graves with three skulls from his collection. He devoted his fatherly passion to his last remaining boy, Edward.

Edward was born on April 16, 1881, at his mother's country home. He was an oversized baby, "quite enormous," his proud father boasted, but with a withered left arm. Another withered left arm once made history. It gave Wilhelm II the inferiority complex that drove the Emperor into bullying and bossing a world whose contempt he feared. The Woods of Yorkshire, in contrast to the semi-Prussian—really Swabian—Hohenzollerns, are unafraid. Edward, the quite enormous baby, remained true to type. Today the ambassador stands six feet five, and has never noticed his slight handicap. Already, in his early youth, he excelled as a sportsman. He became a formidable tennis champion, he is famous as a huntsman, and he was "born on a horse." Indeed, he learned horseback riding before he could walk. His father, meticulously careful in this, as in all things, decided every morning whether gigantic little Edward, should practise walking or riding. It was, morning by morning, an important decision. As a much-beloved only remaining son, the child grew up into boyhood.

Next to religion, politics was his heritage. Politics is a duty as well as a privilege to the ruling classes of England. Inescapably, the country squire must devote much of his life to public welfare, either in his own neighborhood or in the Empire. This benevolent feudalism is under strict democratic control. Even organized Socialists speak approvingly of "those who rule us." Perhaps the war is bringing about a total change in these conditions. But it will take more than an upheaval to separate the Yorkshire people from the Wood family. The local farmers and workers hold Viscount Halifax in high esteem. He responds by feeling closely bound to them. He certainly would prefer the quiet life in his home, Garrowby Hall, to the heavy duties in the newish brick building on Massachusetts Avenue, Washington, D. C., which houses the British Embassy. But the fulfillment of his duty is beyond personal wishes. He once disclosed his private predilection in a sentence that quickly found wide currency: "I would rather be Master of the Foxhounds than Prime Minister." To be Master of the Foxhounds means glorified rural life. Lord Halifax does not overemphasize the glorification. The woods, the forests, the fields and moors of Yorkshire, belong to all Yorkshire people. And the squire belongs to them, too. Lord Halifax likes to chat with his neighbors. He takes his private polls of public opinion. In the days of the Abyssinian conflict, a railway porter who carried his bag, felt highly honored when the Viscount, instead of asking him when the train left, inquired what he thought about the sanctions against Italy. Lord Halifax speaks the language of the people. Although a distinguished student at Oxford, he never affected the Oxford accent.

At Christ Church College, Oxford, after the prescribed number of years at Eton, Halifax took his degree with highest honors in modern history. His remarkable work as an undergraduate brought him a fellowship at All Souls College, where he took his M.A. "All Souls" is that unique college in which there are no students, only fellows—prominent men of state, of affairs, religion and education, who ponder what they like to call "the broader lines" of life and events over a glass of wine, looking thoughtfully into the blue smoke of exquisite cigars. Modestly, never outspoken, they pride themselves on their intellectual dominance of the realm. It was here that the intimate friendship that exists between Lord Halifax and Dr. Lang, the Archbishop of Canterbury, began. Here begin many friendships between the more enlightened youths of the British peerage. The gentlemen are not necessarily Tories. There is a distinct group of Oxford Socialists, representing the freedom of thought and teaching in Britain. Although strict and, if you like, old-fashioned in religious matters, Halifax always showed his enlightenment in Imperial affairs. He never belonged to the uncompromising Imperialists of Winston Churchill's school. He has not, like the latter, molded his mind in the barracks of Aldershot and the garrisons of India—although Churchill, it is well known, did a considerable amount of independent thinking in his "long Indian nights." Churchill has frequently expressed his regret that, galloping through a turbulent youth, he was deprived of the intellectual stimulus of an Oxford education. Halifax, on the other hand, is deeply affected by this stimulus. He was once heard regretting that Hitler and Mussolini had not studied at his own university. "They might still have turned out Socialists, but not outlaws," he said. And he sighed, "The world would have been easier to manage." Among all the honors in the course of his rich and fruitful career, Halifax prizes highest the Chancellorship of the University of Oxford that was bestowed on him in 1933, for both his scholarly and statesmanlike achievements.

In September, 1909, the then Mr. Edward Wood married Lady Dorothy Onslow, daughter of the Earl of Onslow. Half a year earlier, so the story goes, this marriage was predicted when Lady Dorothy was consulting a fortune teller, who read the name of her prospective husband in the palm of her hand. The seer also predicted a model marriage, and his prophecy came true. Lady Halifax belongs among those great English ladies, like Lady Baldwin, Mrs. Annie Chamberlain, the widow of Neville Chamberlain, and Mrs. Churchill who are their husbands' active collaborators. She made a tremendous success as a diplomatic hostess and Vicereine. She is said to read her husband's speeches before their delivery, and to express a very independent and sound judgment on them.

It might be inserted here that Lord Halifax's speeches do not kindle the flames of eloquence. Perhaps this explains why the people of England, while always respecting him, took a long time to warm up to him. His unimaginative style is partly due to paternal influences. Although the second Viscount Halifax was extremely formal in his manner, and has bestowed a rich heritage of Victorian politeness on his son, he distrusted words. "If a thing is right, it is simply done!" was his creed. Verbosity seemed undistinguished to him. This paternal influence has tended to increase Lord Halifax's natural shyness. He is too shy to admit this shyness. Although not the popular type of after-dinner speaker, he is not above beginning his speeches with an anecdote and interspersing them with jokes. His humor is typically English. It expresses wisdom in terms of everyday trifles. Among Halifax's favorite appeals to unity is the story of the inquisitive old lady, about to board a steamer, asking a sailor if he could tell her which end of the boat would start first. "If all goes well, Madame," the sailor replied, "both ends start together." And the Viscount rarely forgets to add: "The example of this boat is one we may all follow with advantage." This philosophical remark invariably invites a salvo of applause.

Yet one is aware that he is not always perfectly at ease when standing in the limelight—that is, until his conscience or simply his stubbornness is aroused. Hecklers don't have it all their own way with him, particularly when he feels that there is bad will in their questioning. Then his elaborate sentences suddenly become terse; he no longer minces words, and even his face shows the strain of the self-imposed discipline that alone prevents an explosion. For the rest his speaking is unexciting. His temperate habits govern his tongue. But his voice resounds with a genuine ring that is more convincing than dramatic accents would be. His speech is not loaded with burning passion, but there is in it a determination indicative of unbreakable strength and uncompromising courage. It is the strength and the courage an otherwise conciliatory personality derives from his deep attachment to the Christian way of life.

In 1910, at the age of twenty-nine, and a few months after his marriage, he was elected Member of Parliament for Ripon in the West Riding of Yorkshire. He kept his seat for fifteen years until he was shifted to the House of Lords. (Twenty-seven years after his first election to the Commons, his son, the Honorable Charles Wood, then twenty-five, was elected to the constituency of York.) He was a modest back-bencher in these years of political grooming, conspicuous only on account of his uncommon height, which he obviously sought to conceal by a slight stoop. This droop of the shoulders, even in front of the camera, is still characteristic of Lord Halifax. It looks almost as if he wanted to descend to the average height of his fellow men.

At the outbreak of the first World War he formed a troop of Yeomanry of the country people. His Yorkshire Dragoons were among the advance guard of the B.E.F. in France. Their commander was promoted to the rank of Major. He left the front-line only once, in 1916, to fulfill an important parliamentary duty. He sided with the Conservative malcontents who expressed their dissatisfaction with Mr. Asquith's fatigued conduct of the war. It was the first time but not the last that an emergency turned the quiet friend of compromise into a determined fighter. Edward Wood pleaded for a smaller, but stronger, war cabinet, and advocated immediate conscription. Some members of the government were reluctant to introduce this measure, and Sir John—now Viscount—Simon resigned on account of it. Already, as a young back-bencher, Halifax, then Mr. Wood, stood high above party strife. Although a true-blue Tory, he announced his readiness to support any party government, even one that included Labour, if it was prepared to carry on the war with more vigor. Considering the distrust with which Labour was still regarded in high circles, this was a courageous statement.

A year later, in 1917, Major Wood took part in the work of the National Service Department, whose first director was a provincial politician, of local rather than national reputation, the Mayor of Birmingham, Mr. Neville Chamberlain. "Appeasement" had not yet been invented. Halifax was one of the two hundred signers of the famous Conservative resolution demanding harsher terms for Germany, when the first World War was over. He urged Lloyd George, at the Peace Conference, to "eschew" clemency toward the vanquished.

Lloyd George was not particularly impressed by this appeal. Yet it brought the young back-bencher to his attention. Here was a newcomer, remarkable for his assiduous behavior and for the sincerity of his attitude. Lloyd George, always a fisher of souls, gave him, in 1921, the minor job of Under Secretary for Colonies. In the same job Winston Churchill, many years earlier, had embarked upon his governmental career. Coincidentally, he was at the head of his

old department when Edward Wood moved in as number
two man. But Churchill soon switched over to the War Ministry so that no intimate collaboration had time to develop.

The newcomer made a remarkably good job of his first
assignment in government. He quickly familiarized himself
with the extremely complicated material, and won unanimous applause when he formally moved the Vote of Supply
of his department, in July. With Mr. Ormsby-Gore, afterwards Lord Harlech, he spent two months in the West Indies
and British Guiana. This was both his first visit to the Western Hemisphere and the first time that members of a British government had visited these colonies. He wrote a report of his survey, which rapidly became a best-seller in the
West Indies. The constitutional changes in the statute of
these colonial dependencies which followed in 1922, were
based on this report. Even the Labour spokesman called
them "winged words of wisdom."

The only man in England to express his displeasure with
the promising young statesman was his discoverer, Mr. Lloyd
George. The Tory revolution that upset the coalition government and led to the establishment of the short-lived
Bonar Law cabinet, in October, 1922, promoted some of the
Conservative Under Secretaries of the defunct coalition to
full-fledged cabinet members. Edward Wood was among
them. He was advanced to the Presidency of the Board of
Education. All England welcomed the choice of this scholarly man for the position. But Lloyd George could never
forgive those who decided to join the new masters, even
though this course was prescribed to them by party affiliation.

Many years later even, the old Celtic wizard had not
learned to conceal his grudge. Walking through an orchard,
he remarked bitterly to a friend, pointing out a particular
tree: "Observe its rich foliage. See how magnificently it casts

its shadow. But it bears no fruit. I call this tree—Halifax."

Lloyd George, who won the first war, was a bad loser
where his personal vanity was involved. Stanley Baldwin,
now Earl Baldwin of Bewdley, who helped England to lose
the peace, has, on the other hand, a winning personality.
He soon established close contact with Edward Wood, whose
virtues, and still more, whose high birth irresistibly appealed to the businessman from Sheffield. Forming his own
government, Mr. Baldwin re-appointed him to the office he
had held under Bonar Law.

Although the Board of Education was not concerned with
foreign affairs, Halifax soon had an opportunity to make
his debut in international politics. In 1923, Mr. Baldwin
chose him to represent Great Britain at the League of Nations meeting which was to settle the complicated problem
of the Saar. It was a difficult job. The first wave of the strong
pro-German feeling that blinded England throughout the
following years was just then mounting. Versailles had only
deprived the Reich of French and Polish settled districts.
The small Saarland, however, whose fate Geneva was to decide, was overwhelmingly German. Halifax felt convinced
that it belonged "home to the Reich." On the other hand,
French feelings were to be considered. The French began to
distrust the reliability of their English partner. Furthermore, German strong-arm gangs, predecessors of the Nazis,
terrorized the Saar electorate, which did not help the German cause in the atmosphere of Geneva. Halifax threw his
weight on the side of moderation. He made an excellent
impression on his diplomatic audience. But when he returned to London, everybody knew that the Saar would return to the Reich.

Baldwin was elated with his choice. In his second cabinet, in October, 1924, he made Edward Wood Minister of Agriculture and Fisheries.

The offices of President of the Board of Education and Minister of Agriculture were traditional gentlemen's jobs; the one, held by an outstanding scholar, the other by a big landowner. Halifax was both. But he was more. Already, he was a man of rare and refined qualities who stood, as it were, on a lonely peak. Critics retreated before his impregnable character. They could not measure him with their customary yardsticks. To them he was more convincing than compelling. Yet no one could escape the impression of his absolute unselfishness, of his devotion and candor. He was a serious-minded man who could occasionally be a witty conversationalist. He lived for his task, his country, his ideas. Still, one sometimes felt that to him politics were something external. His conception of mankind was brotherly, but his innermost self was impenetrable. He was a junior cabinet member, obviously destined for a great future, when the first whisper of his "enigma" arose. It is the enigma of the English character.

Harold Begbie, who wrote under the pen name "A Gentleman with a Duster," a shrewd judge of men, pierced this enigma in describing Viscount Halifax, who at the time— 1924—aged forty-three, was still Mr. Edward Wood. "Men of all parties recognize in his personality something that is admirable," he said. "I call Edward Wood the highest kind of Englishman now in politics, for the following reason: He is a man whose life and doctrine are in complete harmony with a very lofty moral principle, but who has no harsh judgments for men who err and go astray. . . . He believes without a shadow of doubt that Conservatism is the truest and most enduring form of politics, but he can see the good that is in Labour, and in the sorrows and sufferings of the depressed classes he can perceive at least some excuse for the wild words of the extremists."

A harmonious mixture of stubbornness and tolerance— that is how Halifax, the typical Englishman, appears in this description. And this mixture explains why the English are putting up such a glorious show in this war.

Promising English politicians with the right background, the right connections and affiliations are for half their lives the object of untiring guesswork. Will he become Prime Minister? is the inevitable question that disturbs their sleep and spoils their appetite. There are at least three coming men in every government, and some of them have been "coming," from their Eton days to their seventieth birthday—the day when the successful British statesman retires into the peerage.

The Honorable Edward Wood was a much-favored speculation for Prime Minister. But in his forty-fifth year it seemed as if the door leading to the highest office in the Kingdom would suddenly be slammed in his face. Baldwin was looking for a new Viceroy of India. Someone was needed who would impress the Indians with English sincerity. A man with knowledge, culture, gentleness of manner was badly wanted; one who knew that all God's children have invisible wings. Baldwin's choice fell on "the noblest Christian in politics." He never regretted his choice. Even then, Halifax was deeply marked by his creed of human brotherhood. He never thought of racial differences or of class distinctions. There was no forced descent from lonely eminence to men of low estate. If any man could bring peace to India as Viceroy—here was the man. But the Viceroy must be a peer. And a peerage means the House of Lords for the rest of one's life. A Prime Minister must have a majority in, and be answerable to, the Commons. So the vicious circle closes, choking from then on, whatever ambitions Mr. Baldwin's lucky-unlucky choice might nourish for ultimate Premiership.

Fortunately, the man who is now Viscount Halifax did not nourish personal ambitions. His admission that he would rather be Master of the Hounds than Prime Minister is probably the deepest expression of his innermost urge. However, it was a difficult decision that Mr. Baldwin forced on him. It meant the end of a promising political career, and, worse still, five years' separation from his aging father. A Viceroy is not supposed to leave India during his term of office. Moreover, the confused situation in India demanded a special type of guidance. There was not much choice as to the successor of Lord Reading, "the greatest Jew in Christianity," who was then retiring.

Halifax consulted his father. Matters of transcendent importance, both for the Empire and for the men involved, were at stake. "Let us pray," the old Viscount suggested. Father and son went to church. Afterwards the old gentleman said quietly: "I think you'd better go!" "I think so, too!" his son answered. He extracted a promise from his father to live another five years that the two might meet again. The Viscount, already in his eighties, gave the promise which was faithfully kept.

The formality of creating Mr. Wood, Lord Irwin of Kirby Underdale, after a little hamlet on his Yorkshire estate, was negotiated. And off he went with his courageously smiling lady at his side, to India.

India was always, and still remains, a stumbling block in American understanding of the problems of the British Empire. In establishing new order in India, giving the vast sub-continent an interim constitution, and breaking the ice that had separated Gandhi from the British, Lord Irwin contributed enormously to Anglo-Indian co-operation. Immediately upon assuming his high office he tackled the problems courageously. He made a strong first impression on the Indians when he, a rigid Sabbatarian, refused to disembark when he happened to arrive on a Sunday. This gesture appealed to the deep religious feeling that the Indians share with "the tall, thin Christian," as they soon called the new Viceroy. Unfortunately, simultaneously with him, arrived a group of young men from England—British Communists, delegated by the Comintern to disturb, and if possible wreck, the great work of reconciliation on which Halifax was bent. During his entire term in India, the Communists proved their nuisance value. At that time Gandhi was still patient with those of his followers who were Communists. The Mahatma's patience has since then been exhausted, admittedly a little late.

At the time of his arrival, Halifax was entirely untried in the difficult and complicated art of Anglo-Indian administration. But with his deep piety, he was likely to succeed where spiritual values enter into every phase of life and politics. His object stood clearly before his eyes. "From the day I landed in India I knew that my main task would be concerned with the investigation which was to be the first step in the building of a new constitution for India and the subsequent stages through which these grave matters would have to pass," he recalled, in reviewing his viceregal term. Again there sound no trumpet calls in his recollection, but one can hear an honest man's decision to do an honest job of work.

After a few days in office he sent for Gandhi. The Mahatma was then the prophet and leader of the Hindu Civil

Disobedience. He was reluctant to accept the Viceroy's invitation. But he came. The first meeting between the two men passed without ceremony and drama, without mutual recriminations and polemics. However, it left a strong mark on both. Halifax's bold humanity did not go unnoticed with Gandhi. He inspired the Indian leader with confidence in his spiritual earnestness and good faith. The talk about a compromise constitution and the attainment of Dominion status for India could begin. The first result was the approach to the conference table and an immediate decline in anarchy.

From the outset Halifax recognized that only full equality could keep India within the framework of the Empire. "Partnership, not subordination!" he proclaimed as the aim, and on November 1, 1929, he issued an official statement: "His Majesty's government authorizes me to declare that in their view the attainment of Dominion status is the natural completion of India's constitutional growth."

Of course there were two prerequisites to be fulfilled before the goal of full self-government could be attained. First, India, disrupted by internal struggle, must achieve domestic unity. Second, the Indian people must acquire a certain measure of political education.

The Indian Princes in conference in London agreed to become part of the Dominion-in-the-making. Halifax, proud of this success, called it a turning point in India's constitutional history. But no one could end the traditional feuds between Hindu and Moslem. The unity of India, it must be remembered, is only geographical. For the rest, the sole factor that holds many of the parts of India together is their common allegiance to Great Britain, officially termed their "loyalty to the Person and the Throne of the King-Em-

peror." The English language is the only means of understanding between various Indian peoples. Paradoxically,
even the very rebirth of Indian national spirit is due to the
English language.

"An educated electorate is the only sure basis of democracy," Lord Halifax said. The Communists tried to educate the Hindu electorate in their own way. Into the fur-
thest valleys and mountain villages, forgotten by history,
they carried their war-cry that the individual counted for
nought, and the "class" for all.

Determinedly the Viceroy resisted Communist infiltra-
tion, which offended his fundamental humanitarian feeling.
"We shall very certainly fail if we permit ourselves to forget that individual personality is the strongest and the most
securely rooted element in all human nature," he declared.
The bills which he introduced in the Indian Parliament in
1929 provided for energetic measures against men and money
from Moscow.

But these prohibitory measures were only part of the reforms he introduced. He believed in fighting communism
by fighting poverty. As an agrarian expert, he was shocked
by the primitive methods of farming that still prevailed in
India. He established the Central Council for Agricultural
Research, which subsequently did a great deal for the improvement of farming conditions. But soil cultivation was
not enough. India should not remain forever a mere pro-
ducer of raw materials. Lord Halifax did a great job in pro-
moting the industrialization of India.

He ruled with firmness and energy, yet he considered
himself primarily as a trustee for both sides: the Empire,
and the Indian people. He developed his English genius for
compromise to new heights. But he never tried to dodge
difficult problems. "It is better to be blamed for saying un-

pleasant things, if they happen to be true, in time than to be condemned for saying them too late," he put it.

Sure enough, he did say unpleasant things. When he first addressed the Indian Princes, in 1926, shortly after his arrival, he frankly criticized their opium policy, which had led to disastrous consequences. Moreover, he candidly blamed some of the princes for their exaggerated lavishness and their squandering of money which, of course, aroused the underfed masses. It was a breach of sacred Indian tradition to disagree with this provocative luxury, and it might have been politically unwise to antagonize the princes, who are the pillars of the British system in India. It was politically still more dangerous to antagonize the diehards at home, as Halifax did when he, in 1928, openly discussed the claim of Indian nationalists for complete separation from the Commonwealth of British Nations. Of course he refuted the claim with good reasons, but even its serious discussion by the Viceroy aroused horror in polite society.

"The general note of British criticism," Halifax answered in 1930, "was that anyone who even talked of Dominion status in connection with India must be mentally affected, and that the idea was almost too fantastic to merit serious discussion. What wonder that Indian national feeling was offended and a real chance thrown away!"

It was largely owing to Halifax's untiring work that the chance was not thrown away. Today all England is resolved to accord to India full equality as a self-governing Dominion, as soon after the war as circumstances permit.

But Halifax did not forget to educate also his India listeners. He reminded them: "Throughout all her own history Great Britain has been the pioneer as regards the application of representative institutions to the science of politics. It is a commonplace to say that this, indeed, is the principal fact that she has contributed to the thought and practice of the world."

To a large degree Halifax's ultimate success in India depended on his relation with Gandhi. They recognized and esteemed each other's spiritual values. They spent many hours praying together. They both liked to tackle their problems from the moral point of view, discreetly drawing political conclusions. Once they spent a whole night in Gandhi's "mud hut" in a distant village, examining the question of whether there are conditions under which a man may righteously be permitted to break his word. Incidentally, the Viceroy had come by car to Gandhi's village and had walked on foot through the muddy streets. This was not quite without danger in a time of teeming unrest in India. But it was a grand proof of humility. When Gandhi's advisers showed their dissatisfaction with the outcome of the philosophical night, slightly tinged with politics, the Mahatma asked them: "Could you argue with Jesus Christ?"

A few months later, unfortunately, Gandhi could. The Simon Commission had found a rough reception in India. The first Round Table Conference ended in failure. So Gandhi revived his crusade for civil disobedience. He and his followers marched to the sea and there manufactured salt, thus infringing the State's salt monopoly. He was arrested and jailed. He entered his cell, blessing his followers and greeting his "noble, Christian friend."

In London the opposition grew restless. Lord Rothermere's *Daily Mail* denounced Halifax as the man who opened the gates of India to revolution. He was called a "second Kerensky." Nor did Winston Churchill like what he then believed to be Halifax's hesitations. And Winston has a way of expressing his dislikes in Parliament. However, the Labour

government, then in office, backed up the Viceroy. Mac-
Donald felt deep affinity with what appeared to be Halifax's indecision. Apparently, he failed to understand that
Halifax was not undecided at all. The Viceroy had, on the
contrary, made up his mind to steer a middle-of-the-road
course. No less than 46,000 Indian lawbreakers, most of
them Communists, were locked up for political crimes. But
Halifax's contact with Gandhi was never interrupted. On
March 5, 1931, both men had the deep satisfaction of sign-
ing the agreement that led to the second Round Table Conference. Gandhi attended it, and the foundation was laid
for India's self-government, subsequently embodied in India's Charter of August 2, 1935.

A towering white marble statue in New Delhi commemo-
rates the tenure of office of the man who was Britain's
greatest viceroy. No single man could solve the vast com-
plexities of the Indian problem, but probably Halifax has
saved the sub-continent for the Empire. Certainly it was his
personal influence which determined Gandhi's attitude in
this war. The Mahatma keeps his restive followers under
control. England, he explains to them untiringly, is a much
better bet than Hitler or Stalin.

Indeed, Halifax has well deserved the resounding praise
of Baldwin, then the spokesman of the National government, who declared in March, 1931: "Such a conclusion as
has been reached could not have been reached by any other
Englishman. It is a great tribute to his character—a character that has given him a prestige in India that nothing
else could have afforded him. The great work of Lord Irwin
is that he has, after many years of suspicion, closed the gap
between Great Britain and India."

On his return from India he was a tired man. The droop
of his shoulders had visibly increased. His plain, open face

had grown thinner. In consequence his nose, his ears, his mouth—all a little beyond classical proportions—appeared still larger than they were. The hair receded and the forehead expanded formidably. His bright, wide eyes, however, retained their friendly, benevolent smile. Kindness and wisdom marked his appearance.

Here stood a man at the summit of his life. He was created a Knight of the Garter. The highest decoration of the realm had been bestowed on him. There was nothing more left to wish for.

Nothing? In 1932 his old dream came true. He was appointed Master of the Foxhounds. "A gentleman, a foxhunter, a friend!" congratulated Winston Churchill. The position, to which a singular distinction attaches in England, was supposed to be his last one, and it was supposed to last for his lifetime. Little did Viscount Halifax know that this innocent office would bring him into the most difficult situation in his career, and that six years later pressure of more profane business would force him to resign it.

All he now wanted was a little rest. But the National government wanted his help and the support of his prestige. Patiently, he consented. He again accepted his old office of President of the Board of Education, a great proof of his modesty. He shifted to the War Office, when Baldwin followed MacDonald as Prime Minister. After the Conservative triumph in the 1935 elections, he was relieved of departmental duties. He became, first, Lord Privy Seal, then Lord President of the Council and Leader in the House of Lords. His utterances in the Upper House were unexciting. "He'd make a good bishop!" was the unanimous opinion. The old story was recalled of the noble Lord, who dreamed he was speaking in the House of Lords—and when he woke up, he was.

Never has Halifax been as enigmatic as in these years

when he was regarded as a governmental figurehead. In truth, he was one of the most influential, if certainly the most unassuming, members of Baldwin's last cabinet. His influence increased under Neville Chamberlain. Only outsiders could seriously believe that a man of Halifax's caliber would be half asleep when fate closed in upon England.

Was he aware of the menace of Nazism? Only history can answer this question, the most puzzling in his rich and eventful life. Contemporary chroniclers have tarred him with the brush of appeasement. Was he an appeaser? Undoubtedly he took his courage in both hands when he plunged into the desperate battle for peace.

In 1937, Neville Chamberlain dispatched Viscount Halifax to Germany. Halifax's position as a Master of Hounds was used as a reason for the journey. He was to meet Goering, Master of the Hunt in Germany. The protocol afforded an excuse.

Certainly Halifax did not feel at ease in undertaking a mission which looked like an infringement of Eden's rights. He had always backed up his younger colleague in cabinet councils and had helped him with the full measure of his experience. However, it might be supposed that he felt himself the better man to deal with the Nazis.

In Karinshall, Schorfheide, Goering's hunting lodge near Berlin, the Marshal played host to Halifax in the grand manner. Unfortunately, according to a widely circulated story, there was a slight hitch during the gala dinner. Lobster was served . . . a strange-smelling lobster. Viscount Halifax lifted a bit of it—not to his mouth, but to his nose. It is inconceivable that his Lordship in all his life has ever used the expression: "It stinks!" He just made a polite gesture of apology. Whereupon Goering pushed his broad nostrils right into the lobster plate. Indeed, it stank. This was not Albion's perfidy. This was the fault of his own kitchen staff. Goering is a just judge and he executes his sentences rapidly. He had the entire kitchen staff, numbering some twenty men, brought to the dining hall. He roared at them in front of the English visitor. He had them arrested, stripped of their liveries. The chef, he yelled, would be sent immediately to the concentration camp. Then he turned smilingly to his guest. Wasn't he a fast worker?

It is not recorded whether Lord Halifax continued his meal with unspoiled appetite. Both slightly disgusted and a little amused he returned to London.

He misjudged Goering, as did, incidentally, almost the whole world. Confused by his own goodness, he did not see the megalomaniac, the blood-crazed founder of the Luftwaffe. What Halifax did see was a fat, oversized, naughty boy who wanted to be humored and to have his sense of ostentation, his gross witticisms, admired. In Halifax's opinion Goering had a soft spot in his heart. Why, he called the deer in his forests by names and spoke to them. "The least objectionable member of a government of criminals," Halifax said. This judgment reveals more about the judge than about the culprit. It is an English understatement.

Early in 1938, he again visited Germany. This time his mission took him to Berchtesgaden.

Hitler shouted for hours. When Halifax left Berchtesgaden, a gentleman of his entourage said: "The Reichskanzler and the Viscount spent two hours together. Herr Hitler took two hours and a half to explain his point of view." Halifax was most uncourteously received and was tucked away in a special train to Berlin one hour before Hitler boarded his own special train in the same direction. The distinguished British visitor was still in Germany when Hitler delivered a rambling speech in Augsburg. "These

English don't want to give us back the colonies they have
stolen," he yelled within, so to speak, Halifax's hearing.
"Well, I am building such a strong army that they will have
to listen in three years. And in another three years I don't
care whether they listen. We will simply take what rightly
belongs to us!"

It was a calculated insult. This was no longer Goering's
crude hospitality. Certainly Nazis number one and two
played hand in glove. Hitler's role was the holy terror,
Goering's the white hope. The Nazis dared the British Empire with the same methods they later used to disrupt Belgium or Bulgaria—offering a choice between horsewhip and
bribe. It was so incredible that Viscount Halifax has probably never understood it.

At that time Halifax could probably not recognize the
slime which produces a Hitler. His own lifework had been
an unbroken search for the good in every creature. He had
concluded his Indian travail with the words: "I should permit myself to hope, if difference there must be, it shall be
such difference as will not make us unwilling to admit the
sincerity of those whose views differ from our own."

True, Hitler was a difficult case. But so had Gandhi been.
A devout believer in God never loses his hope of man. Not
overoptimistic, but in a hopeful state of mind, Halifax succeeded Eden, in March, 1938, when Neville Chamberlain
dropped his Foreign Secretary the very day that Hitler attacked Eden in one of his customary boorish execrations.

The earth had begun to tremble. The first eruption of the
earthquake was Hitler's rape of Austria. Halifax had seen it
coming for a long time. But since his visit to Hitler he knew
that war was inevitable should the Western powers try to
stop the assault on Vienna. He did not yet know that war
with Hitler was inevitable however far the democratic world

was ready to bend back. But even had he known it, he could, as early as 1937, have convinced neither his country nor the world.

Hitler had discussed Austria with his English visitor at Berchtesgaden. It is not known whether Halifax's deep insight where human feelings are involved warned him that here was a maniac obsessed by an *idée fixe*, nursed since boyhood. But it was well known that no one in England wanted war for Austria. Nazi influences, particularly successful in society, had sold to insular England the idea of Austria as a "German" country. Furthermore, the English sense of fair play was abused, in that many in England were made to feel that Germany, after all, had not received anything as long as she was politely asking. Little wonder, Englishmen concluded, that criminals had come to power in frustrated Germany. These criminals, after all, stood for a good cause. So perverted was English thinking during the first years of Hitler. World democracy, for its part, did not think at all. True, democracy had lost one little country after the other. But that was not worse than having a few teeth pulled. It was painless; Nazi propaganda served as a perfect local anesthetic. It was nothing to get excited about—unless blood-poisoning followed.

Nobody lifted a finger in London, when the second World War began with Hitler's assault on Austria. Democracy was paralyzed. Leaders and followers underbid one another. Neville Chamberlain decided to pull England out by her bootstraps. Unfortunately, he mistook Hitler's famous rhinoceros-skin whip for the English bootstraps as his hands frantically searched for a hold. The Prime Minister brushed aside his Foreign Office. Trusted and experienced advisers like Sir Robert Vansittart, Permanent Under Secretary and Britain's diplomatic expert number one, were superseded by yes-men.

Mysterious, shy, publicity-shunning Sir Horace Wilson, soon to become the co-author of Munich, was suddenly the power behind the umbrella. Halifax had just assumed the Foreign Secretary's responsibilities. Why did he fall in line as England marched down the road to near-suicide?

Again he puzzled those who believed they knew him best. Harold Laski, brain-truster of the Labour Party, quickly found an explanation for the enigma that was Halifax. After paying due tribute to the Viscount's outstanding human qualities, he analyzed the gentleman-appeaser. "At bottom he is a mystic. He likes that twilight world of intuition in which fine sentiments are uttered which all men can approve. He is all for 'atmosphere' and 'understanding the impalpables' which leave you a way out in either direction. Hitler, he believes, can be taught the language of the gentleman. Hitler and Mussolini can build their empires without touching Britain's vital interests. Halifax will carry us over into what is effectively the Fascist camp in the simple faith that he is fighting the battle of democracy."

Of course this explanation is tinged with a radical intellectual's distrust of the old-fashioned cavalier. Its conclusions are utterly wrong, as the development proved. Today Halifax belongs among the outstanding fighters in the democratic camp. But Laski's analysis rightly points out the cardinal weakness of appeasement—the delusion that Hitler's and Mussolini's empires could possibly exist without touching the vital interests of democracy. This delusion for a long time blinded America as well. In England it had been nourished by the Chamberlain government with Halifax's active assistance.

But Halifax was deluded by Hitler for honorable reasons. He was deluded, because in the purity of his own soul and mind he could simply not grasp from the outset the perversion of Hitler and his gang. When it dawned on him what beasts he was up against, he sided with his Prime Minister, partly in order to stiffen him, and partly because he would have considered it desertion to retire in the moment of England's gravest plight. He certainly did not possess Churchill's scent for the Nazi virus, but he had no less courage.

Although he carried out the policy of appeasement unequivocally, all London knew that he remained the center of whatever resistance was left within the cabinet councils. Almost immediately after the fall of Austria Hitler looked for the first time longingly on Czechoslovakia. The Czechs answered with mobilization—on Halifax's confidential advice, Prague whispered. Indeed, on one of those critical days, the Foreign Secretary sent his ambassador five times to the Wilhelmstrasse, to indicate London's interest in the Central-European development. Since Hitler was not yet quite ready, the development was interrupted for a few months. Goering vouched with his word of honor as a German officer that the Nazis would never attack Czechoslovakia.

Hitler played for time. So did, in a certain sense, the government in London. Unfortunately, it was not in a military sense. In spite of Winston Churchill's historic warnings, the days after Munich were blindly squandered. But this was not Halifax's fault. As Foreign Secretary his job was to use whatever power and influence Great Britain possessed; not to build up power for defense. Devout believer as ever, he was confident that moral powers would ultimately decide. He used the last pre-war year to demonstrate to the people of the world, and particularly to the American people, that no effort should be spared and no sacrifices compatible with national honor and human obligation refused, to ensure peace in our time. Perhaps this sacrificial policy corresponded to his innermost tolerance, his Christian love for the enemy, his humility.

But it must have aroused his English pride. It became increasingly difficult for a responsible British statesman to walk with head erect.

Munich was the ultimate sacrifice. Halifax did agree with the settlement, because he regarded it as the lesser of two evils. However, he soon called it "humiliating." He did not accompany his chief to Munich; undoubtedly his appearance would have disturbed the atmosphere. When Hitler broke the pact and sent his hordes into Prague, appeasement was smashed into fragments. Munich had cost the allies the co-operation of Russia, for what it was worth. Stalin would probably not have needed the fate of Czechoslovakia as an excuse to double-cross England. Munich and its aftermath gave Hitler tremendous military and economic advantages. But to the plain people of the world, and to the Americas above all, it was clearly demonstrated that the now inevitable war was indeed a struggle between day and night. The clean moral bill of health England could now present outweighed for Halifax forty-odd Czech divisions that everybody knew were lost—and perhaps also the terrific indirect losses that followed Munich.

Hastily Halifax dispatched to Rumania and Poland guarantees against aggression. He was determined to stop Hitler now. Five days after the German occupation of Prague he spoke in the House of Lords, which was still the stronghold of pro-Nazi sympathies—with the Labour Lords, in their pacifism, closely allied with Fascist-minded peers. He explained: "No member of His Majesty's Government has failed at any moment to be actually conscious of the difference between belief and hope. It was surely legitimate and right to have hopes." But now the hopes were gone. On June 29, 1939, he addressed the ninth annual dinner of the Royal Institute of International Affairs. "In the past we have always stood out against the attempt of any single power to dominate Europe at the expense of the liberties of other nations. British policy is therefore only following the inevitable line of its own history, if such an attempt were to be made again. Our first resolve is to stop aggression. If Lebensraum means action by one nation in suppression of the independent existence of her smaller and weaker neighbors, we reject it and must resist its application . . . Today the threat of military force is holding the world to ransom and our immediate task is to resist aggression. Let us therefore be very sure that whether or not we are to preserve for ourselves and for others the things we hold dear, depends in the last resort on ourselves, upon the strength of the personal faith of each one of us, and on our resolution to maintain it."

With a confession of a moral creed Halifax shelved all that tattered appeasement. He no longer had to be enigmatic. The skies were clear. The fight was good.

But it was not until the second year of the war, in the spring of 1941, that Viscount Halifax found what he considers the crowning task of his life. An unprecedented assignment brought him to the United States. He is the first Foreign Secretary to relinquish the Foreign Office for an ambassadorship, although he remains a member of the Inner War Cabinet. He is the first ambassador whom his Prime Minister accompanied to the ship at his departure, wishing him Godspeed, the first to cross the sea in a battleship, and the first foreign diplomat to be welcomed by the President of the United States at the American shore.

Lord Halifax's task is to harmonize the English and American efforts to assure victory in common. The outcome of this war depends largely on the success of this synchronization.

And this success, in turn, depends largely on the spirit in, and the skill with which Halifax approaches his job. No other man's personal responsibility is greater. He has to live down ever-ready prejudices. Americans saw a gentleman in correct black with the inevitable bowler hat but almost untidy in his appearance, as if he lived chiefly among books and were entirely careless in practical matters. They expected a feudal Tory, representing the ruling classes. In fact, Halifax welcomed labor into politics and government, long before the New Deal was thought of. In England his statement is not forgotten: "Many of the newcomers are disorderly, many seem essentially violent minded. Yet our debates are richer for their presence. Not all of us are as near to the sufferings of the working classes as they are. They bring, however misguided some may be in their opinions, and however violent they may be in publicly expressing them, home to the House of Commons the gravity of our social problems and the importance of getting fundamental things right."

Americans made the acquaintance of a serious man who in private conversation has a touch of heart-warming gaiety. Under a strong forehead his eyes are deeply set, looking upon life very quietly, kind and thoughtful. His large and flexible, sometimes critical mouth shows good humor. His expression is sometimes grave and scholarly, but the wisdom that marks him is always gentle.

Those who expected a severe High Church dignitary were agreeably surprised when the new ambassador, on his first Sunday in Washington, went into a poor quarter to attend a service for children. His deep religiousness is entirely unpolitical and is permeated with a social conscience. "Christianity," Halifax said, "can never be made the touchstone of some detailed policy. Christianity is essential to right action

LORD HALIFAX   45

toward the problems of the world. The virtue of the Christian attitude consists in gentleness and compassion."

Most surprised were those Americans who expected to meet an appeaser. Halifax speaks with utter contempt of Britain's and civilization's enemies. To him the Nazi system is bondage, bodily and spiritual, political and economic. According to Nazi philosophy, he explains, the State both may and must claim the whole allegiance of man's body and soul. Truth, conscience, mercy, honor, justice, love; where these clash with what is held to be the over-riding interest of the State, they are regarded by Hitler as offenses.

Lord Halifax, the appeaser, is no longer afraid to offend Hitler since he understands that Hitler has offended God's commandments. All Britain, he asserts, laughs off Hitler's threats of invasion. American help, the ambassador says confidently and unhesitatingly, will not come too late. True, the English laughter is not always far away from tears. But it explains why England will never go down.

Prince Charming

ANTHONY EDEN

FEW INFANT PRODIGIES HAVE SUCCESSFULLY STAGED A COME-back. The Honorable Robert Anthony Eden has. He was a celebrated beauty at three, a war hero at nineteen; at twenty he was gassed at Ypres and given up for dead. At thirty he was the coming man in England. At thirty-four his name meant hope and promise to all the world; no other statesman between the wars ever stirred the people's imagination to quite the same degree. At forty-one he was an elder statesman. He preferred polite resignation to the scramble for the British premiership which might have been his for the asking. Since history suffers from a bad memory, he quickly became a forgotten man. A year and a half later another forgotten man came to wake the Sleeping Beauty.

As Winston Churchill's Foreign Secretary, Mr. Eden again occupies the Foreign Office, where the most important years of his life have been spent. It is not quite the Foreign Office of past days. Diplomats need no longer comply with the property qualification which previously required a private income of two thousand pounds a year. The foreign service is now open to all. Merit alone decides the career. It is no longer absolutely necessary—although it still does no harm—

ANTHONY EDEN

to be of aristocratic lineage, to have written Latin verse, to
have rowed at Eton, and to have played football for Oxford.
The Foreign Office no longer keeps aloof from the life of the
nation as it did a few years ago. To a large extent these
changes have been brought about by a chief who does come
of aristocratic lineage, has written Latin verse and rowed at
Eton, and did play football for Oxford. In our age of mass-
production Anthony Eden stands out like a precious antique.
But he is not getting dusty. His rich dark-brown hair is only
slightly greying at the temples. The stoop of his shoulders
has visibly increased. He carries heavy responsibilities. The
times are gone in which the success of a Foreign Secretary
was fully vindicated by the King's traditional phrase to the
Commons: "My relations with other powers continue to remain friendly." The new times ask for courage, vision, sacrifice. Anthony Eden has many outstanding qualities. But he
is best known for one—for his personal charm. Thousands
of his friends and acquaintances call him, tenderly, "dear
Anthony." He has had to spend half his life living down his
silly reputation as a play-boy, another Beau Brummell. His
rare refinement is above all spiritual. He belongs among the
few responsible men who have heard the distant thunder
of the new deluge from the first day. He will emerge from
the turmoil as a man of vision and loyalty.

Robert Anthony Eden is of the old English breed. He
descends from a North Country family which dates back to
the fifteenth century. His father, the late Sir William Eden,
baronet, was a conspicuous Victorian. Some called him a
virile and violent individualist, others simply an eccentric
Englishman. Undoubtedly, Anthony Eden's quiet tastes, his
horror of showmanship, even his sartorial earnestness, have
been formed by a conservative rebellion against his some-

what eccentric father. Sir William was famous for his grey velvet knickerbockers and his dinner jacket made of silk handkerchiefs. He was well known both as a fox-hunter and a painter. Some of his water-colors have survived him. Anthony, his third son, has inherited the predilection for brush and palette. Painting is his only hobby—a hobby, incidentally, which he shares with Winston Churchill. But whereas Churchill indulges in strong oil-colors with aggressive red and blue as his favorites, Anthony Eden confines himself to almost transparent aquarelles. Perhaps this contrast explains the difference between them.

"My sons shall learn painting," the late Sir William decreed. "But they shall also know how to drive a team, ride across country, box and shoot." As far as Anthony was concerned, his father's last-mentioned wish was not fulfilled. Mr. Eden despises the cruelty of hunting. He showed considerable courage in indicting the English gentleman's favorite sport, fox-hunting, as bloody slaughter. There is only one hunting story about him on record.

In 1934, as Lord Privy Seal, he paid a state visit to Sweden. Of course an elk-hunting party was arranged for the distinguished guest. When the elk came within shooting range his companions politely dropped their guns to give His Britannic Majesty's Lord Privy Seal the honor of the catchball. But dear Anthony also dropped his gun. He looked into the elk's tender brown animal eyes, and turned around to his party: "Isn't it a beauty?" The elk, it is reported, shook his horns and trotted comfortably away. It had a new lease of life—until another diplomatic visitor came to Sweden. Hermann Goering, among other things Master of the German Hunt, expressed with a shout of laughter, his desire to "shoot Sweden empty of elk."

Anthony was born on June 12, 1897, at his father's country estate, Windlestone Hall, near Bishop Auckland. His mother was known as the fairest lady in the land. The boy inherited her looks. Indeed, at the age of three, from when his first photographs date, he looked like a beautiful girl, thick dark hair tumbling on to his forehead, and enormous black eyes illuminating the round face with the cherry-lips.

His formal education began at the age of nine at Sandroyd Preparatory School, near Cobham. Perhaps there lies more than a mere coincidence of names in the fact that he passed two years later into Churchill's House at Eton. In his black Eton suit and silk hat he looked like a miniature gentleman. Only his protruding teeth and an incurable habit of thrusting his hands deep in his pockets indicated some signs of youthful stubbornness. He achieved no eminence at Eton either as a scholar or an athlete, although he played some football and was even slated for Eton's rowing team. He was a quiet boy, intended to pass quietly into the Church.

But Wellington had not said in vain: "The battle of Waterloo was won on the playing fields of Eton." Early in 1915, aged seventeen, Anthony went straight from school to join the colors as a lieutenant in the King's Royal Rifles. He proved his heroism on the Ypres front in 1916. He was in command of a trench raiding party out to capture a few Jerries. His party encountered terrific German fire in no man's land. One of Eden's men was hit; Eden carried him to safety. The wounded man had to remain two years in the hospital; today he still corresponds with his lifesaver. A year later Eden again risked his life to save one of his non-commissioned officers. He received the Military Cross for bravery. His fame grew in the army. On June 4, 1917, just over twenty, he was promoted to the rank of Brigade-Major.

Winston Churchill once confessed that he no longer had

enough patience for the quiet halls of Oxford after having heard the bullets whistle around his ears. Anthony Eden could muster the required patience. He returned from the war and entered Oxford. The war, it seems, had removed his inhibitions. As a retired major, the once indifferent pupil at Eton excelled in oriental languages at Oxford. He became a scholar in Arabic, wrote Persian verse, and took first class honors. His linguistic gifts are brilliant. He is one of the few Englishmen who speak French like a Parisian. German was more difficult for him. He endeavored to learn it in later years, when he wanted to impress the masters of Germany with his sympathetic understanding of their cause. But being by then a very busy man, he found time to study the intricacies of German grammar only during his morning shave.

His familiarity with oriental languages came in very handy in the recent past. In the spring of 1941 he visited Ankara to prepare the Turkish leaders for the German onslaught, then in the making. A crack regiment paraded before him. He surprised the troops by addressing them fluently in their own vernacular. The soldiers were stunned. Then they cheered. They had never before seen a foreigner who was able to say "Give Hitler hell!" in Turkish.

Fresh from the university, Eden ran for Parliament. Politics was a gentleman's natural vocation; and besides, the lesson of the war had sharpened his sense of social obligation. In 1922, he contested a mining district, the Spennymore Division of Durham. It was a three-cornered fight between the young Tory, Eden, and his Liberal and Labour competitors. The miners of Spennymore turned down the Tory. They elected the Socialist candidate—the Countess of Warwick, a red millionairess, related by marriage to Anthony Eden.

Subsequently greater events have proved that Eden is immune to adversities. A few months after his defeat, he stood again for Parliament, this time for the safe Conservative seat of Warwick and Leamington, which he holds to this day. His busy campaigning left him just enough time to marry dark, graceful Miss Beatrice Beckett, daughter of a local banker who was also the owner of the influential *Yorkshire Post*. The marriage was performed at St. Margaret's, Westminster. In his morning coat and light waistcoat, broad silk tie and top hat, the milk-faced bridegroom looked almost grown up. Unfortunately, dear Anthony could only spare twenty-four hours for his honeymoon. Mrs. Eden soon learned to become "diplomacy's widow," as she used to call herself during the years her husband was Europe's most constantly traveling diplomat. She rarely accompanied him on his journeys. Golden silence is her rule. She is not as democratic as Mrs. Annie Chamberlain or Lady Baldwin used to be. Perhaps she is a little jealous of politics. The marriage was blessed with two boys, Simon and Nicholas, today both youngsters in their teens. For England the marriage was a blessing since Eden now had a mouthpiece of his own. In the heyday of appeasement, when even the old thunderer, the *Times* of London, bent back, the *Yorkshire Post* assumed the role of England's conscience: until the *Daily Telegraph* joined it, it was the only conservative paper which uncompromisingly fought appeasement.

The Edens soon moved to London, where they established themselves in fashionable Fitzhardinge Street. They lived comfortable, if by no means extravagant, lives. Mr. Eden's income has been assessed at £2,500 a year—not so very much for Mayfair high life, but enough to assure his complete independence and lack of any personal interest in politics. He was never compelled to seek office or to write his memoirs.

Three fortuitous qualities started him the smooth way. First, his gentle birth, his material independence and high connections. Second, his great knowledge and intelligence. Third, his intense seriousness of purpose. One is not allowed to add his good looks to his natural endowment. Anthony Eden does not resent any reproach as much as he does a compliment to his handsome appearance. One way to arouse this very quiet man's wrath is to call him a glamour boy. He is nothing of the kind. He is very definitely Anthony minus Cleopatra. Proudly he points out his protruding teeth and the fact that his eyes are a little too close together. He is aware of his peculiar gait; he rolls slightly as he strides along. His chin is rather small. He has difficulty in discovering other faults in his appearance. He is a bit above the average in height, on the slender side. His face has classic lines. His thick hair falls over a high forehead. As the years go on, he is getting a little short-sighted. Sometimes he wears horn-rimmed glasses behind which his large dark eyes seek cover. Well-groomed, mostly in conservative black, and with his "Guardee" moustache, he is precisely the aristocratic young Englishman—Milord to foreigners. He looks like an officer, thinks as a patriot, and feels like an artist.

His facile approach to important people considerably eased his career. Although some time has elapsed since he was the center of world attention, his name and fame carry on. Students of the University of Paris, accustomed to go hatless in the Latin tradition, now wear Anthony Eden hats—the black fedora—to demonstrate their pro-British feelings. A little incident, both sad and funny, shows his prestige even among the enemy. A few weeks before the rape of Austria Dr. Gouido Schmidt, then Foreign Secretary in Vienna, an ambitious, handsome young man, had not quite made up his mind to become the Quisling of the Danube. Herr von

Papen cut short his wavering. "If you play with us we will make you the continental Anthony Eden." This vision sufficed to make Dr. Schmidt betray his country. The turncoat, of course, confused Anthony Eden with Sir Oswald Mosley. But when Schuschnigg, awaking too late to the dangers around him, finally discovered that he had been double-crossed by his Foreign Secretary, the latter tried to vindicate himself with the confession: "Papen told me that I have what it takes to become the continental Anthony Eden. Could you have resisted?"

No one could resist Anthony Eden's image. Still less the man himself. Yet it was not the personal relations, it was the masses who made him. As a young progressive statesman he was the people's choice. His public popularity was unparalleled, when he expressed the average man's dream—eternal peace through a league of nations. Unfortunately, his friendly personal relations made him abandon the dream for a time. In this most tragic interlude in his life, dear Anthony was just a little too nice a chap.

After three years as an unassuming back-bencher, Eden became Parliamentary Private Secretary to Commander Locker-Lampson, then Under Secretary in the Home Office, and a veteran friend of Churchill's. The job carried no pay, but it gave the young M.P. intimate insight into the functioning of the government machine. It also brought him to the attention of the bigwigs. Mr., now Earl, Baldwin was always looking for new talent, particularly for gifted vote-getters. He was well aware that the female vote in England outnumbered the men's vote by hundreds of thousands. This was an important factor in Eden's favor. Besides, his elegant appearance and easy manners concealed much hard work and seriousness of purpose. Baldwin appreciated these qualities the more, as indefatigability did not belong among his own outstanding virtues. He flashed the green light when Sir Austen Chamberlain, then Foreign Secretary, made young Eden, after a year of apprenticeship in the Home Office, his own Parliamentary Secretary. Eden entered the Foreign Office at twenty-nine. His stay was twice interrupted. Yet he had found his place in life.

True, he again held a job without pay, but once more it was an unrivalled opportunity for inside study. Older M.P.'s recall that Eden at this time was a somewhat frail fellow with a marked stoop and the tired eyes of an overworked student. Neither will-power nor drive was obvious. He developed slowly. He was the typical representative of the generation that had been shattered by the war. His idealism was blended with pacifism, or rather with hatred for war. He believed in a new order and peaceful negotiation. The English were easy-going at that time. Nobody suggested the perils of unilateral disarmament. Nobody questioned whether luxurious social services were indeed more important than military prepared-ness. The Conservatives outbid the Socialists to preserve shaky majorities that involved ever costlier concessions to the electorate.

In these surroundings Eden was fortunate in having Sir Austen Chamberlain's sympathy and advice. He learned from his chief that France's military supremacy alone held Ger-many at bay. As a student of history he foresaw Germany's rearmament at the first possible moment. As an insider in the Foreign Office he knew that the Germans had never ful-filled their disarmament obligations.

He soon proved also a good pupil of Mr. Baldwin's. He learned the old statesman's inimitable art of making friends. He learned the trick of asking even the dullest companion for his opinion. Such dull companions often forgot in front of Eden that they were speaking to a man of deep knowledge and wide experience. Talking to him they could let off steam. He was sure to congratulate second-string speakers on their most abysmal orations. Frequently he had a bit of information for politicians who did not really belong to the inner circle. He never indulged in shoulder-patting, but a very slight and rapid touch with the tips of his fingers made his information appear considerably more confidential. In the grand style of English parliamentary tradition, he maintained genial contacts with his opponents. He often stepped over to the opposition benches to whisper urgently with his most violent critics. After a few years of parliamentary practice he had not a single enemy in the House. His friends cheered his utterances, although these were sparing and not very exciting. His quiet, confident, well-polished speeches, delivered in an unhurried, agreeably modulated voice, which sometimes grew weary or could even sound blasé, produced a stream of well-regulated sentences that meant something and always carried righteous conviction. Everybody could agree with them. In a time of wild talking, uneasiness and unrest, this young Conservative never lost his poise. To him Conservatism was the means of preserving civilization by orderly, regulated progress, with eyes and ears wide open to ever-changing conditions. His moral basis, however, remained unchangeable. Sometimes Eden's speeches sounded like religious rather than political conviction. It became a matter of course to cheer him. A habit was formed to cheer the coming leader.

His strongest conviction rested with the League of Nations. In this field he was the teacher and his chief the pupil. Sir Austen Chamberlain took some time to grasp Eden's idea of the League. But ultimately the success of Locarno convinced him. Intimate personal co-operation with Briand and

Stresemann was established. The friendship among the big three was patterned after Eden's conception of agreeable personal contacts. Of course none of the three statesmen saw the skilful hand, which, if it did not mold their politics, certainly smoothed their collaboration.

Locarno secured, so it seemed, peace in Western Europe. Unfortunately, it was not followed up by an Eastern Locarno, which Dr. Benes advocated. Even Mussolini was ready to behave himself. Thus Eden matured under hopeful auspices. But fate had willed it otherwise. In rapid sequence, Stresemann, Briand and Sir Austen Chamberlain were removed from the scene by death and disease. There is little doubt that the three men, given another few years in full possession of their physical strength, could have established peace in our time. They were irreplaceable. After Stresemann's death there was no man in Germany left to stem the rising tide of Nazism. Briand was followed in France by Laval and others on the same level. In London Sir John—now Viscount—Simon moved into the Foreign Office.

In 1931, MacDonald promoted Eden to the rank of Under Secretary in the Foreign Office, to offset the dissatisfaction caused by his choice of Simon. But this promotion was just one of the ex-red Prime Minister's habitual palliatives; not even Eden's popularity could help. Sir John Simon blundered from his first day in office to the last. His constant indecision was mixed up with a tendency to elude or postpone difficulties at any price. His ice-cold legalistic mind found ever new escape clauses. He was inordinately proud of his "legal brains," a gift that is more highly appreciated in England than anywhere else, and he bothered little to conceal the fact that this shrewd legalism was outweighed by a total lack of political character and courage. He was ever inclined to comply with the powers that be, with a strong Prime Min-

ister at home or with the bullying dictators abroad. By way
of compensation he terrorized his collaborators. He recognized but one handicap—the fact that he belonged to a
splinter group, the handful of National Liberals. In shaping
Britain's destiny he knew but one aim—to smooth his own
way to Premiership, in spite of not commanding a Parliamentary following. Fortunately, he was stopped at the next
to the top rung of the ladder.

The Disarmament Conference opened in February, 1932.
Eden had anticipated it with high hopes, and had done yeo-
man service in bringing it into being. He accompanied his
chief to Geneva. But there the mere presence of Sir John
Simon paralyzed him. Sphinx-like, the mask of Sir John gazed
into empty space. He was a sphinx without a riddle; his only
aim was to avoid committing himself.

To public opinion at home, Anthony Eden rather than
Simon was connected with the Disarmament Conference,
since the English people had come to associate his name with
Geneva. Eden labored untiringly to save what could be saved
from the conference, ill-fated from the beginning. He outdid himself. He became the Prince Charming of Geneva. His
personal amiability was the talk of the Quai du Mont Blanc,
the street of the gossiping, diplomatic hotels. Again, as during his apprenticeship on the front bench, dear Anthony had
a "choice bit of information"—even for the Nicaraguan dele-
gate. He never forgot to send his compliments to Madame,
Her Excellency. "Avez-vous bien dormi?" he started important negotiations. In England such a question would have
miscarried. Foreigners, however, were convinced of its sincerity.

His infectious smile, his multi-colored politeness and his
genuine charm never distracted him from concentrating on

his work. Nor did he abandon hope of a happy outcome. He had to stomach many events that would have discouraged a less fiery believer. He recognized that Japan's invasion of Manchuria would set the style for a series of aggressions. But Sir John Simon remained apathetic to the first arbitrary breach of international agreements in the post-war period. He refused an American offer for joint action in the Far East—America's first and last offer of this kind. He just could not find out which paragraphs of international law Japan had violated. He did not care for right, but only for jurisprudence, with a strong accent on the second part of the word.

Eden was forced to watch helplessly. He could get things done only when he was free of Simon's paralyzing presence. In such a brief interlude of independence, his artful mastery of negotiation averted a Hungarian-Jugoslavian war. But in matters of world importance, he saw that his own chief, frightened by fraudulent aggression, was conciliating the law-breakers and disputing away their illegality. Mussolini was allowed to prepare quite openly the rape of Abyssinia. Hitler came to power in the Reich. Sure enough, after a few months of his regime, in October, 1933, the Germans left Geneva, banging the door behind them. The blow came as a relief to Eden. Now the test was approaching. But Sir John Simon yielded again to blackmail, leaving his successors to pay tenfold afterwards.

Eden's forehead was deeply furrowed when he came back from Geneva. For the first time his hair was touched with grey. His bright smile faded quickly. He used his strong-lensed spectacles more often. Sometimes, with an impetuous movement, he tore the glasses off—as if he did not want to see too much. His voice had lost some of its enchanting ring. He delivered speeches in a high-pitched, tired, sometimes superior tone; not everybody understood that this was superiority enforced by solitude. He did not speak more than was necessary. Above all, he was to carry on, not to revolt.

A strange fate destined Anthony Eden to spend the crucial years of his life in an effort for appeasement, which disgusted him although he was fundamentally peace-minded. But of course for him there was no peace thinkable, save peace with honor, peace with the powers of civilization prevailing, the very opposite of appeasement. This was too natural to need mentioning. Perhaps Mr. Baldwin misunderstood Eden's silence. He chose his slightly fatigued Prince Charming to establish personal contact with Hitler. The year was 1934. The monster was still in his puberty. Perhaps one could polish him up a bit. Eden, if anyone could do it, was the man for the job. To invest him with sufficient authority, he was promoted to the rank of Lord Privy Seal.

Hitler expected to receive a chocolate soldier; he was stunned to see a "Frontsoldat." He rejoiced to discover that his visitor had been at Ypres. Of course Hitler had been at Ypres also, though, it is true, as a dispatch rider at a safe distance from the firing line. The Führer's hospitality reached a high mark when it came out that Eden had been gassed at Ypres. Hitler had been gassed there, too. As a matter of fact, his gas-poisoning was thought by the doctors in the Pasewalk hospital to be a case of nervous breakdown, and it happened almost two years after Ypres. But Hitler could not miss the opportunity of establishing what seemed to him cordial relations with his first distinguished English visitor. His air fleet was still in the making. As soon as the armada was finished, the Führer singled out Mr. Eden for his coarsest and vilest personal attacks.

Was Eden captivated by Hitler's crude amiability at their

first meeting? All the signs indicated that he was both amused and slightly disgusted. But he did his best to avoid a new conflict. In the winter following his visit to Hitler he became a leading figure in the negotiations with Germany, and was instrumental in handing back the Saar to the Third Reich. Some critics believed that the independent, anti-Nazi vote in the Saar territory had not had a fair chance in the plebiscite. But Eden's position at home was unassailable. The ballot in the autumn of 1934 showed a great majority in favor of collective security. The eleven million votes commanded by the League of Nations could not be disregarded. They were, indeed, cast for their hero, dear Anthony.

The dream of a peace with Nazism lasted a few months. In the spring of 1935, Hitler was burning to establish his "equality of status," meaning the formal abolition of the military clauses of Versailles. Sir John Simon wanted to build himself up in the public mind as the man who brought about Anglo-German understanding; in view of the lethargic apathy then prevailing in England, there was no better way to Premiership. He was willing to grant Germany a free hand in the East. His Foreign Office advisers warned him that such a course was fraught with danger for England. Baldwin was warned. Eden engineered a two days' conference with the French cabinet leaders to bring about a compromise and to choke Simon's plans, which were running wild. The outcome of this conference was a new, if modified British advance to Germany. London proposed a "Western Air Pact," together with a status of security for the Eastern States. Politely, Sir John inquired whether Hitler would care to receive him to discuss the matter.

Hitler was "indisposed." He cancelled the English visit after having agreed to it at first. His alleged sore throat, however, did not prevent him from delivering a boisterous and offensive speech, denouncing the clauses of Versailles and announcing that thirty-six German divisions had already been established. Then he had the effrontery to renew his invitation to Simon. "The angel of peace is unsnubbable," Winston Churchill commented when Simon hastened to accept the preposterous invitation. He went to Berlin. Eden accompanied him. The Führer spoke for seven hours. His interpreter, Dr. Schmidt, took half an hour to translate Hitler's peroration. Sir John Simon confessed himself a little tired— too tired to continue the journey. Eden was left alone to go on to Prague, Warsaw and Moscow. His trip to the Eastern capitals was clearly a demonstration on his part. He wanted to offset the general impression that England was helplessly yielding to Hitler. But he was well aware that even this gesture could not affect the fundamental problem. It was no longer to be solved by demonstrations and gestures. A decision was demanded from England—and England remained undecided. A decision was demanded from Anthony Eden, too—and he, too, could not make it. He could neither acquiesce in the spinelessness then prevailing in London, nor could he quit his job, lest the last line of British resistance should break.

Upon his return from Moscow where Stalin, who rarely receives European diplomats, had treated him with the astonished friendliness of a jungle chieftain confronted for the first time with a white man, Eden suffered a heart attack. He had to take to his bed for a rest. The official explanation was that the airplane in which he flew back from Moscow had been so badly battered by air storms that Eden's heart was affected. One may be permitted to believe that it did not take an air storm to affect the heart of a man in Eden's tragic dilemma.

His delicate state of health forbade his accompanying Mac-

Donald and Sir John Simon to Stresa. This, again, is the official version. He would certainly not have consented to the
British delegation's decision not to raise the Abyssinian question. Stresa was widely hailed as a success for the policy of
keeping Germany at peace by encircling her with overwhelming power. In fact Stresa was eyewash. The fundamental difficulty, arising out of the Duce's aggressions, was not even
alluded to. The collaboration among the Western democ-
racies and the Southern dictator was cancerous from the outset. Stresa, in fact, had no other result than the strengthening of Mussolini's bargaining position with Hitler. Mussolini could delude the softy MacDonald and the imperturbable Sir John Simon. He knew that he would not have fooled
Eden. He hated Eden before he ever met him.

Even the patient, sleepwalking English people were fed
up at last with the MacDonald-Simon combination. Reluctantly, Baldwin had again to come into the foreground. He
reshuffled the cabinet. Sir Samuel Hoare followed Simon and
Eden became Minister for League of Nations Affairs. British
foreign policy was now under dual control: it did not work
quite harmoniously. Sir Samuel Hoare inherited not only
his predecessor's office, but also most of his inhibitions and,
above all, his total indifference to the Nazi virus. Eden, on
the other hand, used his newly won ministerial independence to achieve solid international settlements. He proved his
tenacity of purpose and great patience in negotiations, combined with firmness of attitude. At the age of thirty-eight,
which he had by then reached, he was emerging from strokes
of good and bad fortune, a perfectly matured man.

"One man has stood out with courage and consistency for
the translation of the ideals of the post-war peace system into
realities," wrote the *Spectator* at this time. "At thirty-eight,
Mr. Eden has won a position for himself at home and abroad

that no man of comparable age has achieved in our time. The fundamental cause is his deep sincerity. Politicians in England have ceased to believe in anything. Anthony Eden believes passionately in the League of Nations. It is that essential disinterestedness and honesty of purpose that has impressed the foreigners. They feel that Albion could never be perfidious if Eden was in charge of her affairs."

To most of his senior cabinet colleagues, however, he was still the blue-eyed boy, irrespective of the fact that his eyes are dark brown. The elderly gentlemen were isolationist minded. Many of them never left England, and they could ill conceal their slight condescension toward the government's traveling salesman. Why, if the "young man on the flying trapeze," as one of the amiable colleagues called Eden, was hell-bent on personal contacts—why, by Jove, didn't he visit Mussolini? The meeting was arranged. It was doomed to failure, exactly as certain jealous elements in the cabinet had hoped.

Indeed, the interview in Rome went off even worse than was expected. Benito's outstanding quality is his maniac vanity. Now "Il Duse," to use Walter Winchell's unforgettable word, was confronted by a young Hollywood star—or so Eden looked to Mussolini's crude perceptions. This fellow Eden had the truly British impertinence to be neither hard-faced nor overweight. He looked odiously perfect. Edda, the Duce's daughter, seemed to feel differently about Eden's perfection. The Cianos took the English guest to dinner in Ostia. They sat on the terrace of a fashionable hotel, and everyone around them giggled. Indeed, Countess Edda Ciano, conspicuous in her white dress and bright red hat, forgot about her meal as she devoured dear Anthony with her eyes. Her husband remained unperturbed. He is an understanding type, whether it is his wife or his father-in-law who is preparing a conquest.

Demonstratively Mussolini sped up his Abyssinian preparations during the British Cabinet Minister's stay in Rome.
Count Ciano remarked to the playboys in the lobby of the
Hotel Esplanade, out of whose ranks he had emerged to become Fascism's son-in-law: "Boy, oh, boy, you certainly
learn shoulder shrugging!" Maybe he only had the Abyssinian venture in mind, which he, with the sharp wit you
acquire in the Esplanade, considered a dangerous blunder.

Mussolini knew that he could safely disregard Eden. When
the British cabinet reshuffle came to pass, England was already half pledged—and France, under Laval, fully committed—to go back on the League of Nations and support the
aggression against Abyssinia. The new government in London was trapped. Sir Samuel Hoare made an abortive effort
to free his hands. At the September session in Geneva, Britain stated that she was prepared to stand by the League principles to the full.

The attempt failed. Sir Samuel Hoare looked for a compromise to prevent Italy from joining up with Germany. He
did not understand that an abyss divided the peace front
from the gangster front. He attempted to bridge the abyss
with petty politics. After the invasion of Abyssinia had
started, Sir Samuel made a declaration of British determination in Geneva, which nobody could take seriously. Immediately he returned to London, leaving Eden, the League of
Nations Minister, behind to cajole the delegates for six long
weeks and to impress them with England's sincerity and determination. Thus Eden became identified with the sanctions. Mussolini stigmatized him as public enemy number
one.

The French and English governments worked out the
Hoare-Laval plan which conceded to Mussolini the better

part of Abyssinia. It was Eden's duty to lay the plan before the League Council. He did so, but he refused to say a single word in its favor.

This plan of shameful surrender in the end outraged the patient English people. Sir Samuel Hoare, its co-author, had to go. Eden became Foreign Secretary. Baldwin could not well have promoted anyone else. Besides, Eden owed this advancement primarily to the mounting influence of Neville Chamberlain, then Chancellor of the Exchequer, who was already singled out to succeed Baldwin. Mr. Neville Chamberlain had known and liked Eden since both had entered politics, the one in his fiftieth year, the other at the age of twenty-two. Perhaps the distrustful, secluded man with the face of a raven enjoyed dear Anthony's facility. Certainly he appreciated Eden's vote-getting qualities, which had just gloriously stood another test. After the General Election in 1935, many a Tory member shook hands with Eden, assuring him: "You have done me a lot of good in my constituency." Furthermore, Mr. Chamberlain felt sure that he could always handle easily the likable featherweight. Although he had already expressed his opinion that England should not commit herself any further on the continent of Europe, Neville Chamberlain still wanted to cash in on the popular enthusiasm that the League of Nations idea and its chief spokesman aroused.

Anthony Eden took the Foreign Office under extremely difficult circumstances. France was against him, and so were some of the most influential members of his own cabinet. The conscience of the British people furnished his only support, when, by intense personal efforts, he rallied the League of Nations to economic sanctions. But he was not able to put through oil sanctions, the only ones that mattered. The elder cabinet colleagues stopped him. Grown rather cynical during the many years they had observed the European scene, they felt, rightly, that none of the League members would fight a war to enforce oil sanctions. No nation would go to war for the much-vaunted collective security. They would, at best, fight if individually attacked. This scepticism was fully borne out by the events that followed. The tragedy of Europe's neutrals and little nations is entirely self-caused, since they preferred to lie low and be devoured piecemeal. But Eden argued in the cabinet that it was England's task to set the example and act as the center of resistance. He would awake the world's conscience. Unfortunately, he could not even wake Stanley Baldwin who, in his last months in power, used to take a peaceful nap during his cabinet conferences. Eden's own government declined to limit Italy's oil-imports, thus making a sorry farce of the whole business of sanctions. Besides, Laval had promised Mussolini never to agree to this measure. "If Mussolini can't fight in Abyssinia he will make war on England!" he declared. Eden understood that oil sanctions would have broken Fascism. The chain of further aggressions, he foresaw, would be nipped in the bud. But Haile Selassie collapsed while Geneva was split; London super-cautious, Paris treacherous. Eden was defeated, the League discredited, collective security shattered. The small nations had heard from Mr. Chamberlain, Great Britain's coming man, that they could never again count on English help. Mussolini, of course, ended in Hitler's arms.

It was a desperate situation. In restoring it Eden proved that he had grown to full stature. After Laval's fall he reestablished closer relations with France. He even approached Russia. Litvinov promised co-operation; he developed into the chief advocate of "indivisible peace." In his two modest rooms in the Kremlin, which Stalin had converted into an

Asiatic quarter for his private use, tovarich number one may well have laughed about the white men's funny preoccupations. The Spanish War broke out. Together with Léon Blum, Eden proposed a general treaty of non-intervention. Everyone nodded agreement. Then Berlin sent the "Condor" flying-squad to Spain; strong-arm detachments of the Gestapo followed. Mussolini dispatched troopships bulging with human cargo. The wretched Italian soldiers in these bottoms were betrayed. They had been told that they were off for a frolic of head-hunting in Abyssinia. Russia had just a few airplanes to spare, but unloosed thousands of Commissars. "A leaky dam is better than no dam at all!" Anthony Eden consoled himself, and the world. In the midst of adversities and failures he never lost his poise.

Neither the adversities nor the failures were of his making. His powers as Foreign Secretary seemed unlimited since Mr. Baldwin no longer exercised the Prime Minister's privilege of directing foreign affairs. On the surface he let his blue-eyed boy do the job. But this semblance of independence was deceptive. Since the Prime Minister persistently dodged the issues, Eden had to take up all important matters with the full cabinet. Perhaps some critics were right in their repeated assertions that Baldwin had made him Foreign Secretary too early. In the councils of government, Eden could only suggest various courses. He had to leave the decisions to much older colleagues who were all obsessed with the idea that dangers had to be deferred, and never challenged. Eden, and the younger generation with him, believed that dangers could be averted only by showing one's teeth. But England, in her woeful state of moral and material disarmament, had not much to show by way of teeth, anti-aircraft guns and war planes. So Eden was in the tragic position of wanting to conduct a strong policy without the force to back it up.

One must bear this situation in mind to understand Anthony Eden's gravest sin of omission—his silence when Hitler tore up Locarno, after having voluntarily confirmed the treaty, and remilitarized the Rhineland. The German generals who led their troops into Rhenania carried sealed orders to be opened at the first shot. These orders, signed by Hitler, commanded their immediate retreat if they should encounter armed resistance. At that time Germany would not yet wage a war. It was the God-given moment to prevent the mass slaughter of a second World War, and to eradicate the Nazi pest from the face of the earth. "We will clutch ourselves into the German earth, retiring step by step," Rudolf Hess, Hitler's lieutenant, threatened. It was Nazism's maximum threat—and an empty one. The German people—still unwilling Nazis—would gladly have wrung their home-grown oppressors' necks. Only suicidal folly could prevent world democracy from using the unique opportunity. On this very suicidal folly Hitler gambled. His bluff was not called.

At the height of perversion, English public opinion asked why the Germans should not occupy their own soil with their own army. Shrewd Nazi propaganda, largely supported by truly innocent American "liberalism," had aroused their conscience about Versailles. In fact Versailles was the mildest and weakest peace victors have ever imposed on the vanquished. Only a few border-provinces, settled by restive minorities, had been sliced off from the Reich. And for the ten billion marks in reparations they had to pay, they made good in borrowing and embezzling twenty billion from the English, American and neutral money-lenders. Yet, their "moral cause" was accepted by great majorities in England and America.

Sir Austen Chamberlain, for a few years retired, reappeared to warn Eden that England was committing a grievous mistake. The militarization of the Rhineland would definitely shatter France's supremacy in arms. The only solid basis of peace would be gone. Anthony Eden remained silent. He spoke up no earlier than three weeks after Hitler had declared Locarno a scrap of paper. "I am not prepared to be the first British Foreign Secretary to go back on Britain's signature," he stated. But these proud words were not followed by any action. Undoubtedly, Eden could not swim against the current. He had not what Kipling once called "the essential guts" to turn the tide. Up to this day he has never revealed how he thought and felt when forced to acquiesce in an act of aggression that changed the balance of power in Europe. One can only guess that the darling of the gods was a deeply unhappy man—too well-bred, however, to show his sentiments. He was still regarded as the spokesman of the oppressed, the personification of British understanding and decency to small nations, to minorities and refugees. But the great hope in him was fading.

For a last time he could revive something of this hope by his determined stand at the Conference of Nyon, which decided to clear the Mediterranean of submarine raiders of "unknown nationality"—Italian, of course. Mussolini refused to send a delegation to Nyon, but his submarine pirates vanished without leaving a trace. Then Mr. Neville Chamberlain took over the British government.

Anthony Eden received his new chief with undismayed pleasure. The merchant from Birmingham as Chancellor of the Exchequer and strong man of the old government had frequently supported him. He liked to call himself Eden's elder friend. One of his first acts was to relieve the Foreign Secretary of the duty of reporting all important matters to the cabinet. They would settle England's foreign affairs be-

tween them. Although Mr. Chamberlain's experience was
limited to local and financial administration, he decided to
direct foreign policy. Eden, the popular, vote-getting, handsome young friend would advocate it and carry it out. Two
other promising junior members, Leslie Hore-Belisha at the
War Office, and Alfred Duff-Cooper at the Admiralty, had
similar tasks. Lord Swinton, an old follower of Mr. Chamberlain's, would take good care of the Air Ministry, the importance of which increased rapidly since the gadfly Winston
Churchill raised such an infernal racket. Finally, through
retaining spineless Sir John Simon as Chancellor of the
Exchequer, the personal supervision of the Treasury by the
Prime Minister was also assured.

Neville Chamberlain, to whom power had come late in
life, was a dictator, if of the helplessly faltering type. He
was too narrow-minded and unimaginative to understand the
real dictators, but he did not feel averse to regarding them
as good neighbors. One of his first blunders in international
affairs was to write Mussolini, during the August holiday in
1937, a personal letter full of brotherly feeling. If there was
some fooling about these feelings, Mr. Chamberlain must
have erred as to who would be fooled. He was growing ever
more impatient to remove old enmities and establish personal contacts, lest war become inevitable. Disregarding his
dignity abroad, which he stressed so firmly at home, he did
not mind how many snubs he got. He considered it his duty
to accept them and to renew his efforts and offers.

Once more Eden was condemned to watch disastrous dilet-
tantism. He understood that running after dictators only
convinced them that Britain was frightened. His world-wide
personal contacts revealed to him how rapidly England was
losing, first the confidence of her friends, then her friends al-

together. In view of the Duce's systematic and unblushing perjury, he resented Chamberlain's eager professions of friendship toward Mussolini. He soon felt powerless in his office, but matters were still worse when he was not present. Mr. Chamberlain used the occasion of a short visit of Eden's to Paris to give an unfavorable answer to certain confidential suggestions from Washington which he knew Eden would gladly have accepted. He did not even inform his Foreign Secretary of the incident. Eden had to learn of it from documents.

The situation was unbearable. The elder friend had turned out to be a stubborn boss, unflinchingly determined to go his way to ruin without accepting advice from his responsible adviser in the Foreign Office. The open breach came over the acceptance of Mussolini's demand that the English must come to Rome to talk peace "now or never." Eden refused pointblank to be bullied into an agreement that would give Italy direct advantages and, by the same token, expose England to new shame. But this refusal was the very drop that made the bucket overflow. After a prolonged war of nerves, the breach between Chamberlain and Eden might as well have come over the dispatch of Halifax to Berlin or over a showdown of British strength in the Mediterranean, which Eden advocated. In fact, it seems that the ultimate motive that shook Eden out of his painfully preserved complacency was entirely unconnected with Mussolini. In his famous speech of resignation on February 21, 1938, he lifted the veil of diplomatic secrecy just enough to refer to his disagreement with Chamberlain with the words: "Within the last few weeks upon a most important decision of foreign policy which did not concern Italy at all the difference was fundamental." The House buzzed with whis-

pered speculation. Was there a new disaster to come? Three
weeks later Hitler invaded Austria. The series of German
aggressions had begun.

His speech of February 21, 1938, became the most famous
utterance in his entire career. Yet the importance of this
speech lies rather in what Eden left unsaid. His decision to
part from Chamberlain was more than the end of a basically
unsound friendship. It was more than a personal disappointment to both. It revealed the cleavage between England's
older and younger generations. At forty-one, a little worn
out by years of self-imposed, but deeply resented, restraint,
still rigid, if entirely easy in his bearing, in a low voice with
occasionally strong accents, he proclaimed the demands of
those who had not yet resigned themselves to apathy. "I do
not believe that we can make progress in European appeasement if we allow the impression to gain currency abroad that
we yield to constant pressure." But he did not go beyond
hinting at generalities. He carefully omitted any word that
might have been construed as an attack on the man who had
forced him out of office. Neville Chamberlain was no longer
his friend, but as his party's chief he still commanded Eden's
respect.

The speech followed the act of resignation by forty-eight
hours. Once more a private member, Eden spoke from his
seat on the back-bench next to the gangway. On this gangway crouched his Parliamentary Private Secretary, handsome
young Jim Thomas, Jimmy-boy to Westminster. Jimmy listened respectfully to his master's voice. But somehow he
seemed disappointed. He was a youngster of real youth,
neither polished nor restrained, not schooled by years of
responsibility. Dear Anthony seemed a trifle artificial next
to him. Why did Eden not burst out? Why did he not risk

a "damn it all!" It would have been easier, but considerably less cricket.

The most "cricket" family in England, next to the dynasty, is the Cecil clan. Bobetty is a Cecil. Bobetty, of course, was Lord Cranborne, Eden's Under Secretary in the Foreign Office. Faithful to dear Anthony he resigned with him. But now he stole the show.

The House was stunned as Bobetty, of all people, in his "personal explanation," showed the driving force they had been expecting in vain from Mr. Eden. "I am afraid that to enter on official conversation with the present Italian government would be regarded not as a contribution to peace, but as a surrender to blackmail." Fancy Bobetty saying that!

Never would Anthony Eden have used an expression like "surrender to blackmail." He silently tugged at his moustache, as had become rather a habit with him since Hitler's access to power. He had obviously been bettered by Bobetty. But he smiled at his *fidus Achates*. Good boy!

Another back-bencher next to him did not content himself with a smile. On his rotund cheeks the scars of his latest motor accident flashed dark red with excitement. So pleased was Winston Churchill to hear the genuine Cecil ring again. A Cecil—Lord Hugh—Bobetty's uncle, had been his own political discoverer, the most intimate friend he had ever had, and best man at his wedding. Lord Hugh Cecil had meanwhile retired to top a life of exquisite wisdom as provost of Eton, far from politics. But the tradition of the clan carried on. This was the true Cecil touch. Winston Churchill rose to shake hands with Bobetty. Anthony Eden had just delivered the speech of his life. But everybody looked at Churchill and Bobetty.

Anthony no longer tugged at his moustache. His hand was

quiet. Peace was on him. He hates the limelight. He is happy to have the show stolen. He sank into silence.

The most faithful among his followers did not quite understand this silence. A dangerous word went the rounds: Anthony is half a hero . . . Gilbert Murray, famous translator of Greek tragedies and champion of the League of Nations, offered an explanation. "There is one figure in British political life," he wrote, "which stands out from the overtired and slightly discredited cabinet members as somewhat different in quality. There is a feeling that Mr. Eden was right and the cabinet from which he resigned was wrong. He is an object of interest in the general dullness, a hope in the midst of continual bad news. He, at least, tried to stand firm, and to put an end to the long retreat. If only he would speak out . . . If only one could be sure what he wanted . . . If only he did not remain an enigma . . ."

The public shared this anxiety. They still expected a tornado from Eden instead of mild spring breezes. After his resignation he addressed a meeting of the League of Nations Union, in London. Throngs packed Queen's Hall and Caxton Hall as well. A third meeting had to be improvised in the open air. Lord Lytton, the chairman, had whetted the listeners' appetite. But Eden in his anxiously awaited speech insisted that the discussion must remain non-partisan and unpolitical, and evaded any attack on Chamberlain. His utterances were sensible and well phrased. But they failed fully to explain his stand. They did not indicate any plans he might have for the future. Thousands had come to get their cue from him. The nation wanted him to lead. He refused leadership. In concluding, he did not receive more than polite applause, whereas Lady Violet Bonham Carter's caustic sallies, which followed, swept the audience.

Seven months later Munich interrupted Eden's silence.

Now was the propitious moment for a return. Dozens of dissident Conservatives were ready to desert Neville Chamberlain. The government itself was divided. Duff-Cooper resigned in protest. Hore-Belisha was on the brink of resignation. Walter Elliott, Oliver Stanley, W. S. Morrison, Malcolm MacDonald were ready to follow suit. Outside the cabinet Churchill mustered his shock troops: Lord Wolmer, Leopold Amery and a score of others. The Liberals under Sir Archibald Sinclair, and most of the Labourites declared their willingness to fall in line if Eden wanted to lift the banner.

Munich had been signed on September 30, 1939. On the Monday following, October the third, in the evening hours, Anthony Eden rose to deliver the speech that had been overdue for more than half a year. The House was already tiring from the stormy debate throughout the day, yet its nervous attention kindled again when it heard the well-modulated voice, long familiar, and now long missed.

After three-quarters of an hour the House was half asleep. Eden had not delivered a fighting speech; he had preached a sermon. He mixed eulogy, comment and criticism of Neville Chamberlain. His eulogy and comment were outspoken; his criticism was oblique and gentlemanly. The leitmotiv was *Unity*. "If there ever was a time for a united effort by a united nation, it is my conviction that the time is now!" was the pillar of his argument. Next morning the speech read better in the newspapers than it had sounded to an overstrained audience.

But next morning Bobetty, too, was back again. Lord Cranborne looked pale with shame and suppressed passion. He took Munich as a personal insult. "Peace with honor?" he lashed out. "Peace the Prime Minister certainly has brought back to us. But where is the honor? I have looked and looked, but I cannot see it!"

Was it as certain as that that Chamberlain had brought back peace from Munich? Winston Churchill did not conceal his grave doubts. But he carefully refrained from pouring oil on the flames. On the contrary, while a majority in the House was openly disappointed in Eden, the old warrior praised him as the "one outstanding young man of the generation that has been ravaged by the war."

"What about Hore-Belisha?" a Labourite shouted.

For the first and probably last time in his life, Leslie Hore-Belisha lowered his head and hid in embarrassment.

Anthony Eden, England was agreed, had missed the bus. They did not quite understand that a gentleman of such exquisite quality was not in the habit of traveling by bus. Certainly Eden wanted to reach the terminus—Premiership. But he was constitutionally unable to ride the wave of a popular upheaval. It was no secret that Baldwin had changed his political testament, crossing out the name of Sir Samuel Hoare as the eventual successor to Neville Chamberlain, and replacing his name by the two words: Anthony Eden. Dear Anthony might have believed that Earl Baldwin's will would some day get him more safely, and in better company, to number ten. But what might become of himself was certainly not his prime consideration. He could not split the Conservative Party to which, he felt, he owed his entire career. True, all his worries also had always come from the appeasement-ridden Conservative camp. He had slowly formed the habit of swallowing deceptions and carrying on in good bearing so as not to mar the team-work. The crucial question that now confronted him was the logical outcome, indeed the quintessence, of a dilemma that had pursued him all his life in office. He has always had considerably more vision than his friends, his patrons, his colleagues. But he be-

longed to them. With his eyes wide open he belonged to the
blind men. Now was the last moment to make up his mind
whether to acquiesce as a gentleman or to fight as a patriot.

He showed more self-restraint than ambition when he decided not to oppose Neville Chamberlain. It was a grave
decision. He breathed uneasily. He took a trip to the United
States.

His visit to this country in the winter of 1938 was strictly
unofficial. Yet Americans donned their Sunday best to welcome Prince Charming. Eden, unfortunately, had to disap-
point some dowagers and prospective hostesses. He showed
more interest in the social reforms of the New Deal than in
the gaiety of the smart set. This well groomed English gentleman became ever more confusing. He dashed to visit housing projects and exposed his immaculate white tie in nightly
wanderings through the slums. There was much headshaking
over him. Most determinedly the State Department shook
their heads when the discreet question arose, whether Mr.
Eden might be welcome as Britain's next ambassador. There
was no need for him in the capital. Washington has its own
old charmer.

It was widely believed that Eden's trip across the ocean
would be just a cooling-off period. On his return he would
join the Chamberlain cabinet again and use the lessons he
had learned in Roosevelt's America as British Minister of
Labour. The Ministry of Labour is notoriously a political
graveyard. Neville Chamberlain was unafraid of burying his
young friend there. He longed so much to have him back—
in safety, not as an uncontrollable political free-lancer. But
the outbreak of the war disturbed this plan. Now Anthony
Eden was wanted for a job that demanded both his unfaltering patriotism and all his powers of persuasion. He became

Secretary for the Dominions "with special access to the war cabinet."

Again he had an opportunity to use fully his gift for making friends. He invited every Dominion to send permanent representatives to London, thus, by the same token, tying the Dominions closer to the war effort in common and giving them greater opportunity to wield their influence in the councils. When the first Canadian troops landed on English shores, Eden was there to welcome them. Now there were no more inhibitions. Joyfully Eden embraced the Empire-idea.

When Winston Churchill stepped on the bridge, he made Eden his War Minister. In the short time he held this office, Eden played a much more important role than is generally realized. General Wavell came to London to complain about his difficult position in Egypt, which after the fall of France threatened to become untenable. He needed more men, more armaments and munitions, and he needed them immediately. Sir Archibald Wavell is no parlor general. Besides, he holds no brief for politicians. His conversations in Westminster did not go off well. The impression he made in not mincing words and in pointing out the imminence of danger awakened—strange as it seems now—some doubt whether he was the right man for the difficult job in Cairo.

Eden prevented the minor catastrophe that Wavell's recall, then dangerously near, would have brought about. It is hard to imagine two men more different than dear Anthony and the gruff, short, somewhat brusque Sir Archibald. Yet they understood each other at first glance. Eden strongly supported the General's demands. The majority of the war cabinet feared that it would be too dangerous to denude the British Isles of important war matériel, as the invasion seemed in the making. But Churchill, whose delight in action

and adventure remains unrestrained by his realistic shrewd-
ness, decided for Eden. Vital convoys were dispatched to
Egypt. General Wavell could prepare his offensive.

Eden flew to Cairo to watch the preparations personally.
Cairo is a hotbed of axis espionage. The German spy-masters
received hundreds of reports as to the places Eden was going,
the modest number of drinks he had, and even photographs
showing dear Anthony's smile of perfect insouciance. The
German High Command was elated to have a playboy in the
job of British War Secretary. Sir Archibald Wavell confessed
later that he could not have struck without Eden's invaluable
help.

Almost at once a new crisis arose. Greece had entered the
war and was badly in need of airplanes and supplies. Again
Eden acted as spokesman for the Greek demands in the London war cabinet. Again Winston Churchill backed him up.
In spite of the gravest handicaps, England discharged her
moral obligation toward her heroic little ally to the full.

The choice of Lord Halifax as ambassador brought Eden's
career in the War Office to a sudden end. For the second
time he was his Prime Minister's natural choice for the now
orphaned Foreign Office. He was back again in the large
room with the high ceiling and huge windows on two sides,
which is really his home. Both the room and its master look
a little old-fashioned. The predominant colors in the room
are deep reds and browns with touches of gilt on the ceiling
and along the edges of the wall panels. At one end there are
two large oak doors, one leading to the red-carpeted corridor,
the other to the room occupied by Mr. Eden's two private
secretaries. In winter a coal fire burns in the spacious, ancient
fireplace with its marble mantelpiece and overhanging gilt-
framed mirror. Two mahogany tables, a dozen chairs covered

in red leather, large bookshelves and the Foreign Secretary's desk make up the furniture.

Mr. Anthony Eden looks true to type in these surroundings of marble and mirrors and gilded armchairs. Undoubtedly, the young man looks a little *vieux jeu*. They don't come quite so precious in our times. But his face is tense with energy. His carefully chosen words are to the point. His every minute is closely organized. His desk is littered with the small red boxes that flow into his room in a constant stream. They contain dispatches, memoranda, reports from all corners of the world. Studying these papers, writing "minutes" upon them, discussing them—so Anthony Eden makes history. He does not, incidentally, confine himself to his desk. When the war threatened to engulf the Balkans and the Near East, he visited Cairo, Athens, Ankara. Belgrade would not admit him. It was a suicidal mistake on the part of the Jugoslavs. A few weeks after they had snubbed him, their new government frantically asked him to come. But by then they were already done for. Eden's companion on his journey was not some grey-haired dignitary as would befit a Foreign Secretary. It was Sir John Greer Dill, Chief of the Imperial General Staff. This proves that Anthony Eden, wherever he goes, is constantly on Adolf Hitler's track.

This is the story of Eden's private life. It might read disappointingly, since it contains nothing but war activities, parliamentary and military battles, and a rich record of work. There should be more to the story of a handsome young man. Life, after all, is full of possibilities. Once the author asked Mrs. Eden about her husband's private life. "Private life?" she repeated. Then she smiled a bitter-sweet smile. "Of course he has a private life. Sundays he sometimes takes an hour or two off for tennis."

But that was before the war, when he had plenty of time.

Churchill's Man Friday

SIR ARCHIBALD SINCLAIR

ST. GEORGE, THE DRAGON-SLAYER, RIDES AGAIN. IN HIS LATEST reincarnation, the knight without fear and without reproach is a tall, handsome, Scottish nobleman, half American by descent, with a thin, chiseled face, a wealth of black hair falling on to his high forehead, a Celt with the profile of a Roman statue. He stands well over six feet. His Olympic build is not marred by an ounce of fat. He is fifty-one years old, but looks at least a decade younger. A famous American commentator, Raymond Gram Swing, once called him "something of an intellectual version of Jimmy Walker in his prime." With all due respect to Messrs. Swing and Walker, this was distinctly an understatement. The Right Honorable Sir Archibald Henry MacDonald Sinclair has not a touch of Tammany. Nor could one easily imagine him co-ordinating the garment industry in the world's new fashion center. He is out to slay the dragon. He was born for the job. A knight who answers to the name of Sir Archibald cannot breathe the same air with the fat, monstrous, misshapen dragon whose name is Hermann, and whose ambition—don't laugh—is to become Nazi King of England. One of them must be shot down from the air: the founder of the Luftwaffe or the British Air Minister.

81

The gentlemen in the New York garment industry might well smile at Sir Archibald's appearance. He does not wear the season's fashions. He sticks to an old-fashioned outfit that contrasts amazingly with the youthful expression of his stream-lined face, with its pugnacious nose, firm fighting lips, il-luminated by burning dark eyes. He always wears black. He prefers a bow tie and wing collar. He is a trifle stagey, some critics have remarked. But he is not stagey enough. You would, indeed, expect him to appear in shining armor. No such appearance is on record; whereas his German counter-part, given a ceremonial occasion, is wont to cram his three hundred pounds of flesh into white silk with golden breast plates. "Lohengrin . . . Or, rather, Parsifal." His personal mouthpiece, the *Essener National Zeitung,* once adulated him. Hermann Goering, it is well known, devours his paper from cover to cover—before it is printed.

When he is at home Sir Archibald enjoys wearing the kilt. So do his sons, Robin, aged eighteen, and Angus, a sixteen-year-old Eton boy. With their sisters, Elizabeth and Cath-erine, now nurses,—Catherine, incidentally, is both an artist and a trained farmer—they form a happy family group, cir-cling around the sun of the beautiful wife and mother, Lady Sinclair, "the fightingest woman in Scotland," a tireless and enthusiastic campaigner for her husband. There was a lot of hunting and fishing around Thurso Castle, Caithness, high up in the northernmost county of Scotland. On holidays the members of the Sinclair clan enjoyed themselves sawing wood. A good time was had by all.

It is almost a year since Sir Archibald has worn the kilt. He has not been at home for as long as that. He sleeps on a cot in his London office. He sleeps three to four hours a night, air-raids permitting, and providing that Winston Churchill does not have a brain-wave just before dawn. In

SIR ARCHIBALD SINCLAIR

that case, Sir Archibald must, of course, step across to No. 10. He is one of the war lord's closest collaborators, and certainly, among the veterans who shared Winston's path in politics, his most intimate and most trusted friend.

Undoubtedly it is Britain's Air Minister who has the toughest job in this war. The odds weigh 15 to 1 against the R.A.F. if you believe a recent statement issued by the German High Command. And if you don't believe it, which is always wiser, a few months ago it still seemed to the layman that the R.A.F. was outnumbered 1 to 4, or possibly 1 to 5. One must bear this sad relation in mind to understand, not only the tremendous difficulties of Sir Archibald's historic task, but the essence of his activities as well.

Sir Archibald Sinclair presides over the Air Council, a small group of men in whose capable hands lies the management of Britain's air force. They include Captain H. H. Balfour, Under Secretary for Air, Air Chief Marshal Sir Hugh Dowding and another dozen ranking officers of the R.A.F. Their duties are manifold. There are the problems of operations, of offensive and defensive actions against the enemy, and the supplying of everything the force needs in the way of equipment, armament and instruments. Last but not least, the Air Council must see that the supply of airmen keeps pace with the expansion of aircraft production.

It is permissible to divulge some of the major problems that have confronted the Air Council at crucial stages of the aerial war. An indispensable aim of British air strategy is to force the Luftwaffe to vacate their Channel air bases for landing grounds deeper in occupied territory and in Germany proper, thus reducing their striking power. This is the reason for the nightly, and sometimes daily, savage attacks on enemy aerodromes, all the way along the German-occupied coasts of the Atlantic and the North Sea. Of course a healthy pounding of Berlin would be much more spectacular. But the value of strategic attacks is infinitely greater than the wanton destruction of densely populated civilian areas in which the "bandits" indulge. "Bandits" is R.A.F. slang for the German air killers.

Other concerns of the Air Council include the springing of one or two new, secret air weapons on the enemy at the strategic moment. Further, the distribution of available planes in the right proportions to match German air strength from Iceland to Africa. Finally, the devising of a method whereby great numbers of planes may be used at the same time without having the formations too unwieldy. Owing to the numerical superiority of the Luftwaffe, this latter problem bothers the Germans, it seems, more than the R.A.F. Thus far in the war, major air clashes have usually turned into a series of dogfights, in which the British bring their better equipment and their infinitely higher individual courage into play. However, experts on both sides hope for progress in organizing air battles to the point where the formations can act with the precision of shock cavalry of the old-time ground armies.

Next to these grave and great problems, to which Sir Archibald devotes most of his twenty-hour working day, there are a great number of minor, but no less essential, questions to be tackled. He quickly became famous for the aggressive spirit in which he "goes at it." His is the inspiration, indeed, which has converted the R.A.F. into the finest fighting force in England's proud history. Before Churchill brought his intimate friend and follower into his cabinet, the spirit of the R.A.F. was somewhat marred by half-heartedness and indecision on the part of the former government. "Don't hit them, and perhaps they won't hit us!" was the guiding rule—not spoken aloud, but strictly enforced. The boys of the R.A.F. were, of course, anxious to show their mettle. Eager, and sometimes unruly, they demanded permission to raid Germany. The permission came. But they were not allowed to drop anything more dangerous than propaganda leaflets.

Once a British pilot came back prematurely from such a leaflet raid. It happened that Sir Archibald Sinclair's predecessor was at the aerodrome. Somewhat embarrassed, the pilot excused his early return. "My distributor did not work," he explained. "So I dropped my leaflets in whole parcels and made rapidly for home!"

"Did you say you dropped them in whole parcels," Sinclair's predecessor exclaimed. "Goodness, didn't you consider that such a parcel is heavy and that you might have hurt somebody?"

This attitude has completely changed. With the advent of Churchill and his crew, England toughened up overnight, Sir Archibald always a few steps ahead. The measures he introduced to get the R.A.F. working in high gear seem sometimes unorthodox. Bombing practice on living targets is one of them.

The living targets are three men in a little yellow armored motorboat. There are many of these target boats in use. They can be seen all around the coasts and bays of Britain. They do twenty knots, and are smaller than any elusive German craft that might be used for the much-heralded invasion. When the daily practice time comes, they take up their positions. The three men inside each of the target boats are protected by three and a half tons of armor and are equipped with crash-helmets and ear-protectors. The armor covers the wheel-house, the engine-room and the hull. The little boat is packed with a secret, buoyant material that renders it unsinkable. Never has one of them been sunk, but several have been overturned by the force of the bombs from the practising aircraft. The men inside, especially trained for escape, right the craft if it capsizes and, again, they are ready for the next attack. Bombs weighing eleven pounds, enough to dent the armor-plating of the target and give the crew inside an uncomfortable feeling, are rained on them.

The bitter joke is that the aircraft pound the target boats with real bombs. True, the planes have to work hard. The crews in the boats give them a good run for their money. They streak along at full speed, they zig-zag, dodge the bombers, pretending to be German motorboats, the smallest and nimblest objectives the R.A.F. may have to hit in defense of the British coast. The men in the target boats belong to the Marine Craft Section of the R.A.F. They receive the ordinary pay of their rank, and they have contributed immensely in developing the skill of the British bombers. Of course the dangerous game was thought out by Sir Archibald Sinclair himself.

He is indefatigable in inventing ideas, reforming the rules and introducing new measures. His interest embraces the most minute details. He is a strong believer in mobilizing science for the fight. Scientific methods are now widely applied. Sir Archibald has acquired an American discovery— a light that throws out no glare—for reducing the pilot's eye-strain, one of the gravest handicaps in the flying service. Even British pilots are now selected by scientific methods. Whereas until recently it took three months of flying instruction to discover the candidate's personal qualifications, experts on psychology can now tell after an examination of eighty minutes, whether the man is fit for the job. They can even distinguish from the way the candidate behaves when given certain instructions, whether he will make a better fighter or bomber pilot. Some of the tests include grown-up versions of children's games. One test has to be completed in five minutes, whereas the average length of time it takes is twelve minutes. Night flyers, for instance, demand brilliance in everything, plus very special eyesight. The R.A.F. psychology is ninety-five per cent successful.

So was the campaign to cut down accidents. Sir Archibald Sinclair has appointed a Special Research Commission for reducing training accidents. The commission found out that flying aptitude could be discovered before the aspiring pilot ever left the ground. Of all failures to fly, a third are due to the candidate's being "ham-handed" or "lead-footed," which means that he has bad muscular co-ordination, while two-thirds fail for psychical reasons—they simply do not possess the flyer's temperament.

Thanks to this system of precaution, the number of training accidents in the R.A.F. is practically negligible. In the Luftwaffe, on the other hand, where there is no regard for human lives, the relation of casualties during the training period is 4:1. Every fifth German would-be pilot does not live to see his day of action.

How does the R.A.F. know this fact? German casualty lists are never published. Even Lance-Corporal Schmidt's cold-in-the-head is treated as an important military secret. But there are few military secrets the belligerents don't know about each other.

Nowhere is military intelligence so important as in the air war. Sir Archibald, like Winston Churchill, has been an espionage-fan all his life. Under his personal supervision Britain's aerial intelligence has advanced in mighty strides. Photographic reconnaissance is the eyes of the R.A.F., indeed the eyes of the whole British war conduct. Where the bomber goes, the camera went first; recording the building of new enemy aerodromes,. the concentration of German troops, the movements of German warships, the expansion in army plants, the building in shipyards, everything. The omniscient camera used by the British can be adjusted in the air. It is hand-operated and weighs only twenty-eight pounds—sixty pounds less than its German counterpart. It carries film enough for one hundred and twenty-five exposures. The pilot who handles it can take a photograph by flashlight, so sharp that it cannot be distinguished from a similar photograph taken in full daylight. The photographs, incidentally, are usually taken from a height of about thirty thousand feet.

Supplied with all available information, the R.A.F. hammers relentlessly at the enemy's weakest points. Sir Archibald believes in carrying out a "scientific plan of attack." He has neither the disposition, nor for that matter the means, to compete with the German system of wholesale bombing. It takes a great deal of self-restraint to renounce the idea of reprisals when, say, London must suffer terrific blows, and not to have the R.A.F.'s forces diverted to glorious side-shows. Fortunately, Sir Archibald has this self-restraint. He executes a plan which, in his judgment, is slowly but surely crippling the resources of the enemy, and, in its entirety, must inevitably bring them to defeat. German oil storage centers and refineries, aircraft and armament factories, power-stations, dock and railway yards, harbors and lines of communication, are the permanent targets. The German and German-controlled lines of transportation are the weakest link in the Nazi armor. Consequently they get the most relentless battering. Sir Archibald calls it the "blockade by bombs." This crippling of German war resources, pursued with unbreakable determination, irrespective of what Britain must take at home meanwhile, is the first phase of Sinclair's great offensive plan. Once it is completed, the "fighting offensive" will begin, directed at throwing the German and—if they survive until then—the Italian air forces on the defensive, and so preparing the way for daylight operations over Germany—the final phase.

Nobody knows better than the British Air Minister that the execution of this gigantic plan depends largely on American support and supplies. There was, to tell the truth, until a short time ago, a certain amount of grumbling in England over the alleged inferior quality of some American aircraft. Sir Archibald rebuked this unsubstantiated grumbling, energetically. He spoke about the "choicest fruit of American aircraft production," the receipt of which he gladly acknowledged, and he praised "the remarkable performance of the *Martin Maryland* medium bomber, which has shown its ability to outpace Italian fighters attempting to intercept it." He had another word of praise for the "remarkable *Douglas Boston,* which is sufficiently fast and maneuverable to be used as a night fighter as well as a bomber."

His particular interest goes to the Eagle Squadron, this heroic group of American flyers, who have chosen to join the R.A.F. This group is rapidly increasing in numbers. As this is written, two more American-manned squadrons are just being organized.

Sir Archibald has another rather peculiar way of expressing his gratitude and admiration for American help. It is his personal privilege to give the new types of aircraft that come into service, names of his own choosing. He likes to select picturesque names of the Indian and Wild West days of American history. In England, the fighters that are called in the U. S. A. by drab alphabetic and numerical designations, are known by colorful names. Our Curtiss P-36 is their *Mohawk,* our Allison-powered Curtiss P-40 is their *Tomahawk,* our Allison-powered Airacobra, or P-39, their *Caribou,* to say nothing of the pursuit interceptor *Mustang,* or the tubby, squat-nosed, single-seater fighter, made by the Brewster Company, which, to Sir Archibald, is the *Buffalo.* American bombers carry American geographical names as soon as they arrive at their English destination. The Lockheed transport, the first American plane to be used in large numbers by the British, is the *Hudson,* the Martin medium bomber, *Maryland,* whereas its new version will be named *Baltimore.* The Helldiver, originally so called after a Clark Gable picture, has been re-baptized *Cleveland,* and the Douglas DB7 twin-engined medium bomber is the *Boston*—probably because it comes from Santa Monica, California.

Sinclair has another way of popularizing his planes. When a public collection was started to contribute to the building of new planes, he suggested that women and girls with the same Christian names should give "Mary Spitfires" or "Pamela Hurricanes." The idea caught on among British womanhood, as would probably any idea sponsored by the most handsome Minister of the Crown. In a surprisingly short time he has risen nearly to the peak of popularity. He would undoubtedly reach this peak, if he could in the end make up his mind to have Berchtesgaden bombed, just once, for the fun of it.

But here his sense of humor entirely deserts him. "Goering has disgraced his service and his uniform in bombing Buckingham Palace!" he declares.

Sir Archibald's service and uniform have been shining all his life. He is the cavalier, reborn. In his blood the chivalry of the Highlands is happily mingled with the audacity of the New World. For longer than five hundred years the Sinclairs have ruled their lands in Caithness with royal authority. One Sinclair, the Earl of Orkney and Earl of Caithness, was High Admiral of Scotland and, in 1471, presented the Island of

Orkney to the Scottish crown. An eighteenth-century Sinclair, Sir John, first baronet, the first President of the Board of Agriculture, was an agrarian reformer of wide repute all over Scotland, England and Wales. He represented Caithness in Parliament, as does his scion, Sir Archibald, today. During the Napoleonic Wars, Sir John Sinclair issued an inspiring message to the men of Caithness to defend their country, as invasion seemed near. Sir Clarence Granville Sinclair, third baronet, married Miss Mabel Sands of New York. The eldest son of this marriage was born on October 22, 1890. He was christened Archibald Henry MacDonald. To him applies the phrase coined by Mark Twain toward the turn of the century, in introducing young Winston Churchill to a New York lecture audience: "I give you the son of a British father and an American mother—the perfect man."

The heir presumptive to the hundred thousand acres of Caithness was educated at Eton. Afterwards he went to Sandhurst, the English West Point, and was gazetted as a second lieutenant in the 2nd Life Guards, one of the King's most distinguished regiments. But military service to him, as to many sons of the British aristocracy, was a preparation for the real, gentleman's service—the service in politics.

Already, in his early twenties, Sir Archibald took a lively interest in political discussion. He carried on the established Scottish liberal traditions. He was a free-trader by persuasion, and a reformer whose main interest lay in agrarian reform. His personal hobby, however, was in another field. As if he had an early premonition of the supreme task he would one day be called upon to fulfill, he jumped headlong into aviation, which was, in these first years of the century's second decade, still in its infancy. Sir Archibald became one of the first pre-World-War pilots in England.

This was in the heyday of Liberal rule. Mr. Herbert Asquith soon paid attention to the promising newcomer, and another leader in the Liberal camp did more: he offered him his friendship. The friendship of Winston Churchill is a priceless gift. Great men remain utterly lonesome, although, or perhaps because, they are popular favorites. Churchill is reputed to be a convivial, hospitable, jolly good fellow. Yet it is difficult to approach him and almost impossible to keep pace with him. Sir Archibald Sinclair accomplished the impossible. The friendship he struck up with Churchill, when he was in his early twenties and Churchill in his middle thirties, has lasted to this day. It has outlasted tests and blows. Churchill, it is well known, towers above the rules of political "cricket." He quit the Liberal Party, when this group deteriorated into a mere annex of Labour. Sir Archibald did not follow him. Instead, he remained in the party camp and did an excellent inside job in reasserting the last Liberals' independence. Churchill acquiesced in "Imperial protectionism with reservations," since already, at the time of the Ottawa agreement, he sensed that the unity of the British Commonwealth of Nations was what mattered most of all. It is, in the light of what has happened, more than questionable whether this unity, the source of Britain's indomitable strength in this war, could have been maintained, had Ottawa failed to bring the mother country and the Dominions closer together. Looking far ahead of his time, Churchill proudly lowered the tattered banner of Free Trade that he had once waved under different conditions, in a different time, nay, in a different world. Sir Archibald, the gallant Scotsman, on the other hand, felt the necessity of sticking to old traditions. A Scottish baronet does not abandon them— least of all if they happen to be in effect progressive, almost radical.

But the parting of the two men's ways never implied personal misgivings. Gentlemen in English politics remain personal friends even though they may be political adversaries. During his tenure of office as a Liberal Minister, Churchill's closest associate was the Conservative Lord Birkenhead. And when Winston rose to assume the Tory leadership again, there was no man who understood him better than Sir Archibald Sinclair, Leader of the Liberal Party in the House of Commons. This understanding is firmly based on years of personal experience shared in common. Sir Archibald is no blind follower, no yes-man. His Celtic genius has more than once contributed to Churchill's leadership. The relation between the two men has often been compared to that of Socrates and Plato. Indeed, there would be something Greek about them—if both were not so thoroughly British.

When war broke out in 1914, Sir Archibald remembered the message his ancestor, Sir John Sinclair, had given to the men of Caithness. He, too, now sent a message to his friends, exhorting them to resist the Kaiser's hordes at any price and in spite of any sacrifice that might be demanded. The message of the young man, then aged twenty-four, resounded like a trumpet call all over the British Isles. For the first time it expressed that unbreakable determination that pierced the melancholy and anxiety of England's 1914 government. When history repeated itself, Sir Archibald again cut across English indifference. The policy of appeasement found no more determined antagonist—next to Churchill—than the Leader of the Liberal group in the House.

Sir Archibald spent World War number one, from almost the first day to the last, in the trenches. He arrived in France on August 14, 1914. At once he played a heroic part in the skirmishes before Mons. There he gathered first-hand experience in the meaning of a German attack. It helped him in forming a cool and precise opinion when the Blitzkrieg started in May, 1940. In the last war he was in the first line of combat at the Marne, at the Aisne, in the rush for the Channel ports and throughout the first battle of Ypres.

In the spring of 1915, he was posted to the Canadian Cavalry Brigade. Lord Mottistone—then Major-General Sir John Seely—remembers his valor with the words: "I was a witness to the courage, resource and fearless devotion to duty, which won Sir Archibald the Legion d'Honneur and the gratitude of all ranks of the Canadians at the battle of Festubert."

In the autumn of 1915, Sinclair was promoted to Second in Command of the 6th Royal Scots Fusiliers in the 9th Division of Kitchener's First Hundred Thousand. Probably it was more than a lucky coincidence that the Commander of the 6th Fusiliers, at that time, happened to be Lieutenant-Colonel Winston Churchill. They were comrades in arms now, but they did not forget that they were comrades in politics, too. Their fellow officers remember to this day how the Lieutenant-Colonel and his "Second" spent their nights discussing the conduct of the war, and how they regretted that Mr. Asquith's hands were obviously getting too weak to hold the reins. Churchill returned to the home front, the House of Commons, to give this august body a shot in the arm.

Sir Archibald was transferred to the newly formed Cavalry Machine Gun Corps, as Second in Command. He remained there until the Armistice. He was a little lonely now. But a six-foot-tall, dangerously handsome, Scottish laird does not remain lonesome for long. On a brief leave toward the end of the war, he met the girl who ran the British Canteen in Boulogne. Her name was Marigold, and she was the daughter of Lady Angela and the late Colonel J. S. Forbes. The young couple were married as soon as the bugles announced

the Armistice. At Christmas, 1922, Lady Sinclair presented
her husband with a fat, pink baby, nowadays a young knight
of the air, Robin MacDonald by name, heir to five hundred
years of Sinclair glory.

The year 1922 was important to Sir Archibald from another point of view also. He wrested the constituency of
Caithness from the hands of his opponent, and entered Parliament. The exhilaration of the victory over Germany had
just given way to that deep feeling of exhaustion that so
tragically influenced England for the next seventeen years.
But Sir Archibald made his political debut by swimming
against the stream. His maiden speech was devoted to the
necessity of developing a strong British air force, in order to
avert a new catastrophe. The prophet was thirty-two years
old at that time. England was sick to death of war talk, and
Germany still shivered in the throes of a never-accomplished
revolution. The passion for the air that they shared in common brought Winston and Sir Archibald ever closer together.
Churchill, whose driving force had contributed so much to
victory in the war was, so the world believed, in the prime
of his life. Both as Secretary for War from 1919 to 1921, and
as Secretary of State for Colonies, in the subsequent period
from 1921 to 1922, he wielded great power. He shared this
power with Sir Archibald, who was first his Personal Military
Secretary in the War Office, and later his Private Secretary at
the Colonial Office. To Whitehall, he was simply Churchill's
Man Friday. His faithfulness, some critics believed, went a
little too far. Why, did he not even stutter a little, as if to
match Churchill's slight lisp? The lisp has not prevented
Churchill from becoming England's most forceful orator.
Nor did the stutter impede Sir Archibald's irresistible eloquence. He was soon recognized as one of the most skillful

debaters in the House. Today, as then, he shows great courage, at times even aggressiveness, but he keeps perfect control of his temper. He can take punishment smilingly and is never despondent, not even in the most critical moments. His personal charm, his velvet voice and his perfect manners have greatly contributed to his success.

He fought for the revival of the Liberal Party, which, in 1930, made him Chief Whip. It was a losing fight. There was little left of Gladstone's great heritage. Much publicized but mediocre leaders, engaged in constant rivalry, did their best to add to the confusion. The question of supporting MacDonald's first Labour government split the party. The "National Liberals" seceded to the Right. Lloyd George, of course, founded a party of his own, ably and noisily assisted by his son and daughter, both members of Parliament, and by two other members among the six hundred-odd, who still fell victim to his indomitable charm. The bulk of what was left of the Liberals followed Sir Herbert—later Viscount—Samuel. They supported the Labour government; indeed, MacDonald's cabinet was dependent on their vote. Yet Sir Archibald felt that they were treated as the "patient oxen." His relations with Labour, which he officially helped to keep in power, were none too friendly.

His intimacy with Winston Churchill was, of course, not interrupted when the latter went to Canada to breathe a little fresh air and paint the Rocky Mountains, thus expressing what he thought of England's new pink lords. But Churchill, after all, had won his war already and, if he believed that the performance would have to be repeated, he did not divulge it as early as 1929. Churchill's Man Friday was an unwelcome ally to Labour. Much water had to flow under Waterloo Bridge before he and Labour made up.

Today, incidentally, he belongs among the undisputed favorites of the British workingman.

MacDonald took another view of Sir Archibald than did his party. He was tremendously attracted by Sinclair's aristocratic charm. At the peak of his life the ex-rebel and ex-revolutionary was attracted by all that represented traditional British glamour. Nobody represented it more impressively than the laird of Caithness. Besides, both men were Scotsmen first and foremost, Scotsmen above all, both were extremely handsome, if of different types and ages, and both were deeply religious. True, the younger man was born with a silver spoon, whereas the older one had had to fight the hard way. But something in the harmonious climate of England softens such differences. When MacDonald formed his National government in 1931, he offered Sir Archibald the post of Secretary of State for Scotland. It was not a very important job, but one that was close to both their hearts.

For a short time Sir Archibald, it seemed, was wavering. He had not yet made his peace with Labour. But he was afraid that Britain would plunge into grave financial straits, if the Labour influences in the National government were not outbalanced by more sober counsel. Putting the country ahead of party feelings, he accepted MacDonald's offer.

During the almost two years of his tenure of the Scottish Office, he developed that capacity for unlimited work that distinguishes him in the key-position he now holds. He soon proved that he possesses the administrative flair which can pierce irrelevance and reach the core of the essential facts. His department was astonished by his uncanny mastery of details. Yet he did not feel altogether happy. Churchill was on the other side of the fence, and the company in which Sir Archibald now moved was not always an unmixed pleasure. He gladly used the opportunity of the Ottawa agreement, to which as a traditional free-trader he was opposed, to resign from the government. It seemed as if, by taking this step, he was throwing away his political future, since now both the great parties, Tory as well as Labour, believed him to be an unreliable customer. But had not Winston, too, been regarded as a traitor by both the great parties of his time? And was there a better man than Winston? Resigned, but by no means dispirited, Sir Archibald accepted the future as a lifelong, modest back-bencher.

He remained a back-bencher, though not always a modest one, for three years. In 1935, he succeeded Viscount Samuel as Leader of the Liberal group in Parliament. His advancement was not undisputed. Some of his own political friends called him a "likable lightweight, with great personal charm, but minus political reliability." It was exactly the same criticism as that to which Franklin D. Roosevelt was exposed when he first stepped into the White House.

Of course Sir Archibald never rose to the world stature of President Roosevelt. But he made a thoroughly workmanlike job of knitting his party into a tight little group—of not many more than twenty—who made up in honesty and intelligence what they lacked in numbers. Their leader now had an opportunity of making his voice heard as a first-string speaker. He did not miss his opportunity. With all his vigor he switched over to foreign affairs which soon dominated the discussion everywhere. He was still young and had an abundance of physical and mental energy. His judgment, however, was now matured, and everyone understood that here spoke a man who knew his own mind. In England's last years of tragic indecision, this was a rare gift. Sir Archibald's joyous gaiety concealed a keen and resolute spirit. The touch of boldness was always tempered by excellent manners.

His violent attacks on appeasement did not prevent him

from paying tribute to Neville Chamberlain's "courageous social reforms, high spirit of public duty and untiring devotion to the cause of peace." But the spineless toleration of aggression, however, he pointed out, did not make for peace, but for inevitable war.

Winston Churchill was a worried man in those days, deeply conscious of dark forebodings, and lonesome in a country that turned a deaf ear to his "Cassandra" calls. He rarely smiled. But he did smile when his junior partner—a junior, by then late in his forties—launched his attacks in Parliament. Here was another man who developed the Churchill touch. The years of their political intimacy had not been wasted.

Sir Archibald Sinclair's series of incisive speeches on Abyssinia, on the abandonment of the League of Nations, and on what he called the "spiritless" policy toward Hitler, breathed the very essence of modern English radicalism. Suddenly Labour stopped, looked and listened. Here stood a leader in the fight against Neville Chamberlain. He was a young man. He did not belong to the wornout old-timers, who would no longer go down with the working class. Ancient feuds and mutual suspicions were quickly forgotten in the ever-deepening plight of England. There was much talk of forming a coalition government of Liberals, Labour, and rebel Tories, under Sinclair as a "compromise" Prime Minister. But when this talk grew uncomfortably loud, Sir Archibald suddenly retired to Thurso Castle in Caithness; to its last-century romanticism, its endless acres of green pastures and cultivated soil, its cottages of local sandstone. He has never explained why he so suddenly disappeared from the surface—if only for a little while. He did not say: "There is a better man!" Such public resignation would have sounded tactless and obtrusive. But there is little doubt as to the reason why he stepped aside. Six months after the advent of Churchill to power, Sir Archibald jubilantly declared: "Six months of Churchill are six nails in Hitler's coffin!"

Indeed, he played a major part in bringing the Churchill government into being. It was Sir Archibald who unloosed the storm that swept away Neville Chamberlain after the Norwegian disaster. In a speech at Edinburgh he attacked the old government for its "craven and irresolute counsels" and asked a number of searching questions on the ill-fated Norwegian campaign. Historians will some day record that this very speech brought the beginning of Chamberlain's end.

Now Sir Archibald can direct his "gloves off" oratory against the enemy abroad. "Hit the Germans in Germany!" is his slogan. "Many wrecks along enemy coasts and many half-submerged masts testify to the success of the R.A.F." is the account he gives. "The R.A.F. will blaze the way to victory!" is his creed.

Every man in the R.A.F. feels himself closely and personally connected with his leader. Proudly, distinguished officers in the Force may incorporate the Astral Crown, a new heraldic device of Sir Archibald's invention, into their armorial bearings. Sinclair plays no favorites. But there is one group which claims particular intimacy with the chief. It is the County of Surrey Fighter Squadron, whose Honorary Air Commodore for almost five years has been Winston Churchill. Frequently, both in France and in England, old man Winnie inspected his personal squadron, and always in his Air Commodore's uniform. He examined the Hurricanes which the boys fly, shook hands with every pilot, and was, against his habit, mute, when his inquiry after some particular friend met with embarrassed silence. The Surrey Fighter Squadron belongs to the R.A.F.'s shock troops. They have already won a half-dozen D.F.C.'s and another half-dozen D.S.O.'s. When one of these decorations was awarded to a Canadian Flying Lieutenant in the squadron, the lad climbed into his Hurricane and shot down a couple of Jerries in celebration.

As soon as they have shot down their hundredth "bandit," Churchill has promised them he will come to a dinner in honor of the squadron. He will take the evening off, his first free evening since war began. Sir Archibald, it is reported, checks the records of the Surrey Fighter Squadron first, when he receives his daily reports. He, too, will attend the dinner. He will click glasses with Churchill. And for the dream of a short evening, in a bomb-menaced aerodrome mess, it will again be like the old days.

Miraculous Metamorphosis

SIR KINGSLEY WOOD

IMAGINE HENRY FORD ABOLISHING CAPITALISM OR JIM FARLEY entirely abandoning the Democratic Party. If your imagination is equal to it you have gauged the metamorphosis of Sir Kingsley Wood, Chancellor of the Exchequer, the man who forges the silver bullets with which, once again, England will win the war. For fifty-eight years Sir Kingsley has lived the life and preached the creed of capitalism. In his fifty-ninth year he has, to use his own phrase, "liquidated the millionaire." For fifty-eight years he was both product and prophet of dark blue Conservatism, climaxing a career of unquestioning devotion to the Party as one of the highest Tory dignitaries. In his fifty-ninth year he delivered a speech in the House that brought the Labour members to their feet to give him a solemn ovation. On the Conservative benches, however, many a bewildered face expressed its understanding: Now I am broke . . . It must be added, to the lasting honor of Conservative landowners, shipping magnates, business executives, that they don't care whether they are broke or not as long as they are helping to break Hitler. This was not always so. They have changed as miraculously as has their Chancellor.

SIR KINGSLEY WOOD

The fifty-ninth year of Sir Kingsley Wood's life coincides with the second year of the war. On April 7, 1941, the Chancellor of the Exchequer introduced what a highly-placed American observer termed "the most gigantic budget Great Britain has ever faced," a budget, indeed, that takes almost the last penny out of the rich man's pocket and makes England a poor man's country. If a Labourite had done it the City would have suffered a serious attack of jitters. However, since it was Sir Kingsley, everyone understands that war transforms people and problems, and that England must go the hard way into a better future.

Before the war, Sir Kingsley's was the easy way. He and good fortune are on the best of terms. Success is a habit with him. Conditions and circumstances have always favored him. He was the happy-go-lucky type of British politician. Life has made him neither hard nor bitter. On the contrary, he was the softest-spoken man in the United Kingdom, diminutive in stature, Pickwickian in appearance, with some rather comic physical characteristics. Throughout his entire career he has managed to disguise successfully how dynamic he is in action. He is a living English understatement.

Today, he looks plump, rotund, chubby. His white hair is slightly curly. His eyes peer curiously from behind thick glasses. Sometimes they look astonished, and occasionally hurt, at the wickedness of the world. But his double-chin proves that he has not fared so badly in this wicked world. His waistline shows no sign of undernourishment. A heavy gold watch-chain, stretched over the belly, gives a strong impression of solidity.

He looks like a kind-hearted minister of the Church rather than the sharp-witted minister of the Crown he is. Indeed, he was destined for the clergy. His father, a Wesleyan preacher in the south of England, decided on the very day he baptized little Kingsley in his own chapel that the boy should become a soldier of God.

But the boy proved to have few militant qualities either physically or in the spiritual realm. His poor eyesight handicapped him in sports. He was not fit for Eton or Harrow, not to mention the fact that a Wesleyan minister's salary would not have allowed of a public school education for his son. Sir Kingsley Wood is a most unusual character to have achieved Tory prominence. He was a poor boy, he wears no old school tie, he lacks the background of an ancient university.

Yet, after having given up the idea of theology, he excelled in his law examinations. At nineteen he was articled to a solicitor in Brighton. He made a rapid success in the small town. At the age of twenty-seven he married Agnes, the daughter of Mr. Henry Fawcett, a local patrician, and shortly afterwards he was appointed a justice of the peace for Brighton. He had found, it seemed, his natural destination.

But there is an element of restlessness in the dullest of Englishmen. Many an Empire-builder hails from a small-town brick cottage. Young Wood was not really set on re-building the Empire. However, when he moved wife and office to London, he had bigger plans than simply to establish another law office in the metropolis. He had fallen under the spell of Joe Chamberlain. The great old man's imperialism and his high-sounding tariff principles provided just that amount of excitement compatible with the well-ordered life of an assiduous young lawyer. Encouraged by Chamberlain père, he entered politics. In 1911, the working-class district of Woolwich elected him to the London County Council. His clarity of thought, grasp of detail and even-tempered behavior soon made him one of the more important Conservative spokesmen in the Council. He busied himself with housing problems, old age pensions, insurance and separation allowances. In 1915, he was elected Chairman of the Old Age Pensions Committee. A year later the London Insurance Commission, too, came under his rule. He won universal respect as a local administrator. True, there remained this fellow Herbert Morrison, a pain in every Conservative neck, who was bent on snatching control of London from the Tories and introducing Labour into power. Wood and Morrison were ardent rivals for the favor of the big city. For a few years Wood undoubtedly had the better of Morrison. Although he was a Conservative, the man in the street felt safer with him than with the restless intellectual Morrison. Wood spoke in a high-pitched voice with a strong Cockney accent which sounded slightly ridiculous, just as was his minute stature. They called him the "Cockney sparrow" and this nickname was life insurance with the voters of Woolwich. Indeed, they remained faithful to him, sending him to the House even after Morrison had finally succeeded in dethroning Tory rule in London. Today Sir Kingsley Wood enjoys the double pleasure of having one of the safest seats in Parliament and, by the same token, entertaining cordial relations with his old rival Morrison, now Home Secretary, with whom he rubs shoulders in the war cabinet. Wood likes cordial relations. To the war-time Chancellor who despotically holds England's purse-strings, peace is at least as wonderful as it is to Father Divine.

His pacifism is not weakness, but kind-heartedness. To those who don't call him the Cockney sparrow he is the Cherub. Were it not for his glasses and his moustache he would indeed resemble the cherubic Cupid that adorned many a Victorian garden. His predilection for mischief-making fits into the picture. He has had ample opportunity to display his sense of mischief since he entered Parliament for West Woolwich in the khaki-elections toward the end of 1918. At that time he attracted the attention of Lloyd George. In those days a single word from the Welsh wizard could make or break a politician. When Lloyd George playfully called Wood "naughty boy," the career of the young back-bencher was assured. True, Lloyd George did not squander his feelings gratis. Wood, for one, had won his affection by persuading him to establish a Ministry of Health, which soon proved a valuable asset with the electorate. For this piece of good advice Wood was rewarded with a knighthood. He became Sir Kingsley in the same year in which he entered the House of Commons.

Almost immediately he was made Parliamentary Secretary to the Ministry of his inspiration. For four years he served as right hand man to the chiefs of the department, first Dr. Addison, and then Sir Alfred Mond, the later Lord Melchett, head of the Imperial Chemicals. But when Bonar Law followed Lloyd George, Sir Kingsley was marked a "coalitionist" and left out of the new government. He consoled himself with a look at Winston Churchill, who had suffered the same fate. Churchill, however, was made of sterner stuff. He could take it with a grin. Wood does not like to lose. The only setback in his entire career made him think. He learned the importance of party orthodoxy. Never again would he be labeled an infidel. He developed a fidelity to the Tory cause that no one could surpass. There was no Conservative meeting he missed, no by-election in which he failed to support the party candidate, no Tory club he did not join. In 1924, his position as a prosperous city solicitor, coupled with his place in politics, earned him the Mastership of the Wheelwright's Liveried Company. Now he went all out for tradition. He was, it must be stressed, a traditionalist by conviction. Toryism, he insisted, understood and embodied the average Englishman better than Socialism. Liberalism was much too unromantic for the Cherub's taste.

By a stroke of what his friends call the Kingsley luck, Mr. Balfour died after a four months' Premiership. He was followed by Stanley Baldwin, who never overlooked promising youngsters, although he never gave them free rein or full responsibility. Baldwin sent Sir Kingsley back to the Ministry of Health. The department had a new chief, a man known previously only as a local administrator—Neville Chamberlain. Under him Sir Kingsley Wood served the four and a half decisive years of his career. It was a fruitful cooperation, particularly since Mr. Chamberlain had no objection to decorating himself with borrowed plumage. He gladly accepted the initiative and advice of his Parliamentary Secretary. At that time Mr. Chamberlain had already developed a certain high-handedness which later so disastrously influenced the course of events. His Ministry had to bear the brunt of opposition attacks. The attacks arose on account of increasing unemployment and the lack of social necessities for the wives and children of the unemployed. Neville Chamberlain showed grave irritability toward the constant badgering to which he was subjected. Sir Kingsley Wood, however, remained calm and unperturbed. He offered his naked breast to the slings and arrows of the Socialists. Untiringly he answered questions and staved off assaults. His devotion to his chief, whom he protected, outweighed everything else. In 1928, this devotion was rewarded with a Privy Councillorship for his work for the Party.

He knew to whom he owed this distinction, and since he is both grateful and gentle by nature, and not averse to receiving honors, he decided to remain a Neville Chamberlain man for the rest of his life. He had started as an admirer of the great Joe; to him there were two dynasties in England to which he owed his allegiance.

A year later he was again in opposition. When the tables were turned, he gave it back ten-fold to the Socialists who had tortured his idol Neville. The Labour government that followed Baldwin's first cabinet had no more experienced tormentor to deal with. Sir Kingsley had always remained unruffled by opposition while he was sitting on the Treasury bench. Now, whenever an opportunity arose, he jumped up from his seat, elevating heckling to a fine art. He developed a technique of his own in Parliamentary debates that remains unforgotten. His first question was usually asked blandly and innocently, but the one that invariably followed had a pretty little sting in its tail. The effect of his questions was enhanced by his sparrow-like jumping up and down and by the querulous high pitch of his voice. Delightfully he feigned surprise and indignation. His touch was light and impudent, as funny as a tickle, but far more dangerous. He was entertaining and never really offensive. He could also evince deep sorrow at the apparent incompetence of Labour Ministers. When everyone knew that the cabinet was divided on a particular question, he would lean across the opposition front bench and ask with deep sympathy: "No trouble over this, I hope?" In those easy-going times parliamentarians used to single out their favorite opponents. Winston Churchill and Philip Snowden were a famous pair of duelists, with Winston always amusing in his thrusts and Snowden, a hunchback, often unnecessarily bitter in his returns. Sir Kingsley Wood fixed his attention on Miss Susan Lawrence, who used her feminine privileges to earn a reputation as "the mischief-maker of Labour." In a sense she was Sir Kingsley's opposite number. But she did not relish the comparison. "You behave like a schoolboy!" she once accused him. "And you like a schoolmistress!" he retorted. In the House of Commons such repartee was considered witty. Indeed, Miss Lawrence did look very much the prim and haggard authoritarian school-ma'am. He had the laughter on his side.

Even the victims of his attacks could not help being amused. MacDonald made him Parliamentary Secretary to the Board of Education when he formed his emergency National government. Two months later a General Election approved this government. Had it been outright Conservative Sir Kingsley would certainly have been slated for a major job. Since the MacDonald administration purported to be a coalition, although entirely dependent on the Conservative vote, so pronounced a Tory as Sir Kingsley had to be tucked away in a minor post. The Post Office, it seemed, was just about the right size for him. But the Post Office grew with its new boss. Surprisingly, Sir Kingsley Wood became a popular Postmaster General, the first for a generation.

He attributes his success to a very simple formula—to the application of good manners. The sale of stamps and the accepting of telegrams in English post offices had not always been polite and agreeable. Sir Kingsley brought about a radical change. Post Office officials were polished up. They did not object to their new schooling. They knew that the boss was considerate of their own interests; he was just open to new ideas and bent on modern reforms. The public, he decreed, was the customer who is always right. The public wants to be induced to spend its money. The new postmaster introduced the "golden greeting" telegram, which was enthusiastically received. He conducted a tremendous campaign to put a telephone in every household. The services expanded rapidly. The Post Office made a greater profit than ever before.

There were hitches as well. The Post Office, it became known, controlled the correspondence to the Irish Free State containing tickets for the Irish Sweepstakes. Both were illegal: the sale of tickets and the government control. "Does the Post Office need any extra staff to tamper with the correspondence of private individuals?" a defender of human rights asked in the House.

"No, sir," Sir Kingsley replied, smiling benevolently like Mr. Pickwick in person. "We take it in our stride."

His smile did not fade even when Sir John Reith came into the foreground. Sir John was the almighty chief of the rapidly expanding British Broadcasting Corporation. Today he heads a committee for the rebuilding of England after the war. He is a man of big affairs, a big man according to his own conviction. He does not object to being called superman. His deep bass filled the offices of the B.B.C., which is one of the postal services. But it could not subdue Sir Kingsley's falsetto. David and Goliath worked in passable harmony until Goliath chose to quit. No one has ever outroared, outtalked, or outsmarted Sir Kingsley Wood.

A Postmaster General's job is not confined to selling stamps. Just ask Jim Farley about the mysterious relation between post and patronage. Sir Kingsley rose to the position and influence corresponding to those Farley held until the third term. In 1930, he was elected Chairman of the Executive Committee of the Conservative Party. It was primarily to his credit that the General Election in 1931 brought about a Conservative landslide. He was in the very midst of the campaign. Speaking at three meetings a day did not distract him from hard work in office. His meetings were thronged. People wanted to see him on the platform, beaming benevolently through his glasses and uttering agreeable platitudes in a language everyone understood.

Outside England he remained almost unknown. But within the tight little island he became an intimately familiar figure. He was sufficiently a showman to lift elections above the average dull level. Yet he never antagonized the strong English feeling for what was "good form." He knew what was going on, was interested in everything, liked company, occasional jokes and good living. Broomhill Bank, his forty-acre home at Speldhurst, near Tunbridge Wells, became a center of higher middle-class life. The society there was a little mixed. Prime Ministers and post office clerks—of course only those of particular merit—played golf together on the nine-hole course. True English democracy gathered under the blue Tory banner around the country squire whom everyone loved and who, in turn, liked everyone.

Sir Kingsley Wood is not a bookish man, he is not gifted artistically, but he has taste in things domestic and enjoys the beauties of nature, without ever forgetting that West Woolwich, the crowded and poor London suburb which sends him to the House, is nature's most beautiful spot. His wife once said of him: "He lives by the clock and is moderate in everything." Lady Wood, incidentally, has throughout his career assisted her husband in his work. In the evenings he likes to hear light music and she plays the piano to him. He does not care for broadcast music; it reminds him too strongly of Sir John Reith's booming voice. He looks conservative enough in the dark suits he affects. Only the polka-dotted bow-tie and a heavy signet ring on the third finger of his right hand lend a slight touch of extravagance.

His sympathy for his fellow men is well known. In politics it proved a liability at the moment when England needed nothing so much as determination. In his personal relations it has always been a great asset. Although a shrewd connoisseur of human nature Sir Kingsley is ever ready to forgive the faults of others. He has no time for grudges and nothing of the non-conformist severity his descent would suggest. His faith is simple: he believes in England and in tariffs, whether or not they bring about the millennium. He firmly believes that efficient administration can bring order out of chaos. He is quick to grasp a point. But he does not cling to principles. Once a measure has served its purpose he is willing to let it go. There is a romantic touch to him which he is anxious not to display. His faithful adherence to his chiefs exceeds all the requirements of simple loyalty. It is his obsession. He did not hesitate for a heartbeat to serve as Sancho Panza when Neville Chamberlain engaged in his quixotic effort to appease the windmills. When his personal loyalty is involved, Sir Kingsley Wood, the incarnation of British tolerance, can be as stubborn as a mule, which is again a very English quality.

His effective administration won him cabinet rank, an honor rarely accorded to a Postmaster General. When Baldwin returned to power, he immediately elevated Wood to the Ministry of Health. Once more Sir Kingsley's luck proved helpful. The Ministry of Health at that time had to face a barrage of Conservative attacks. The slum-property owners, all of them important, dues-paying party members, protested against the slum clearance drive which, they insisted, had confiscated their property without offering adequate compensation. Sir Kingsley, the humanitarian, who, in addition, had a great many slum residents in his own constituency, approved of the clearance. Yet he could escape the Conservative property-owners' resentment by pointing out that he was helpless; he had inherited this sad state of affairs from his predecessor in office. The blame of the outraged capitalists rested with Sir Hilton Young. The gratitude of the slum residents went to Sir Kingsley Wood.

In February, 1938, he received what he considered the highest prize life had to bestow. He was elected Grand Master of the Primrose League, the Torys' inner sanctum, dedicated to the tradition of Disraeli, and founded by Lord Randolph Churchill, Winston's father. There was no limit to his happiness. "Indeed," he admitted reluctantly, "I think I have made good."

How long does unlimited happiness last? Three months after he had reached the peak, Sir Kingsley fell into the abyss. Neville Chamberlain wanted him as Air Minister. Mr. Chamberlain had a way with his yes-men. Here was the toughest job in England, possibly in the world. Lord Swinton, the predecessor in the Air Ministry, a man of outstanding ability, had antagonized critics through his abruptness and inaccessibility. How should another man work wonders where Swinton had failed? It was obviously impossible to catch up with Germany's aerial armament. The people had begun to hearken to a voice they had shamefully neglected as long as there was still time to stop, look and listen. To many Winston Churchill now sounded like the prophet of doom. It took another two years before he could prove that the word doom does not figure in his vocabulary.

Sir Kingsley took his new office with the resolution to make the heavens hum. He established friendly relations where Lord Swinton had uttered sharp commands. He was brisk without ever being brusque. He allowed no time-wasting. Sometimes he seemed to be the victim of fatigue, but he listened intently to all and sundry. No one ever left him without the proud feeling of having convinced the Air Minister. Few people understood that, on the contrary, the acceleration of their work and the stimulation of their brains were due to the little, white-haired man in the ministerial armchair. It was a triumph of inner forces over external handicaps.

Again, as so often before, good luck attached itself to Sir Kingsley Wood. New factories were completed and came into full production just when he took office. He reaped the harvest that the unpopular Lord Swinton had sown. But it was all too little and too late.

The days of Munich brought the climax. Sir Kingsley was wholeheartedly for compromising with Hitler. He was the most appeasement-minded member of Neville Chamberlain's government. Partly because he did not want to leave in the lurch the man whom twenty years before he had come to consider as his personal chief, and partly because he was very English in not even faintly understanding Hitler and all that he stood for. But first and foremost his heart bled for mankind.

The shameful submission of Munich came to him as a relief. Less subservient colleagues in the cabinet had to remind him that it was a humiliation. "Maybe," he answered. "But war would bring pain and tears."

Amazingly, Munich was hailed by a great part of the English people. True, their delusion lasted but a few weeks before it gave way to the great awakening. But while the enthusiasm over Munich lasted, Sir Kingsley believed it might be good to profit by it. The Conservative Party had assured peace; the Party should cash in quickly. The Tories would win an overwhelming victory at the elections.

The plan was outrageous. It was nipped in the bud by the Conservatives themselves. Sir Sidney Herbert, who had just lost a leg through an operation and was already a dying man, rose to make his last speech. He felt his stomach turn in disgust. He called Munich "a grave and desperate humiliation" and continued: "There are also rumors that if things go smoothly and favorably and comfortably there will be a General Election. Now I don't care at this time about my own party, or any other party. But I know that there could be no greater iniquity in the world than to force a General Election at this moment on the people of this country. At the expense of much dishonor we have gained a temporary respite of peace. In the name of all that is decent let us use that for rearmament. Who will gain by a General Election? There may be some tiny Tammany ring who want it . . ."

It was a mortal blow to Sir Kingsley Wood's scheme. In addition, he was caught by the buzz-saw of airplane production. His personal and party loyalties had led him into shame. But he did not lose his temper. "Never mind, Prime Minister," he encouraged Neville Chamberlain. "We shall come again!" He likes the language of the race-track. He is, in his own definition, a stayer.

When he came again he was a different man. No one can pierce his inscrutable forehead; no one can penetrate his iron mask of friendliness and good humor. One is only allowed to guess at what happened behind his mask and his smile.

His first war measure was to open his country house in one of the most lovely parts of Kent to fourteen evacuated children from Woolwich. Under his personal supervision they annexed the garden, explored the grounds, learned to chop wood, and played games new to town children. Once more Sir Kingsley proved his mental fertility: he adapted a home-made sled to be used for "ersatz" tobogganing. The children were not in Kent; they were in heaven. They cried when it came their turn to make way for newcomers. Two or three little girls cried so persistently that they had to be brought back.

Sir Kingsley rests one day a month among his adopted children. The rest of his time he spends in the Treasury. He has installed a cot in his office where he sleeps. Londoners, with whom he used to mingle freely, see him only on his short way from the Treasury to the Carlton Club, where he has his rationed lunch.

There was a good deal of head-shaking when he took over the Treasury. How, for God's sake, could Winston Churchill have made such a choice? How could the war-lord have entrusted what is generally regarded as the most important government department to a confounded appeaser?

The answer is that Winston Churchill belongs to the select few who can pierce inscrutable foreheads and penetrate iron masks of friendliness and good humor. He is himself a reformed sinner—though, it is true, never a political sinner. He understands what a mighty power atonement is. He always appreciated Sir Kingsley Wood's unique efficiency. He was ready to forgive him his errors. He knows that his Chancellor of the Exchequer simply had the vices of his virtues. Sir Kingsley, a typical Englishman, like all his people, had to learn from the beginning. Foremost, he had to learn to forget. He had to forget party affiliations, personal predilections, all the blunder of inherited doctrines. He did forget. So did the nation. Nothing stands any longer between the British and their cause.

Today the Chancellor, who spent his life in being agreeable to everyone from his district warden to the Führer, demands untold sacrifices from his people. He takes ten shillings in the pound of their earnings, fifty per cent, and they ask: "Why not more?" The man who had the upstart's awe of capitalism taxes big incomes up to ninety-seven and a half per cent, which, he observes with his unfaltering smile, is approaching the taxation limit. His budget is particularly concerned with the suppression of profiteering. He calls profits a "rake-off."

Churchill has given him his chance, and gratefully he makes the best use of it. But perhaps the British miracle of the toughening up of a softy is not due to Churchill's visionary leadership alone. A part of the credit, at least, should certainly go to Mr. Adolf Hitler.

PART TWO

Labour

*B*oss

ERNEST BEVIN

VICTORY IS WINSTON CHURCHILL'S SUPREME AIM. BUT TO Ernest Bevin, second in the war cabinet, victory is not the only goal. It will simply mean another beginning to the man who has reached his fifty-seventh year, having spent forty-seven of them tirelessly at work. He looks like a bull, although his health is in a delicate state. He weighs two hundred pounds—fifty pounds less than in May, 1940, when he took office as Britain's Minister for Labour and National Service. For twenty years he has been one of the three or four most influential men in English politics, outside the government. He is the chief architect of England's Trades Unions Congress, the stronghold and backbone of Britain's labor movement. Three times he has refused a peerage. Standing five feet four, a short, thickset man, he feels that he towers above titles, honors, decorations.

His formal schooling ended in his tenth year. By then he had acquired a working knowledge of reading which was to prove most useful in an early stage of his career. He is one of the selected few who have not the slightest use for money, although there were times in his youth when he was hard put to find food to satisfy his hunger. Undoubtedly, hunger drove

121

him on. When, at last, he could afford three meals a day, he ate seven, and gained his oversized belly. With his habitual ruthless energy, he has reduced it to normal proportions. He probably knows that his life expectation depends on his keeping down his waistline. And his life's expectation is still unfulfilled, although he started at the bottom and is today at the top; next to the Prime Minister, England's most powerful man, dictator in the realm of labor.

He has the right to transfer every man and woman in England to whatever job and whatever place he chooses. Feudal seigniory was never as absolute as are the powers vested in the man whose whole life has been a crusade to abolish what he called the feudal servitude of the old system. He was always a rebel with dictatorial leanings. He was frequently called the Mussolini of Labour. But there remains one difference. Power made the Duce drunk, whereas power has sobered Ernest Bevin. He exercises his almost boundless rights with meticulous care. Indeed, he does not exercise them at all, at least not by force. At the time of his start in politics he threw an opponent, after a spirited clash, into the river. Since his every word can now decide human destiny he has become argumentative and persuasive. Occasionally, if not too often, he is even polite. This transformation is not astonishing. It is an old English miracle. Ernest Bevin, the product of poverty, is as British as the King.

He takes the good with the bad, demonstrating the indifference to adversities and the indomitable stubbornness that at present carries his nation through the darkest and finest hours of its history. But Ernest Bevin is not one simply to carry on, come wind, come weather. His eyes, restless behind heavy, horn-rimmed glasses, pierce the fog. He is, by the same token, a shrewd realist and star-gazer. Hitler's defeat is not to him, as to most of his harassed compatriots, an aim

ERNEST BEVIN

in itself. It is simply the inevitable condition for building the kind of world that the man who has built the house of labor wants to live in.

Bevin is perhaps the only one among England's responsible statesmen who rarely misses an opportunity to state his war aims. He does not express them in terms of boundaries, treaties, alliances. His stern determination to carry out the job at hand is curiously intertwined with his vision of a better world order based on justice and freedom for all. He has been fighting and feuding throughout an eventful life. Now he is hungry for peace. But in his hunger for peace he is just as resolved as is Churchill in his bellicose genius, first to blow up the stumbling block on the path to human happiness—Nazism.

Bevin's task will not be completed when Hitler is finished. His life begins at sixty. Then only will it be real life. Every human being will have his opportunity. Why shouldn't Ernest Bevin have the opportunity of moving into No. 10 Downing Street? England will need a reformer to bring construction out of chaos. No. 10 with no liveried lackeys hanging around; state dinners of roast beef and beer.

Ernest Bevin is not a revolutionary; he is, rather, a pathfinder. He had always to find his way through the dark. His father was an agricultural laborer; both his parents died when Ernie was eight years old. Perhaps that explains the solitude which somehow shrouds this leader of the masses. He has an untold number of followers, devotees, collaborators; but few friends. Having been through hell and high water, he remains hard-boiled and not easily approachable.

He was born in the hamlet of Winsford, in Somersetshire, in 1884. At ten, after living two years with an elder sister in Devonshire, he left school and began working as a farm-

hand for sixpence a week. He soon had the nerve to demand
a raise to ninepence. He was fired, but he fell upstairs; he
found a job at a shilling. Of course he had to work seven
days a week. However, in the new place he got jam on his
Sunday pudding. He earned this preferential treatment
through his ability to read. In the evenings, the neighbors
gathered around his employer's fireplace while Ernie read the
newspaper to them. English newspapers in those days carried
endless accounts of the speeches in Parliament. Ernie never
missed a word. It took him almost another fifty years to reach
the House. But he was sovereign master of the situation,
when he first bowed to the Speaker. He had served his parliamentary apprenticeship as a boy in Winsford.

Looking for a station in life where there would be jam
every day, he moved to town—to Bristol. He became first a
page boy in a restaurant, then a shop-clerk, and finally a
tram-car conductor. He did not last long in any of these
jobs. He was too restless. Menial work did not interest him.
His curiosity for life was absorbed by the teeming, sweating
dock-life. He hung about with dockers, packers, longshore-
men, and soon they accepted him as one of themselves, although, professionally, he had meanwhile reached the dignity
of a ginger-beer cart driver. Of course he acquired the mentality of the docks; and their manners. Soon, he was running
for the City Council. It so happened that his cart drove dangerously near an open-air meeting where his fellow contest-
ant was speaking. One of Ernest Bevin's shortcomings has
always been his dislike of contradiction. The only man who
may safely contradict him—and who uses this privilege frequently—is Ernest Bevin himself. He has not yet quite overcome this dislike. But now he controls it; he compromises.
In his youth his argumentative methods were simpler. He
stopped his horses, flung himself on his opponent, and threw

him into the Avon. The burgesses of Bristol did not approve, and failed to elect him. But the dockers were unanimously agreed that he had acquitted himself well, particularly in view of his small size. He had wrestled his way to local fame. Even Ben Tillett heard the boys talking about him.

Ben Tillett, now long retired, and British labor's grand old man, was the hero of the dockers' strike of 1889, the biggest of the century. He was always on the lookout for promising newcomers to help him in building up a mighty labor movement. He gave Bevin a small job in the local dockers' union and thus determined the rest of the young man's career. Bevin became a professional union-man. At twenty-six he founded the Bristol Unemployed Union, and was elected its secretary. The unemployed had no insurance at that time, so, quite naturally, there was no salary. Yet Bevin stuck it out with them for five hard and troublesome years. He is entirely unashamed of his antecedents. It was the fault of the system, not his own. Perhaps it was even a blessing in disguise. Not many of the English leaders have actually experienced the seamy side of life.

The sun in those somber days was the plain-looking Bristol mill-girl who is now Mrs. Bevin. She has kept herself in the background while her husband has made his career. "People should be interested in my work, not in my private life!" is one of Bevin's gruffer maxims. Mrs. Bevin did not become one of the country's leading ladies when Ernie rose to the stature of one of England's leading men. She is no celebrity. But she is known to some old friends as his good companion in life and work, sharing her husband's views and endeavors.

She keeps a photograph of Ernest taken at the time they met. In this picture he looks square-faced; tough and pugnacious. He is wearing a workman's cap and a cheap mackintosh.

In Bristol he took part in all the struggles of the period of industrial unrest before the first war. Ben Tillett, pleased with his "find," watched his development and entrusted him with a particularly difficult job. Bevin was singled out to unite the Bristol dockers with the dockers' organizations in other British ports. It was the birth of the National Transport Workers' Federation, which Bevin throughout the following years regarded as his favorite child. It was a painful birth. It proved hard to unite the dockers in different ports. In 1911, Ben Tillett and Bevin risked their first showdown. They organized a national strike which succeeded to some degree, but they suffered a terrible setback when, a year later, the dockers in London struck again, and their comrades in the other ports refused to support them. Bevin emerged from this turmoil with the firm conviction that strict centralization of the trades-union movement was the only solution of the social problem.

By then he was a national officer of the dockers' union. He soon became their assistant secretary, rose steadily through the ranks of the labor bureaucracy, and in 1922, founded the Transport and General Workers' Union. Today this is a combination of forty-five formerly independent unions, with a membership of 850,000, and a reserve fund of four million dollars; the largest trade-union in the world. Although Bevin modestly contented himself with the post of secretary-general —which he held until he joined the war cabinet—he has been recognized for years as Britain's Labour Tsar. As the head of the most powerful single union in the country, he controlled the Trades Union Congress which, in turn, decided the policy of the Labour Party. Transport House, Westminster, where Bevin established his headquarters, was widely known as the Labour Kremlin.

As a successful trades-unionist, exclusively interested in

raising the living standards of his membership, Bevin early learned to look down on professional politicians, and most disdainfully on those of his own party. One explanation might be that he twice unsuccessfully contested a seat in the House. Yet he tried his hand at politics. He made his debut in 1920, when Winston Churchill, then War Secretary, wanted to send some implements of war to the White Russian generals engaged in their death struggle with Trotzky's Red Army. Bevin, like all of England after the first war, was sick to death of military adventures. He founded the Council of Action to prevent the shipping of ammunition to Archangel. His London dockers fell into line; the English supply ships were tied up. It is not known whether Bevin regrets today the success he scored. Perhaps Bolshevism might have been choked in its initial stage. This would certainly have meant an easier life for Ernest Bevin. The helpful friend of the Red Army developed into the man whom the Communists hated and slandered more than Hitler before the Moscow pact. He returns their feelings. To a large extent it is owing to his influence that fellow-travelers are unwelcome in the Labour Party.

Public attention was focused on him when he, in the same year, 1920, acted as spokesman for a hundred thousand London dock workers who were striking for a minimum wage of sixteen shillings a day and stable conditions of employment. The Ministry of Labour set up a court of inquiry, the Shaw Commission, to decide on the merits of the case. Bevin argued, pleaded, and tortured the employers' witnesses for twenty-one days. He raised the local, if grand-scale, strike to the level of a fight for generally better living conditions for the working class, thus appealing to a country-wide audience. Professor Arthur Lyon Bowley of Cambridge, then the foremost statistician in England, testified that one could very well live on the dockers' established wages. He had made the experiment, living and feeding himself for three weeks on a docker's earnings. Bevin, however, forced the professor to admit that he had not done any physical work during this period beyond cultivating his garden. Then he rose to make his final speech. It lasted eleven hours. It reviewed the entire social problem in England and ended with a dramatic coup. Bevin unfolded a parcel containing bread, margarine and tea. "That is what our dockers get for their work!" he roared. "That is exactly what one can buy with their money. Can you live on bread, margarine and tea?"

He won his case. His friends shook hands with him. "You should read for the bar!" they agreed. Bevin looked at them, incredulous. "But I don't understand law. I could never learn it. I can only argue with conviction when I am sincere." Of course this was an understatement. Sharp-witted, hard-hitting Bevin with his precise matter-of-fact intelligence would have cut as good a figure as anyone in the Temple. It was simply that silk did not tempt him. It was much more of a temptation to give a popular answer that would resound in every worker's cottage in England.

"But you would certainly become a K.C.," his friends insisted.

K.C.—King's Counsel—is the highest rank at the English bar.

"P.C., if you please," Bevin retorted. "P.C.—Counsel for the Proletariat." It is more than twenty years since he coined this expression. He does not use the word "proletariat" any longer. He detests it. He remains true to his cause, but his terminology, indeed his whole aspect, has considerably matured.

The case for the London dockers was won by a man without any legal training, whose discussions until then had been confined to Socialist debating clubs and union haggling. But again Bevin amazed England by his grasp of highly technical and complicated problems when Philip Snowden, then Chancellor of the Exchequer, appointed him a member of the Macmillan Committee to inquire into the affairs of British finance. Montagu Norman, President of the Bank of England, mystery man of world finance, had an uncomfortable time of it when he was forced to run the gauntlet of Bevin's pertinent questions.

Bevin was then still considered a dangerous radical. His record made him appear dangerous. The black spot on this record was the leading part he had played in the abortive General Strike of 1926. This strike was broken by Winston Churchill, who stiffened the attitude of Baldwin and his fellow cabinet members and smashed the upheaval. Bevin resented Churchill's victory. "It will be a Godsend for this country," he said, "if Churchill is out of office for ever. It is not that he is not brilliant. But it is not safe to leave the destiny of millions of people in the hands of a man with an unstable mind." This very criticism, cheap as it was, in adopting the once widely accepted notion of Churchill's "instability," discloses the real Bevin. His prime objection to an adversary is the latter's alleged instability. This is a remarkable reproach on the part of a radical. Of course Bevin has never been a radical at heart. He is a balanced Englishman, accidentally born with a predilection for roaring.

Perhaps his balance is the result of inner contradictions. He disturbed public order for the last time in calling out 25,000 drivers for a bus strike in London at a time when it hurt most—during the festive days of the Coronation. He argued for better working conditions for his bus drivers. He pointed out the health-impairing character of their jobs and climaxed his speech by the accusation that most of them were swindled by the salesmen of worthless, even dangerous, patent medicines. "My bus members are extraordinarily good customers of this trade," he said. "I don't think they are getting very good results for their money." Nobody could remain untouched by such a heart-rending plea. On the other hand, Bevin, iron-fisted, ejected the Communists who wanted to muscle in on the strike. *The Daily Worker* slandered him mercilessly. Of course he won the inevitable libel suit. Right and Left attacked him. But the working hours of his drivers were cut down to seven and a half.

Practical results—that's what he wants. All that talk about "social significance" is as odious to him as it was to Samuel Gompers. Although he was an indefatigable campaigner, criss-crossing all England, speaking to villagers from push-carts and packing the largest halls in the big cities with organized union memberships, he loathed what he calls political babble. In 1931, when MacDonald, Snowden and J. H. Thomas sought refuge in the Conservative camp, he washed his hands entirely of political leaders. He did not join the leftist choir that accused the converts of treason. He simply understood that the betterment of working-class living conditions could not depend on partisan and parliamentary poker.

More and more he retired into his shell, Transport House. He became obsessed with his work there. Admiringly, his staff used to call him a slave-driver. One Monday morning he entered his office with the ominous words: "It was a rainy Sunday yesterday. I spent all day thinking about the union." The staff shivered. If Ernest thinks all Sunday, the staff has to work overtime for a couple of months.

The more he barricaded himself behind the walls of Transport House, the further his influence spread. The party became ever more dependent on the boss who controlled the unions; that is, the votes and funds. They had to come to him when the *Daily Herald,* then a struggling partisan sheet, seemed on the point of death. Bevin took a hand in reorganizing the paper. He persuaded one of the press-lords that a newspaper with the backing of all organized labor could become a most prosperous undertaking, provided that it did a good job of journalism as well. His lordship agreed. The *Daily Herald* acquired all the aspects of Beaverbrook's and Rothermere's penny press, which had so far been anathema to socialist intellectuals. Bevin decreed that the party should retain only political control of the paper, leaving its shaping, style and make-up to the publisher. He accepted, personally, the vice-chairmanship of the reorganized paper. Today the *Daily Herald* sells two million copies a day. It is second only to Beaverbrook's *Daily Express* in circulation.

Only once did Bevin desert Transport House, Westminster. He went to Geneva to work at the International Labor Office. Mr. Winant, director of the I.L.O., now United States ambassador in London, hailed Bevin's work as "invaluable." In Geneva he recognized the necessity of bringing science into closer relationship with the labor movement. Back in London, he instituted the Scientific Advisory Committee, to which twelve of Britain's most prominent scientists belonged. Bevin showed his new collaborators the greatest respect. To him scientists are not "intellectuals."

His contempt for the latter category remained unchanged. Although he seldom took a hand in politics proper, it delighted him to knock out philosophers and labor theorists as fast as they stuck their necks out. The movement, he insisted, must be purged of its intelligentsia. Higher wages and shorter hours were labor's only permitted aims.

This uncompromising attitude did not increase his popularity with the minor Labour leaders. His personal seclusion added to the difficulties. Bevin stuck close to a handful of unionmates. He kept aloof from his party's officers' corps. At Labour conferences, where easy social contacts develop between delegates who are constantly meeting, Bevin was only seen hurrying to and from his seat. He never indulged in patting shoulders and offering cigars. He smoked his pipe thoughtfully and silently.

The pipe brought him uncomfortably close to Baldwin. Both looked restful, peaceful, middle-class men. When the rumor circulated that Baldwin had offered Bevin a peerage, Labour youth almost revolted. It was, incidentally, the third offer of this kind, and Bevin rejected it with the query: "Shall I call myself Lord Bevin, of Winsford?" To English hearers that would sound much as Lord Flynn, of the Bronx, would to Americans.

Repeatedly radical youth tried to get rid of Bevin. He was, they said, more conservative than Neville Chamberlain. They insisted that he was satisfied with the progress Labour had made since his own youth. Now he had definitely become middle-class.

But ever again when Bevin arose, his domineering personality, his control of the vote, his ability to explain his case, his logical and emotional appeal to the masses proved that here stood the most formidable figure of British Labour.

Had he indeed gone middle-class? The volcano slumbered; that was all.

A spark set Ernest Bevin in eruption. The advent of Nazism did it. The time to eradicate the nuisance of the intellectuals, until then his foremost political predilection, was over. Hitler was not just a nuisance. Bevin belongs among the first men who understood how dangerous the paperhanger was. Soon after Hitler's access to power, Bevin, who up to that time had never shown any interest in foreign affairs, declared: "Nazism will lead to war and disaster, for it does not offer any solution for the economic problems of the people. Its principal weapons are tyranny, corruption, depressing the standard of life, destruction of freedom."

It was from the outset more a social than a national conflict that Bevin saw in the making. He was determined to defend human rights rather than the supremacy of the Empire. His patriotism was earthbound. It was love for his suffering fellow-men and nothing of Winston Churchill's glorious vision. But Bevin's insatiable hunger for freedom and for the betterment of the conditions allotted to the toilers on this earth was added to Churchill's all-embracing patriotism. It was Bevin's conviction that if war came, it would not be an imperialist war, but a war to save the British working class from Nazi serfdom. The workers would have the biggest stake in this war. They had to be prepared.

At the Conference at Brighton in 1935, he fought for the Labour Party's soul. It should not be forgotten that this party, which subsequently produced the most vociferous critics of appeasement, was deeply pacifist by tradition, and must shoulder a large share of the responsibility for Britain's wavering in the interval between the two wars. Even the wavering of the Tories is, if not excused, largely to be explained by the fact that they had to underbid the then low standards of the Labour Party in the appeal to an effete electorate. Baldwin's promise that there would "be no armament race" was the inevitable consequence of the race for the *grand prix* of appeasement which both the parties were running. George Lansbury, who succeeded MacDonald as the party leader, was the pillar of downright defeatism. At Brighton he moved a resolution not to support the policy of sanctions against Italy. The old man, whose personal sincerity was beyond question, deeply impressed the conference. Mussolini stood at the threshold of a new triumph, due this time to his rabid Socialist antagonists.

It was a highly critical moment in which Bevin rose to speak. He is no spellbinder. But his voice, heavy with the accents of his native West Country, deflated those socialists who wished to give the enemy the right of way. He delivered a terrific peroration, passionate in its hatred of dictatorship, contemptuous of the weaklings in his own ranks. Indeed, the slumbering volcano was in eruption. The conference was swept off its feet. A few defeatists remained isolated in their corners; old Lansbury slumped in his seat. Immediately he resigned from the party's Executive Committee. Broken in body and spirit, he left the conference.

Had Bevin not been a little too harsh with the old man? "George Lansbury has been dressed up in the robe of a martyr for years, waiting for somebody to set fire to the faggots," Bevin said. And he continued with his inimitable terseness: "Well, I've done it!"

He has done more. He has brought Labour back into the house that is England. But in exchange Labour, he decided, should be comfortable at home.

Silently he watched the Munich crisis. The Socialist Lord Lieutenant of Northumberland, Sir Charles Trevelyan, egged him on to call out his men on strike in protest against Munich. But Bevin has never called a strike for political reasons. "You want me to call out a million of my workers?" he answered Sir Charles. "And whom are you going to call out? All the Lords Lieutenant?"

Bevin maintained his silence when the war broke out. Largely under his influence the Labour Party had promised not to take any action that might impair Neville Chamberlain's conduct of the war. But his eminently practical sense revolted against a conduct of the war à la Chamberlain. He spent months in anguish, disgust, and near despair. The fact that he did not speak up during this time is perhaps the strongest proof of the power of self-restraint he has developed.

On May Day, 1940, however, the flame burst out. His speech at Stoke-on-Trent struck home. He compared his country to an old boxing champion who had won so many times that he asked: "Who is this young challenger? I can knock him out in my own time!", and then woke up in danger of being knocked out himself, with a new champion risen.

Had the party rebels ever considered Bevin as middle-class? "I am afraid that kind of middle-class mentality has little knowledge of the new psychologic and organizing ability of those in charge of the totalitarian states," he continued. "Let them never forget that the forces we are fighting are governed neither by the old strategy, nor follow the old tactics. The mechanism of this war is such that we can neither afford mistakes nor incompetence. Our position is critical and violent. It will require tremendous energy. We have no right to allow the lives of our soldiers and sailors to be played with," he concluded, indicating the stand he would take. "The British working class want this war won. They know what is at stake. It is their liberty. But they want a government that is going to place the nation before its friends and private interests." He breathed deeply, and wound up by coining the slogan that from then on was to be the battle-cry of the English people: "Give 'itler 'ell!"

When Bevin had finished Neville Chamberlain was doomed. The Prime Minister would have fallen even if no Blitzkrieg had struck. He resigned a fortnight later.

Bevin was attending the Labour Party Conference at Bournemouth when he received Churchill's call to take the

Ministry of Labour. Thirty years of political enmity were wiped out in a minute. Later when friends asked Churchill why he had chosen Bevin of all people to share his responsibility, the war-lord answered: "He is the ablest figure in British industry!" And Bevin paid back the compliment by publicly testifying to Churchill's forthrightness and frankness, which, he insisted, he admired highly.

To his own people in Bournemouth he declared: "I hope the war cabinet will not allow vested interests, profits or anything else to stand in the way of maximum production. If this is the policy of the government, I will ask my people to work like 'ell!"

He is working like 'ell himself since he moved into Montagu House, the seat of the Labour Ministry. He was bombed out of his old-fashioned apartment in West Kensington and now stays in a modest hotel. At home his working day begins at 5.30 A.M. At 9 A.M. he is at his desk in the office, having finished his correspondence for the day. At 9 P.M. he is still at his desk. Meanwhile he has had appointments, conferences, cabinet sessions, almost every hour. In addition he must answer questions in the House. After he joined the government, a seat was found for him by elevating its Labour holder to the peerage. But Bevin obviously does not enjoy Parliament. His practical and domineering mentality considers much of the parliamentary procedure a waste of time. He has none of Churchill's innate respect for the House in which Winston has lived so much of his life. Bevin feels that he is an outsider in the Gothic hall. He is apt to feel so anywhere outside his union, but most of all in Parliament, which he entered so late. He shows his disrespect even to his own Party. When Labour once insisted on a second reading of a minor bill, everyone could hear Bevin's remark from the front-bench: "They behave like dogs with a bone, hating to let it go, although there is nothing left to gnaw."

He rarely sits through the sessions. He prefers to go home to his evening work. At midnight Mrs. Bevin sometimes asks her husband who the man is who has spent a lifetime fighting for shorter working hours. Ernest—true to his name—is not equipped with any great sense of humor. Undisturbed by his wife's quips, he burns the midnight oil, bent over papers and documents, hell-bent on sending Hitler right to that very place. A lesser man of his age would break under such a heavy burden; Bevin, like Churchill, thrives on it.

He demands as much work from his collaborators. The staff at Montagu House insist that their office no longer resembles a governmental department. Instead, it has become a sweat-shop. The niceties of the English civil service are banned. Snappy orders over the telephone have replaced the old-style office memos. And when Bevin is in need of a little money for his social services he does not start the once pre-scribed unending correspondence with the Treasury. He simply steps over to Sir Kingsley Wood, the Chancellor of the Exchequer, with an unabashed grin on his broad face that will cost the British tax-payer some ten million pounds.

"We are to produce order out of chaos, and chaos it was when we went in," he said in taking over office. He said it in the presence of his predecessor, Mr. Ernest Brown, who joined the new government as Secretary for Scotland. Personal considerations, it seems, do not deter Bevin from speaking his mind. "The system based on monopoly and big business has failed to deliver the goods in our hour of trial."

The hour of trial was not yet over when Bevin stepped in. He did not lose a minute in carrying out his reforms. His speeding up of munitions production was an enormous job.

He set up a Labour Supply Board with himself as chairman. Each side, employers and employees alike, had to accept the referee's decision as final. Strikes and lockouts were outlawed. Bevin forbade the "stealing" of labor by employers and ordered the workers to stick to their assigned jobs. He declared wages pegged as a further deterrent to wasteful job-shifting. With such sweeping measures he went a long way toward socialized production, but the output in most English plants rose one hundred per cent within a fortnight after Dunkerque. "I want to shorten the war," he stated as his aim. "I believe it can be shortened. But nothing but metal will do it."

Hitler, too, wanted to shorten the war. During the first months the Churchill-Bevin government had to carry out its duties under a constant hail of German bombs over London. It was suggested that certain ministries might leave the capital. Churchill did not bother even to answer this suggestion. Bevin, less poised, roared: "When I leave London it will be with a bayonet in my back!" He counter-attacked Hitler in his own Germany. It is little known that it was Bevin who organized the co-operation with the German underground movement. Nothing but this simple fact can be told; it is well known to the Nazis. It is the reason why the German radio abuses him with its torrents of slime. They hate and fear him no less than Churchill.

Bevin had but one fear: the British workers might misunderstand him as he was compelled to ask them to give up almost all the advantages, securities and privileges they had won in generations of struggle; and, during the present generation, mostly under his leadership. There is an element of Greek tragedy about the man who must shelve the sum of his life's work in a moment of direst peril. But England's workers understood magnificently why they were burdened with the task of winning the war. It was first of all to save their own skins, and second to establish, through victory, an order that would definitely bury the iniquities of the past. They trusted Bevin's word: "When this war is over, the task of rebuilding the world has to be done by the working class. In the past it was a matter of settling frontiers, sorting out minorities, preserving the balance of power. This time it must be the economic reconstruction of the whole foundation of society." Another of his popular sentences showed clearly how he imagines this reconstruction. "If a boy is good enough to handle a Spitfire, he is also good enough to govern his country." The logic of such a sentence is debatable; the honest conviction it expresses is not.

His language is more colorful than distinguished. He despises prepared speeches, euphemisms and English understatements. "You must all work like hell!" is his favorite expression. When broadcasting a written speech on one occasion he interrupted his delivery with an unprintable oath. It seemed that he had mislaid a page. Addressing a group of big businessmen, he lost his patience with his well-bred audience and subjected his hearers to a violent peroration. Amazingly, the gentlemen from the City applauded him heartily. A number of society ladies whom Bevin addressed on another occasion, remained terror-stricken when he had concluded. "He spoke to my friends as if they were mill-girls looking for jobs," a Viscountess complained. His authority allows him to do so. If he chooses to exercise his power, he may walk right into the Savoy grill and ask the merry-makers: "Just what are you doing to win the war? Tomorrow you report to your labor agency. They will give you a pick-and-shovel job. And don't you present yourself in tails, either!"

This is what he has done: He got his workers to carry on at their machines seven days a week, entirely forgetful of the forty-hour week he had won for them. Closed shops have had to admit non-union, unskilled labor and even female labor. Strikes are barred; the workman has lost his right to choose his job. Whatever the job, in whatever place, he must accept it. The employers, on the other hand, are forbidden to cut down wages for the duration. On the contrary, the general scale of wages has been raised to match the rising cost of living. A great many other benefits for workers have been established. One of Bevin's measures takes care of the unemployable. There are none, Bevin insists. At worst they have lost their skill, and perhaps their strength, through long years of idleness and semi-starvation. At present, no man who has been out of work for any length of time may be fired before he has undergone a test period of three weeks. Three weeks of regular employment and healthy diet will restore his full capacities. Bevin takes care of the feeding of British labor. Of course food rationing is a serious handicap. But every workshop that employs two hundred or more people must establish a canteen that provides food according to the new scientific methods, and a medical center as well that looks after occupational or bombing casualties. A Welfare Board, which he instituted at his Ministry, sees that none of these regulations is neglected. Another council of advisers, the Board of Labour Supply, helps him to distribute Britain's man power fairly.

Ernest Bevin derives his greatest power from an act which Major Attlee, Lord Privy Seal and Leader of the Labour Party, introduced in July, 1940, and which was accepted in less than five minutes, although it brought about a complete reversal of England's established social order. This act gives the Minister of Labour absolute control over civilian jobs. He can decide which industries he considers essential to the war effort and which he chooses to close down as non-essential. Every man and woman in Britain outside the fighting forces is subject to his orders. Indeed, he has shifted thousands of workers from other industries to armament production. But he does this with the consent of those involved. From the very moment his civilian dictatorship was assured he no longer made use of it. He prefers to fall back on his gift for persuasion and negotiation. British Labour has followed him enthusiastically. To this day only one case of dissatisfaction has been reported. In April, 1941, six engineering apprentices in Manchester—six out of six thousand—went on strike for higher wages. The dark-blue veins on Bevin's temples grew purple. The six strikers were immediately arrested. This case has not been repeated. Bevin is proud that his national arbitration tribunal has so far handled and solved 368 industrial disputes. In the midst of the turmoil of war, he has brought domestic peace to his country.

Peacefully the veteran fire-eater collaborates with Churchill, his principal antagonist in the fight for re-shaping England. Peacefully, too, Bevin works with Lord Beaverbrook, whom he has considered all his life a labor-baiter, and peacefully, or at least, without audible clashes, he coöperates with Herbert Morrison, his competitor for labor leadership and an intellectual type into the bargain. With one man alone there can be no peace—no peace with Hitler.

Bevin certainly belongs to those who are determined to fight it out to a finish. Fraudulent peace offensives don't take him in. When Herr Hess dropped from the skies, the angel of peace, bent on saving humanity, Ernest Bevin dissipated all the confusion that might have arisen, with one word: "Murderer." He does not weaken, but the thought of what shall come, once victory is achieved, is foremost in his mind. "I feel that now is the time for thinking people to be considering the real social obligations of this war," he states. "If Hitler wins we should have rule from the top, a social structure in which the masses of the people would be looked upon principally as soldiers for fighting. But lasting peace and security can only be obtained if the people themselves are the only ones to determine the final issue of security—self-government, the issue of war or life and death itself. . . . Life must have a motive. I want to suggest a new motive. I suggest that at the end of this war we accept social security as the main motive of all our national life. That does not mean that all profit or surplus would be wiped out. It does mean that the whole of our economic finance and science is directed to give social security to the community as a whole. To find the motive of our life in social security is my war aim. The British Commonwealth is looking for something like this. America is looking for something like this. The old days have passed. The new age has to be built? We must begin now, even while the heat of war and the din of battle are on. Let the citizens direct their aims and energies to contributing to the common good, for, after all, the youngest of us has not a long road to go; the youngest of us has not a long time in which to contribute."

This last sentence sounds like a testament. Like Moses looking at the promised land in which he will never set his foot. But Ernest Bevin is rarely in a mood of resignation. Calling on him you meet a busy yet perfectly calm man obviously thrilled by the hardships of life, contradictory in his outward appearance. He is clean-shaven, and his greying hair is carefully cut and brushed. But his never-pressed clothes hang untidily around his large bulk. They are stained with ashes. Incidentally, he is the only cabinet minister to wear colored shirts. He is a conservative gipsy; one can still expect the unexpectable of him. He is deeply aware how time flies, and he is driven on by the knowledge that his business is not done. His high sense of duty is not untouched by ambition. Perhaps, in a last eruption he will jump into the foreground. To be Prime Minister of Reconstruction is not a bad ultimate aim. But Ernest Bevin is about to understand that no man's business is ever done. When the nightmare of this war vanishes, the slumbering volcano might just as well enjoy what he has been missing all his life—a good restful nap.

Lord of London

HERBERT MORRISON

FIORELLO LA GUARDIA MEANS HERBERT MORRISON IN ENGLISH. The two gentlemen have probably never seen one another, nor is it even likely that they know very much about each other. Yet, if there ever were Siamese twins in politics, here they are. Their similarity is striking. It is a similarity not only in outward appearance; Morrison looks like a lean La Guardia, and Fiorello, in turn, like a paunchy 'Erbert. It is a startling similarity of temperament and, most amazing of all, a similarity of destiny. They run the world's two biggest cities, respectively; each is entrusted with the civil defense of his country, and both hanker after a place in world affairs. Both, incidentally, use the same idiom in speaking of Hitler.

Hitler will not wait until he is cornered. He will unleash the new deluge before his bombers lack oil, before his troops are worn out by hollow victories that spread them ever thinner over the globe, and before his people break under the stress of a decade of war and war-like regimentation. At any moment he is likely to let loose hell. Neutral observers "who ought to be in a good position to know" have said publicly that Germany is making active preparations for a

HERBERT MORRISON

gas attack. This statement comes from Herbert Morrison, British Home Secretary and Minister of Home Security, who is responsible for saving forty-five million of his compatriots from choking and perishing by German science.

"One of the likeliest reasons for the enemy to use gas would be that he might regard it as the last hope of doing what he has tried without success to do in so many other ways—stampeding the civil population and causing panic," Herbert Morrison says. But as long as his right eye—the left one was permanently damaged on the third day of his life —watches over the British Isles there will be no stampede and no panic. Confidently he expects that the German gas attack "which might be deadly and decisive against a defenseless or ill-prepared people" can be rendered "little more than a serious nuisance." The protection he has already made available to everyone will save body and mind. The gas mask, when it is properly put on and used, is complete protection against every form of war gas vapor we know of, he declares.

To stave off Hitler's supreme deviltry is but one of Herbert Morrison's jobs within the wide range of his responsibilities. In addition to the execution of a hundred other duties, he is responsible for the shelter system that protects millions, and for another sort of underground work—digging out the Fifth Column. On his watchfulness and efficiency depend the morale, the spirit, the safety, the actual existence of Great Britain.

One would expect a police tyrant to be entrusted with this somber business. But Herbert Morrison is an utterly civilian type who looks more like an artist, and not alone on account of his calculated sloppiness. Many influences, incidents, struggles and strivings have left their mark on him. Hunger, ambition, failure, success, intelligence, cynicism and faith have made him what he is. He is a man in his early fifties, short in stature, with a deeply lined, somewhat chaotic face that grows broader as the years go by. A billow of unruly hair, parted to the left and mixed with grey, tops his high, slightly protruding forehead. His eyebrows are amazingly thin. His face is clean-shaven. Tortoise-shell glasses, thin lips—the underlip jutting out a trifle—and a sharp nose give it the expression of an intellectual. A pleased and sometimes self-satisfied smile flashes across his face. When he feels himself unobserved it suddenly fades. Then he looks in deadly earnest, business-like, as if he were entirely absorbed in his thoughts.

But such moments are rare, since he is seldom unobserved. He lives in the crowd, and is the unrivalled favorite of the masses. Undoubtedly, he is the most popular of the Labour leaders, although in party councils both the Right and the Left opposed Herbert. Herbert who? No one would ask that question.

Above all he is a Cockney. London-born and London-bred, he carries London in his heart and expresses London in his accent. His voice is the echo of the streets he represents. The King of the Cockneys, they used to call him. But there remains a slight difference. When the King goes to Town, His Honor, the Lord Mayor, challenges the Sovereign at the City's threshold before giving him the right of way. It is one of those ancient formalities to which the English stick. It makes both their independence, which is expressed in the Lord Mayor's action, and their loyalty to the Crown, taste doubly sweet.

When Mr. Morrison goes to Town, no Lord Mayor with a golden chain on his chest appears. Bobbies, drivers, newspaper vendors, messenger boys, passers-by, women shopping, all wave their hands: " 'Ello, 'Erbert!"

He comes from Lambeth which, fifty-odd years ago, was not yet a rhythmic walk but an overcrowded, teeming, slum district in the South of London. His father was a policeman, his mother a housemaid. He got his formal education in an elementary school which he quit at fourteen without having achieved any prizes or distinctions. He started as a delivery boy for a grocer. After four years he became a shop assistant. Following an old English custom, he had to "live in." He was only allowed to leave the premises between 9.30 and 11 P.M. Half an hour of this time he could spend at a near-by Lockhart's, drinking a cup of cocoa for a ha'penny. If he wanted to prey on Lockhart's hospitality for his full time off, he was expected to add a penny for a tea-cake. Three ha'pence was, it seems, the minimum check for patrons who wanted to tarry. Young Herbert was one of these. Feverishly he read Marx, Engels, Spencer, Darwin at the table—his room, of course, was unheated—keeping body and soul together with a cup of lukewarm cocoa.

When he discovered the early writings of H. G. Wells, Shaw, and above all, *Riches and Poverty* by Sir Leo Chiozza Money, he decided to turn Socialist. He did not mind informing his neighbor at the table at Lockhart's, an elderly man, and a perfect stranger, of his decision. The stranger seemed not at all amazed. Indeed, he was a wise judge of men. He introduced himself as an itinerant scientist, and encouraged the boy with a prophecy. "If you study hard enough, you will become Prime Minister of England." Herbert was seventeen at that time.

Both hunger for knowledge and personal ambition set him on his way. He certainly studied hard enough to become Prime Minister. He haunted all the libraries looking for books on economics, history and sociology. *Riches and Poverty*, his personal Bible, he even bought in a second-hand shop for five shillings cold cash, which meant no lunch for a couple of weeks.

A healthy youngster need not eat much, ran one of the disciplinary maxims current in his early days. Drinking was altogether a sin. Meanwhile, Herbert had chosen the profession of switchboard operator in a brewery to be able to read all day long. Exposed to the smell of beer, he acquired a distaste for alcohol. Evenings, he used to stroll along the streets of Streatham and Brixton which, unfortunately, were crowded with sinners. Hundreds of drunkards stumbled out when the pubs closed. Herbert watched them with disgust. How shameful to waste one's evening with just another pint, when one might so much better listen to the debates in the town hall. Herbert listened frequently. The public gallery of the town hall became his real home, more so than Lockhart's had ever been.

One evening, while walking through Brockwell Park, poor man's Hyde Park in the South of London, he came upon a crowd of people gathered around a soap-box that was minus an orator. With furious speed, lest another evangelist should forestall him, he jumped upon the box. He harangued the crowd with an oration in which elements of socialism and temperance were queerly mixed. The thin-faced, ardent youth impressed the listeners with his intelligence and honesty. He repeated the feat a few thousand times afterward. But he never forgot his first platform. When he became Chairman of the City Council, in fact Lord of London, he opened a swimming pool where once his soap-box stood.

He entered politics by joining the National Union of Clerks. Soon he was an active and energetic member. But he was not of the stuff of a union man. Intellectual problems appealed more strongly to him than the mere struggle for working hours and wages. He was leftish, and engaged in constant haggling with the Fabians, then the intellectual center of British socialism, whom he accused of moving too slowly. The fact that he did not fit into the unions proved something of a handicap in his later career. He never had a solid bloc of votes to dispose of, nor could he finance his campaigns with money collected from dues. Ernest Bevin, a competitor from the very beginning, could best him easily when it came to exercising influence in the Party. But no one could best Morrison's unfaltering devotion to the cause. In 1912, when he was twenty-four, the *Daily Citizen* was founded. He joined the staff as an assistant circulation manager. It was a still-born venture. London's first Labour daily had to fold up after three years. But this did not injure Morrison's prospects. He became secretary of the London Labour Party, at a pound a week. He still holds this job, although, for the duration, he does not exercise it. His salary has increased almost tenfold. Now it is five hundred pounds a year, still rather a modest sum. But he has conquered London. Under his leadership, disguised as secretaryship, the Labour M.P.'s for London have increased from two to twenty-seven, and the Borough Council majorities from five to seventeen. The London County Council is ruled by a majority of seventy-five Labour Councillors and twelve Labour Aldermen.

Morrison served his parliamentary apprenticeship in the Lambeth Borough Council. It was a modest beginning, but it proved a most fruitful one. For the first time he had to deal with agenda and minutes. Drafts of bills made him lyrical. He packed his mind with facts. His political aspect changed unintentionally. No longer was the reconstruction of the universe his aim; he was set on bettering conditions in his own ward. "Socialism must come out of the clouds

and become more concrete!" was a phrase he coined in these
early days, and to which he has stuck for the rest of his life.
Indeed, he did a great deal to bring socialism from the lofty
realms of vague aspirations to practical application, always
dissociating it from bureaucracy and power politics.

In 1923, he entered Parliament as Member for South
Hackney, in the East End of London. In the following year
he was defeated in his constituency, and since then he has
time and again contested South Hackney with varying success. After the inglorious end of the MacDonald government,
Labour candidates found the going rough in London. No
less than fifteen safe seats in the country were offered to
Morrison, but with truly Quixotic faithfulness he preferred
to stick to London in general and South Hackney in particular. Again he was defeated, but he took it philosophically.
A great love like South Hackney has the right to be unfaith-
ful. Love is above all changeable. Sure enough, in 1935,
South Hackney again elected Herbert Morrison and since
then the harmony between the constituency and its M.P.
has not been disturbed.

His stubborn adherence to the slums is the only romantic tinge in Morrison. For the rest, he prefers to be recognized as a matter-of-fact man. Even his critics recognize him
as such. The late Lord Haldane said: "He has a cool head
in a crisis, he knows his own mind. His administration is
competent, clean, and effective. He won't let us down."

He wants to be regarded as the builder of socialism, not
as its philosopher. He became a specialist in administration,
finance, transport, electrification, town-planning. Politics
proper did not attract him even when he was elected chairman of the Labour Party in 1928. Holding this position and
being a witty debater—rather than a great orator—he was,
in the next years, frequently mentioned as a possible suc-

cessor to Major Clement Attlee, the Parliamentary Labour
Leader. But this job would have been incompatible with his
position in London, which, of course, he would never have
given up.

National rather than local affairs preoccupied him—until
this war brought the great turn-about—only from 1929 to
1931, when he was Minister of Transport in the first Labour
Administration. But again his love for London was his driving motive. His first act as Transport Minister was to coördi-
nate all London's transport services into one body, the London Passenger Transport Board. This Board was in charge of
traffic that on normal days carries two and a half times as
many people as the population of Norway. The increased
efficiency of London's traffic is of great value now that the
maintenance of transport facilities has become so vital in
keeping London going under bombardment.

Morrison's other important reform was the Road Traffic
Act, which became law in January, 1931. This act abolished
the speed limit of twenty miles an hour, but increased the
safety of the roads by stipulating that no employed driver
should remain at the wheel longer than five and a half hours
without interruption. The mobile police was formed, which
subsequently reduced traffic accidents by fifty per cent. The
passenger bus service all over the country was reorganized
to prevent wasteful competition. Nobody knew at that time
how important correct traffic regulation would prove some
day in beleaguered England. But everybody noticed the
drive and efficiency of the Transport Minister. He became
a Privy Councillor and was the youngest member of the government to join the inner cabinet. When the MacDonald
Administration faltered, Herbert Morrison was widely recognized as its only success. The Electrical Development Association offered him the post of Chairman at an annual sal-

ary of five thousand pounds. He preferred to retain his job as secretary of the Labour Party. It paid only a tenth of the income that had been offered to him, but it held the promise that some day he would run London.

The day came early in 1934. It was a serious day. All over Europe Fascism was on the march. Hitler had recently established his regime in Germany. Herbert Morrison did not relish the first news about Nazism. To him labor-baiting brownshirts were not the harbingers of a new order. It seemed a good thing that London was so far away from the German turmoil. In London he would prove that democracy —with a slightly pink tinge—could work.

The 1934 local elections brought Labour to power in London, until then a Tory stronghold. It was Morrison's personal success. His quick and incisive speaking had swept the town. When a learned Tory opponent, debating against him, objected to his accent, his riposte was: "Pardon me, sir! I am 'Oxton, not Oxford!" referring to Hoxton, a poor district in the East End. He does not like to be called a campaigner, but his disciplined and flexible mind forms telling sentences with ease. As if playing with words he switches quickly from major to minor matters and from big issues to details. This fertility of expression, incidentally, made him one of the most prolific writers in the party. Beside his standard work, *Socialism and Transportation,* he produced an unending stream of articles. He likes speaking and writing, but he despises claptrap. He is a typical Englishman in his preference for understatement. Ballyhoo is physically odious to him. Even in the heat of campaigning he makes no extravagant promises. His actions, he insists, not his statements, shall be spectacular. His actions are carefully planned before being rapidly executed. Fighting for power over London, he was surrounded by a brain-trust of journalists, advertising experts, commercial artists, public relations counsels. But he attributed his final victory to "Lord Beaverbrook's violent attacks on Labour."

The votes had barely been counted when Morrison moved into the modern, completely un-gothic mass of London County Hall, right across from the Houses of Parliament, at the opposite end of Westminster Bridge. He established his headquarters in room 116. No. 116 soon acquired the same fame in London that No. 10 enjoys all over the British Isles. Every Cockney knew that the Prime Minister of London resided at No. 116.

Neither his looks nor his bearing revealed that the dream of his life had come true. On the surface nothing had changed. He still wore the unassuming brown tweed suit in which most Englishmen are dressed. Perhaps his movements and gestures became a little more abrupt, impatient, quick and energetic as he entrenched himself in power. He gave the impression of a business-like and practical person who got what he wanted. What he wanted was work. He set the example himself. "Quintuplets" soon became his nickname, because he did the work of five. He slept on a cot in his office. Pretty, dark, sports-loving, Mrs. Morrison felt somewhat deserted in the modest flat in Eltham in the South East of London, particularly since their daughter Mary had become her father's secretary and constant companion. The sight of Morrison and his daughter crossing Westminster Bridge from the County Hall to Parliament became a familiar London street scene. Unfortunately the harmony— except for his marriage probably the only harmony Morrison has ever enjoyed—ended in the spring of 1941, when daughter Mary met a particularly fiery fire-brigade fighter,

Mr. Horace Williams. Father Morrison shrugged his shoulders. "Better married than bombed!" was his congratulation as he had to acknowledge his loss.

Ten days after Morrison had taken office in 1934, Londoners rubbed their eyes. They could hardly believe what they saw. Indeed, workmen were beginning to pull down old Waterloo Bridge. Thereby hangs a sad tale of ten years' haggling over the rebuilding of this bridge which had long been closed, disrupting the city traffic, and jamming in particular the Strand, one of London's busiest thoroughfares. For a decade everyone was agreed that Waterloo Bridge must be rebuilt. But neither Parliament nor the local administration could agree on how to share the costs. With a gesture of impatience Morrison defied Parliament by simply ordering the work to be done. This energetic measure awoke the House; the Commons decided to appropriate what until then they had considered too large a share.

He was a happy man. He had, so he believed, found the supreme task of his life. The task was simple. Poor people should enjoy what he himself had missed as a poor boy. He announced his Green Belt scheme and began buying land on the outskirts of London for parks and open spaces. Half of the eight million citizens of London, now under his care, sleep in the suburbs. To better the untold hardships of suburban life became his endeavour and his pride. In the old parts of London streets were widened and improved. Blocks of workers' houses, long unfit for habitation, were pulled down and replaced by modern apartment buildings. The ambulance service and the fire brigade were overhauled. Six years later Morrison's spring cleaning of London proved a blessing. The widened streets allow ambulances and fire-fighting equipment to race to their objectives. The modern

apartment buildings withstand bombardment better than
the rickety houses of the slums. The A.R.P. services emerged
out of the fire brigades, streamlined by Morrison. By relieving the congestion at the town's center, building workers'
housing estates on the outskirts, erecting new schools and
social centers, which are now used for the homeless, Morrison proved to have more than foresight. He had intuition.

Great as were his reforms, he never lost sight of the smallest details. He supervised the spending of thirty-six million
pounds a year, more than the annual budget of Switzerland.
The London County Council buys forty-three thousand
doors a year, ten million eggs, two million buttons, nineteen million envelopes. It manages the services of seventy-
two hospitals—two-thirds of all hospitals in London, and the
largest hospital system in the world—it keeps twenty-six hundred men engaged on constant repair work on houses owned
by the Council. Fifteen hundred men are at work maintaining parks and seven hundred tennis courts, three full-sized
golf courses, three hundred and fifty cricket pitches, four
hundred and thirty football grounds, nine quarter-mile running tracks. Seventy bands play during the summer in the
public parks.

Morrison took care of everything. His three main interests were: first, the school system, which cares for children
between the ages of three and seventeen; second, Police and
Fire Brigades; third, his merciless persecution of graft. City
Councillors were forbidden to maintain social relations with
city employees, lest friendships should develop from which
the latter might profit. The merit system of employment was
strictly enforced. No one could get a job through pull or personal relations. To all job-hunters, who pursued him by the
hundreds, Morrison gave the same advice: "You can apply

like any other bloke. But don't tell anybody that you know me—or you'll be fired before you're hired."

The world's biggest city never had a more deeply devoted boss. A single time Morrison left London to take a look-see at America. What he saw on this side was not entirely to his taste. Certainly he was duly impressed by the magnificence of the new country. But America, he later confessed, was "too conservative" for the man who is in love with ancient London. Not that he was still a "dangerous" radical. "The Conservatives," he stated, "have assisted in bringing about many issues of progress. It is surprising how much can be accomplished by suggesting things in words that don't sound too radical." Herbert Morrison has gone all the way from a reddish left-winger to an average Englishman.

The Tories, however, did not quite trust his reform. The fault lay neither in them nor in him, but rather in the Communists, who interfered. The City Council was to be re-elected in 1937. Unfortunately this re-election coincided with much talk about establishing a popular front in Parliament, a Communist transmission-belt only thinly disguised by the loudly proclaimed aim of ousting Mr. Neville Chamberlain. Labour was torn by discussion. With almost the entire leadership Morrison decided against an alliance with the Communists. He had by no means switched to the Right. His class-consciousness remained as strong as ever. He proved it in his personal conduct. Weekends he never spent in hotels, but in the guest houses of the Workers' Travel Association, where he mingled freely with the crowds. He took part in all the modest excitements of guest-house life; dancing with his wife and carpet bowling with the other guests. Carpet bowling, of course, is not quite so distinguished as playing golf. Morrison keeps a set of golf clubs, but he has used them only about ten times in his life. When he had to slip into dinner jacket, he wore it with studied negligence. Once Mrs. Morrison admonished him to tidy up. "I am tidying up London!" he answered stubbornly. He stressed the fact that he was a poor boy who had made good. After the General Election in 1935, he circulated a document among the newcomers to the Parliamentary Labour Party, warning them against the temptation of wasting time on niceties and social life at Westminster. But for British Moscovites he showed nothing but contempt.

Nevertheless, the Conservatives were afraid that continued Labour domination in London would open the gates to the Reds and their fellow-travelers. "Get rid of the hooligans!" was the slogan with which they led the campaign to oust the Labour administration from County Hall, when its first term elapsed in 1937. Contrary to all tradition, even Mr. Baldwin took a personal part in the local electioneering. His efforts backfired. Morrison was returned to office by a great majority, after he had rejected any sort of Communist help, declaring that Bolshevik support would only lose the election for Labour. When the Councillors reassembled in County Hall, Morrison publicly attacked and rebuked the Popular Frontists in his own party.

In the following year he took a hand in expelling from the Party Sir Stafford Cripps and other Communist sympathizers. He had to override considerable opposition led by red-haired Ellen Wilkinson, M.P., now his Parliamentary Secretary in the Home Office and the only woman member of the government. Another sort of opposition came from Scotland and the North Country, which always felt a certain rivalry against predominant metropolitan influences. He was too much of a Londoner to play an important role in matters that concerned the whole country, certain delegates from Liverpool and Edinburgh insisted. But he convinced them of his sincerity of purpose. Even left-wingers hailed his switch to national affairs as the crisis threatened England. He soon became invaluable as a debater in the House. He sharply attacked the Conservative government, he chaffed Ministers, but he never hurt anyone's personal feelings. In his fiftieth year Herbert Morrison had become civil. When he said, "The Tory party are the apologists of pride and privilege, we are the champions of honest toil," the whole House laughed at this nonsense, and no one took offense. As a self-teaser he soon rivalled old masters like Lloyd George, Baldwin and Churchill. His speeches attracted a full House, although he never developed to full parliamentary height. His character, vision, energy, and astuteness made a terrific impact. "Morrison the unbreakable," he was labeled.

One day he appeared pale and shamefaced in the House. "These young blackshirt rowdies have paraded in the East End shouting 'Down with the dirty Jews!' " he said with strong emotion. "What a shame for London! What a shame!" He was now committed to fight Fascism and Nazism. For a true Londoner it was the worst of all evils—a local disorder.

It did not remain long a local disorder. It was a fight for human rights. They were doomed if their guardian—the Commonwealth of British Nations—should fail. Morrison, extremely sensitive in spite of his hard-boiled behavior, immediately understood the full scope of the incipient struggle. The veteran in the fight for liberty could not stand aside. This was his war, the little people's war. Millions of British workers understood it; they closed the ranks.

But other millions, all over the world, did not understand what it was all about. The small neutrals bent back to feed the crocodile. American back-seat drivers coined the word "Sitzkrieg," the phony war. The leading men in the British government decided to wait and see.

Morrison exploded. His explosions start with a crack and end in a bonfire.

"This is a queer war," he observed. "So we are all saying to our neighbors in the train. First we had four years of a peace that was anything but peaceful, now we have a war that, so far, isn't nearly as warlike as we expected. But suppose we made peace now? How do we know that when Hitler's strength was renewed and our preparations were dissipated he would not launch his blitzkrieg out of a clear sky and crush us before we could start? Now a handful of people urge a super-Munich. It is not that I overlook what this war may mean. I am no warmonger. I have spent a lifetime struggling to help make a better life for the mass of our people. But I do not overlook other things either. I know that the Nazi regime is, as it has always been, a poisonous growth, a wholly evil thing. A leopard of this kind cannot change its spots. A victorious Nazi government insists on setting up, in its conquered territories, governments of its own kidney. Think of it, you people of our cities and towns and villages! Government by uniform, by the rubber truncheon, the gun and the concentration camp. Parliament abolished. Political opinion and unions suppressed. The legal system turned into one more instrument of brutality. Every child a potential spy upon its own parents. The free life crushed under the jackboot of Adolf Hitler's Gauleiter!"

The vision obviously tortured him. The nervous strain increased as he had to watch Chamberlain's inefficiency in staving off peril. He had agreed to the Labour Party's truce with the government so as not to disturb the conduct of the war.

But the failures of the Administration aroused his common sense. He felt that the grave problem of munitions was incompetently handled. Many M.P.'s agreed with him. Feelings ran high when, on March 15, 1940, the credit for the Ministry of Supply had to be voted. Amidst general uneasiness, which was increased by rumors of corruption, Morrison rose to ask a few pertinent questions. "In particular we should like to know the position as to machine tools, jigs and gauges. Before the war it was admittedly very unsatisfactory. It was a somewhat disgraceful thing for this great country, perhaps as highly skilled in engineering as any country in the world, to be dependent to an enormous extent upon foreign importations." The situation, he continued, had not materially changed during the first months of the war. It was, indeed, worsened by red tape and lack of initiative. Morrison explained the plight of the small manufacturers and sharply attacked the commission system which had developed in securing orders from the Ministry of Supply. He did not stop at criticism, but proposed valuable suggestions, among others the introduction of a black-list covering undesirable contractors and intermediaries. The lion showed his claws. Still, he retained his attitude of patience and restraint for a few more weeks.

But as with millions of Englishmen of all parties, the Norwegian disaster tried his patience too far. On May 8, 1940, he opened the second day of debate in the House with an attack from which, to England's great good luck, Neville Chamberlain never recovered. There was no partisanship in his speech. "I hope the Prime Minister will believe me that if he were the man who played the great part in winning the war, I would sing his praises," he stated. Unfortunately, there were no praises to be sung. Morrison quoted the *New York Herald Tribune,* which he called "fairly consistently a friend of the Allied cause." The *Tribune* had written that the British were outmaneuvered, and got to Norway too late "just as Mr. Chamberlain has been consistently outmaneuvered and has arrived too late on so many occasions." Morrison put his finger on the sore spot. Chamberlain, he insisted, did not understand Hitler. "I really begin to wonder how much experience of him we are to have, how near we are to get to the disaster before Ministers will try to understand the psychology of this man. It is part of the war operations that we should understand his psychology and estimate his possible actions. . . . The fact is," he concluded after having surveyed the long list of sins of omission committed by Chamberlain and his clan, "that before the war and during the war we have felt that the whole spirit, tempo, and temperament of at least some Ministers have been wrong, inadequate and unsuitable . . ." And he named the three grave-diggers: "I am bound to refer, in particular, to the Prime Minister, the Chancellor of the Exchequer, and the Secretary of State for Air."

Mr. Chamberlain rose. His notorious poise failed him entirely. He was a broken man when he stuttered a few words ending with a help-seeking look in the direction of Captain Margesson, the imperturbable Chief Whip of the Tory Party: "At least we shall see who is with us and who is against us. I call on my friends to support us in the lobby tonight." Sir Samuel Hoare, Air Secretary, engaged in a lengthy argument in which the outraged opposition, Conservative members and Labourites alike, got much the better of him. The third of the three guilty men, Sir John Simon, Chancellor of the Exchequer, remained silent. The House was raging with fury and shame. Speakers arose by the dozen. But Herbert Morrison had won the day. Now the boy from the London slums was England's holy terror.

Two days later, Winston Churchill formed the government to save England. Morrison was appointed Minister of Supply. After seven weeks his first account left the House satisfied that the Ministry of Supply was at last functioning with some success. The increase in the output of tanks as compared with April, the last month of the Chamberlain administration, had risen 115%. Production of guns increased from 50% for two items to 228% for another item. The small arms showed increases ranging between 49% and 186%, ammunition of various kinds showed gains ranging from 35% to 420%. Very large quantities—millions—of a "certain weapon" were produced to the tune of 250,000 a week, that is to say, between four and five times the previous production.

Everyone was pleased—everyone but Morrison. "The last thing I would wish the House and the country to believe is that things are satisfactory. They could not be satisfactory in the circumstances of the case. I can only say that they are coming nearer and nearer to being satisfactory as the days pass." This he attributed—himself declining all credit—primarily to the fine response of the working people in industry, who had "understood the situation in France and the actions of Herr Hitler."

Indeed, no one has contributed more than Herbert Morrison to make the working people understand what an enormous stake they have in the war for liberty, and how by defending the democratic way of life, they are defending their own skins. His heavy government duties left him time to write a pamphlet *Mr. Smith and Mr. Schmidt* which compared the situation of the working class in democracy and under dictatorship. This pamphlet is the unrivalled bestseller in England; since the problem is exactly the same for American labor, it deserves the widest circulation in this country as well.

It describes the conditions of life of the average German and British worker, respectively. "Mr. and Mrs. John Smith have their troubles," Morrison writes. "I am a child of the working class. I am a Socialist. I know." Their resources are limited; they do not enjoy all the reasonable comforts of life, and certainly not the luxuries. A considerable proportion of them know poverty at first hand. They risk the worries of unemployment. But their standard of life is decidedly higher than it would be under dictatorship. Mr. and Mrs. Smith have inherited certain rights and freedoms. They enjoy many advantages of a long period of social progress. If they have complaints, they can "start a row"; they can write to their representatives in Parliament; they can ventilate industrial grievances through the unions. Ultimately the people control the government by the vote. "We have not achieved the perfect society," declares Morrison, a Socialist even though also the King's Privy Councillor, "but the standards of life and degree of security, the progress in health and education of the masses of our people have effected an enormous change as compared with the dark days of the nineteenth century."

In Germany, Morrison continues his parallel, Herr and Frau Johann Schmidt have lost their freedom. They are subjected to harsh and extreme tyranny. Unfortunately for the German dupes they cannot get back the liberty they helped to lose. "Let there be no nonsense about the Nazis at the beginning conducting an honorable experiment, or of its leaders starting out with fine ideals. Both in domestic and external affairs the Nazis were blackguards, are blackguards, and, as far as I can see, will be blackguards until they are liquidated. The fundamental aim of these gangsters was to create a vast war machine by the ruthless use of which they hoped to become masters of Europe and of the world." With strong words he draws a picture of the untold sufferings German labor has to endure to feed the insatiable war machine. Quoting official German figures, he proves the heartrending decrease in consumption per head in Germany, "but the bulky form of Field-Marshal Goering still shows no signs of rationing." He concludes: "If the Germans like this sort of thing within their own borders—and I doubt it of most of them—that's their business. But when their government seeks to impose it on the rest of the world it becomes everybody's business."

It is largely due to Herbert Morrison that the war became everybody's business—at least in the British Isles. The people understood his language, which in fact was their language too. In London, particularly, there developed true intimacy between him and the man in the street, who put his complete trust in him. The Ministry of Supply, although formidable in importance, is somewhat remote from the daily life of the nation. Again Winston Churchill proved his knack of putting the right man in the right place. When London was mercilessly bombed and civilian morale became all-important, he shifted Morrison to the Ministry for Home Security. In this job the ex-left-winger, ex-radical, ex-revolutionary shows his true quality. He is paterfamilias; loving, careful, strict, and when need be, severe.

The Communists were the first to challenge his severity. He had already uttered his contemptuous dislike of them before joining the government. In April, 1940, still in opposition himself, he said: "The Communists are a contemptible body of servile instruments of a foreign government. They now share with the Fascists the miserable task of finding explanations for the evil deeds of Hitler & Co." Of course the Reds heaped abuse on him when he took his new office. After this abuse of a single government official developed into persistent treason against government and country, Morrison was compelled to act. He closed down the *Daily Worker*, Stalin's mouthpiece in Hitler's service. He did not take this measure lightly. In Parliament he apologized for tampering with the liberty of the press. But the Bolshevists, having perverted liberty into license, found few advocates even among the extreme left Labourites. Morrison was congratulated on his firmness.

On the other hand he endeavoured to carry on the necessarily strict war-time regulations with the least possible infringement of human rights and dignity. This is no empty phrase to Morrison. Although by no means a sentimentalist, his driving motive is his strong social feeling and his sympathy for the underdog. Of course his humanity also is business-like and to the point. He does not spin fine words. His first statement as Home Secretary read simply: "Internationally known experts are working at Whitehall, studying at the Home Office the machinery for dealing with aliens. They will shortly have devised methods for speedy handling of some 200,000 foreigners. The War Office was the first department to recognize the value of business experience in simplifying Whitehall methods. We are following suit." On January 4, 1941, indeed, 90,000 of 270,000 interned aliens were released, and so were about half of the 15,000 imprisoned British Fascists. An amazing brotherhood of illegal Blackshirts and Communist agents are currently starting a boisterous campaign for the release of Sir Oswald Mosely, Hitler's appointed Gauleiter for England. Unfortunately for the trouble-makers, Morrison seems to be deaf in one ear. The other one he keeps carefully to the ground.

He loves all and sundry, but one could not say that he

trusts everybody. When asked by Colonel Wedgwood, Labour M.P., if it would not be possible to treat Americans like British citizens, Morrison promised to ease the restrictions for American residents. He was entirely agreed that a most liberal policy should be followed. "But as a matter of fact, I cannot treat every British citizen as though he were above suspicion, and it would be clearly wrong if I were to say that every citizen of a nation of a hundred and thirty million was above suspicion."

The conditions of civil defense have greatly improved since Morrison became responsible for maintaining the water, heat, gas and light services; for distributing food; for putting out incendiary bombs and removing time bombs; for the care of the injured and homeless, and for the burial of the dead. His main interest is the constant improvement of the shelter system. Again he argues for it, appealing to reason rather than to sentiment. "Victory depends on keeping the people in the shelters happy." But his gruff manner does not deceive his East Enders, crowded in frequently pitiful caves. They feel that his heart is with them. " 'Erbert will 'elp!" they say. " 'Erbert won't let us down! 'E belongs to us!"

Herbert does help. He devised the new individual shelter, a rectangular steel box six and a half by four feet, with side walls of steel. Flat on top, it may be used in daytime as a table. At night people can sleep in it, safe even if two stories of brick and masonry collapse on them. There is space for two adults and two children in these shelters. Winston Churchill's large bulk needs a little more than normal space. Yet the Prime Minister asked to have a Morrison shelter, "when my turn comes."

For the public shelters in London Morrison has ordered a million bunks, and another couple of million for the shelters in the provinces. He took good care that the shelters were heated, made as dry, healthy and comfortable as possible, especially in winter. He built a spur-tunnel system, attached to the subway, for use as deep air-raid shelters. Yet he recognizes the preference the average Englishman has for his home, his castle. "Eighty per cent of the people prefer to take a chance in their own homes," he says. It is, in its broader implications, a recognition of English individualism that will never give way. After surveying personally the relief work being done in Coventry, he said proudly: "And those are the people Hitler wants to beat!"

His stubbornness is of truly British fiber. It is not resounding heroism; it holds no promise to mankind. All that is Winston's business. Herbert Morrison's part is the cool, considered argument. Yet he cannot extinguish his own flame, expressing like a cold calculation the confession of his creed: "We either go through with it or surrender. We are not going to surrender, because surrender would mean something for many years much more terrible than the experience through which we are now going."

The Gentleman Vanishes

CLEMENT ATTLEE

YOU WILL NOT FIND THE TRUE GENTLEMAN IN DRAWING-room comedy. You need not look for him in the sanctuary of an exclusive West End club. He lives among the small people. He is devoted to the cause of the poor. To be a gentleman is foremost a matter of morale; on his earthly pilgrimage the Redeemer was mankind's greatest gentleman. It is, secondly, a matter of manners, even if the poor don't quite understand it. Sometimes they are bewildered by the gentleman's calm delivery of very outspoken theories on their behalf. They whisper that he belongs to the other side, that birds of a feather . . . Only a few notice how, speaking about the poor, he twines his fingers until the knuckles show white. If he did not control himself he might lose his balance. Balance, of course, is the gentleman's third asset.

But since his poor are English they don't really mind following a leader who is not only a gentleman but looks it to an embarrassing degree. English Socialists used to regret that they could not cast their votes for Earl Baldwin, whom they regarded as a very decent chap. So they accepted "Clem" in his stead, the poor man's Baldwin.

True, radical youngsters and party delegates from the

E. O. Hoppé—London

CLEMENT ATTLEE

slums occasionally objected to the Oxford accent which he does not manage completely to disguise. They were inclined to scoff. He never hit back. Fair-play is the first article of his creed. The underprivileged must necessarily resent his well-to-do descent and his Oxford accent; he understands it perfectly. Besides, he bears the black mark of a distinguished World War record as a highly decorated front-line officer. There was only one way of convincing his followers of the honesty of his Socialist purpose. He had to sound a little more combative than nature had intended a gentleman to be. So it happened that occasionally he lost his way in the fog of politics.

Take his attitude toward war. At Gallipoli he had led his men into an attack, unmindful of the Turkish bullet that struck his hip in the first minutes of the fight. He was just as unconcerned about the fact that his gun jammed; he had no weapon but his officer's baton when he flung himself into the enemy barrage. But when, not many years later, the Labour Party was deluded by wishful thinking of eternal peace at half an hour's flying distance from Goering's first air bases, he became a conscientious objector. Long before most Englishmen he recognized the menace of Nazism. He did his best, and not quite unsuccessfully, to awaken his party to that menace. Yet, he still opposed conscription four months prior to the outbreak of the war in order not to mar the Party's pacifist record. In private life his sharpest word of censure is "odd." In the House he questioned the personal honor of a Prime Minister whom his party opposed. He was their leader, so he had to follow them.

He is still the leader of the Labour Party. Perhaps he is not a great leader; certainly he is not a forceful one. But his devotion to the cause of human dignity is unsurpassed. He has sacrificed his life for the underdog and still retains the gentleness of the upper class. For twenty years he was in the thick of every fight, but he rarely took the gloves off. All England is agreed that he did a good job against heavy personal odds. He is still doing it. However, he is well aware that he owes his influence in the war cabinet primarily to his seniority. Tougher types came to the fore: Bevin and Morrison. Another man with his proud record would not content himself with remaining the front-man. He would probably bang the door behind his back. But a gentleman makes no such dramatic exit. A gentleman enjoys no last curtain call. He does not even sigh when he resigns. A gentleman vanishes.

The Right Honorable Clement Richard Attlee, "Clem" to his three or four friends and to a few million voters, Lord Privy Seal, M.P., belongs among the few born and bred Londoners in British politics. He was born on January 3, 1883, in a comfortable Mayfair flat, furnished with plush armchairs and gilt mirrors. His family boasts a long lineage of lawyers and officers. Both his father and grandfather were distinguished gentlemen in His Majesty's armed services. Clem got his education at Haileybury College, an exclusive "public" school, and at University College, Oxford, where he studied law and took his degree with the highest honors in Modern History. He left Oxford as confirmed a Tory as any of his ancestors. Colleagues from his University days remember him as "extremely unimpressive." They obviously did not understand the very young gentleman who excels in unobstrusiveness. The best dressed man is he whose clothes you don't remember. The most polished speaker convinces by his cause, not with his phrases. In speaking and writing, his colleagues admit, Clem revealed a well-stored mind. He had read widely. But he anxiously avoided learned quotations.

In 1905, at the age of twenty-two, he was called to the Bar of the Inner Temple. Everyone expected him to embark upon a profitable career in the law. For the first time he disappointed expectations. He rented a modest room in the East End, the slums of London, and soon got mixed up with a crowd that would have puzzled and horrified his aunts. He associated himself with the Webbs in their Poor Law work. He went to the Social Science Department of the School of Economics. Occasionally he lectured at Toynbee Hall. He was drawn into the local affairs of the East End. He never revealed how his first realization of the conditions of poverty affected him. A gentleman does not explain how he feels on the pilgrimage to Damascus; an English gentleman least of all. Family and friends were forced to accept his decision to take down his shingle and to become an underpaid lecturer at the London School of Economics. The year was 1913. He held his teaching job for a decade.

His hold on his pupils was as complete as was his hold on the rank and file of Labour in later years. Today he could still pass for a schoolmaster. In politics he applies the methods of a teacher. He shuns rhetoric as if rhetoric were not quite gentlemanly. He argues with the weight of his logic. Besides he knows well that emotional fanfares would make him look silly. Through heavy glasses he looks thoughtful and considerate at a thoughtless and inconsiderate world. He is of medium height, slender and mild-mannered. His bushy moustache contrasts amazingly with his baldness. He invariably wears a black, conservative suit, but his gay, striped shirts make another bold contrast. Not even the perfect gentleman, it seems, can entirely iron out the odd contradictions of nature. Clem Attlee, to give another example, is the most orderly of men. Yet his handwriting would frighten a graphologist and force him to the most somber conclusions. It is completely illegible. Fortunately, American genius can go nature one better. An American invention, the typewriter, accompanies Attlee everywhere. He dictates sentences that sound like translations from Latin. He is never impatient with his secretary who, in turn, can never follow Attlee's stream of words rapidly enough.

The first war interrupted Attlee's scholarly revolution. He hated war. He was fed up with the stories of the Crimean and Boer campaigns, in recollecting which, his grandfather and father, respectively, had never omitted the minutest detail. Besides, his philosophy forbade the use of arms with the intention to kill. So he strolled along the streets of London, dropped into the first recruiting office he found, and volunteered. It was an hour and a half after the declaration of war. He enlisted in the South Lancashire Regiment where he served both in the infantry and the tank corps. He spent the entire war at the front, fighting in France, Gallipoli and Mesopotamia. He was twice wounded, at Kut-El-Amara rather badly. He was one of the last men to be demobolized. He did not muster out before 1919, as a Major, decorated with the Distinguished Service Order. He never afterwards used his military title in private life. He is a hero against his own volition. Of course all England refers to him as Major Attlee.

Immediately on his return to civil life he entered active politics. As if to atone for having been a gallant officer he ran for Alderman, in Stepney, the humblest office in the humblest London borough. He was elected and at once chosen Mayor. After two years his preoccupation with national affairs forced him to resign the office of Mayor. But he remained faithful to Stepney, serving the Borough as an

Alderman for another six years. He practised what he later preached to the world—the policy of the good neighbor.

Attlee entered Parliament in 1922, as Member for the Limehouse Division, which he still represents. MacDonald, a Socialist who liked the flavor of the English gentleman, found him to his taste. Poor MacDonald was not always fortunate in his aristocratic leanings. In his first administration he had a well-born and highly connected Chancellor of the Duchy of Lancaster who looked like a panther, he was so lithe and black and shiny, and who behaved like a hyena. The gentleman was then the son-in-law of Viscount Curzon. He had antagonized Britain's Four Hundred by joining the Reds. Today, he is reported to be the most unruly jailbird in Brixton Prison. He is, of course, Sir Oswald Mosley, Hitler's appointed Gauleiter for England. Already as a fiery-red young M.P. he was an incorrigible trouble-maker. MacDonald had to drop him. He was so fed up with colorful, imaginative and utterly irresponsible fellows that he chose the most uninteresting, unimaginative but most reliable among his back-benchers as successor to the fallen angel. Owing to his faithfulness and to his distinguished war record, Attlee did not long remain Chancellor of the Duchy of Lancaster. He was made Under Secretary to the diminutive Stephen Walsh at the War Office.

He outlasted the first Labour Administration as a parliamentarian of increasing importance. He soon became known as a middle-of-the-road man. His gift for straightening out differences both of internal party strife and conflicts between the parties made him a most valuable Member, often with the weight and dignity of an umpire. Like Winston Churchill on the opposite bench, Attlee always maintained cordial personal relations even with political antagonists. Similarity of tastes brought him close to Mr. Baldwin, the Conservative chief. Both men understood and liked things English; both exercised and appreciated utter simplicity; both were pipe-smokers. Their literary appreciation, their knowledge of what is good language, their contempt for artificial class barriers were much alike. But Attlee never attained Baldwin's ability to speak for England, nor did he reach the Tory chief's real understanding of the workingman. Ever again the question popped up whether or not Attlee spoke with the authentic voice of Labour.

Referring to a great Liberal Prime Minister, "Bob" Cecil —Lord Cecil of Chelwood—declared with undiluted Cecilian authority: "There is in Attlee a Campbell-Bannerman. The question is whether he will get responsibilities and whether they will bring out the vital qualities in him." A similar judgment, both benevolent and a little cautious, came from the highest authority in Attlee's own Labour ranks. The veteran Arthur Henderson said: "Attlee has large hidden reserves. I wonder will they be used."

The cautious note in the appraisal of Attlee by a wise man like Bob Cecil and an experienced politician of Arthur Henderson's standing hinted at Attlee's central quality, an essentially English quality—his shy reserve. The fact that the greatest Englishman alive, Winston Churchill, is by no means burdened with this quality does not upset the rule. It rather confirms it. Outstanding leaders frequently appeal to the masses of their people through a foreign touch. Thus Lloyd George is the only Frenchman in Britain; Poincaré was the only Prussian in France. Winston himself, the reincarnation of John Bull, is more than half American.

Clem Attlee, a youthful Labourite when Premiership was half predicted and half denied to him by the shrewdest of old Tories, had not the slightest tinge of strange magic. He never developed it. He remained English of the English, a familiar and popular type, but unexciting. "I would not walk five yards to hear him speak," his secretary said. The young man could say it and go unpunished. Probably Attlee, a mild-mannered boss, agreed with him.

His pipe became more famous than his words, although on non-controversial matters he speaks better than anyone else. He knows that Englishmen like unity better than dissension. Referring to Lenin's aristocratic descent, an observer called Attlee "a lean Lenin in a non-revolutionary community." He remained the product of his academic background, temperate of spirit, painstaking, modest to the degree of asceticism.

Such was the picture the public had of a man who grew from politics into statesmanship. The picture was wrong. It failed to take into account the true explanation of all Clement Attlee's assets and liabilities. The explanation is simple. He remained hopelessly a gentleman.

A gentleman must necessarily be reserved. His reserve is the source of his strength. He can, at worst, express it in irony. This, to many people, spells standoffishness, coldness, unresponsiveness. The contrary is true. Clem is a human being full of warmth and understanding. He is only afraid, perhaps unconsciously, lest strange eyes pierce his shell. He lives, after all, among and for people from whom he differs widely in background, education and position in life. He remains secluded. Hence, he does not sweep his hearers off their feet. He hates demonstrativeness in himself and others. But he makes his listeners think. What he says is close-knit, sharply argued; it serves a purpose. He dramatizes neither himself nor his topics. He digs himself into his material, never speaking before he has definitely made up his mind. The tenacity with which he clings to his opinions sometimes sounds grim. But his inner fire rarely breaks out into open flames.

His main quality is extreme sensitiveness. Of course that is easily mistaken for unapproachability. His manner encourages the misunderstanding. He seems sharp when he is simply defending his solitude. He prefers listening to speaking in public. In private life he is a brilliant conversationalist, lonesome again, since brilliant conversationalists don't grow on trees on English soil. Among the very few friends who know him intimately the "dullest Englishman in politics" is renowned for his keen and sharp wit. During parliamentary debates he frequently dashes off devastating rhymes and limericks. No one ever sees them. The only sign of unrest one can notice from the gallery is his continuous scribbling. Hunching himself on his bench, crossing his legs and letting his glasses slide down to the tip of his nose, he goes through all the motions of writing. In fact, he does not always write. He is an incurable "doodler," covering sheet after sheet with the most intricate patterns. These patterns, senseless on the surface, reveal more of his inhibited and yet explosive nature than the most vitriolic socialist pamphlet he ever produced.

A grave test of his self-restraint came in 1927, when Attlee went to India as a member of the Simon Commission. Sir John's empty vanity and excesses of self-satisfaction, which flourished tropically in India's oriental atmosphere, made Attlee physically sick. He took his revenge by coining a few of the most biting jokes. You would hardly believe what unprintable expressions a gentleman can use when his good taste is offended. His party friends loved it. They rejoiced that in the end the dignitary had become human. It was highest time for him to break the ice. The Party needed him.

Labour prepared to stage a comeback: Attlee was wanted for the second MacDonald administration. In 1929, he was made Postmaster General, the job that, next to the Home Office, most strongly influences elections. That he could not deliver the goods when the General Election was held, in 1931, was not his fault. It was the famous panic election that all but swept Labour from the House. Attlee, however, was one of the small band of Labourites who retained their seats, if only with a battered majority of a few hundred votes. Owing rather to the lack of other successful candidates than to his own popularity, he became deputy leader of the Parliamentary Labour Party. Circumstances largely beyond his control had brought the great turn-about in his career.

The official leader of the Labour group in the House was old George Lansbury, a veteran highly respected for his personal honesty, but a danger both to the Party and to England on account of his biblical pacifism that demanded Great Britain's outright submission and subservience in the face of every insult. Attlee was the right man to steer the middle course. He humored the old shepherd Lansbury and, by the same token, kept the flock together. Although he was rightist in style and tendency he never sided with the outspoken right wing of the party, with the trades-unionists of Ernest Bevin's and Sir Walter Citrine's type. On the contrary, he delivered a few speeches in, as it seemed, an unnecessarily sharp vein. Only Attlee himself knew how necessary this sharpness, so unpalatable to him, really was. It kept him in the race for leadership to which he aspired, certainly not for personal reasons but through the conviction that he was the best man to keep the party together.

Just before the 1935 Election the question of sanctions

against Italy disposed of Lansbury and a couple of quasi-Bolshevist fellow-travelers, among them Sir Stafford Cripps. The issue of leadership now lay between Attlee, Herbert Morrison, London's favorite son, and Arthur Greenwood, another party veteran. Attlee, as deputy leader, had to conduct the campaign. He managed his job very successfully; the Labour vote was restored to normal proportions. After the poll he was elected leader, and as Leader of the Opposition he was England's "alternative Prime Minister."

Two years later, in 1937, a statute known as the "Minister of the Crown" act accorded a minister's salary—then £2,000 a year—to the Leader of the Opposition. Attlee was embarrassed. He liked the fact that his position was recognized as a constitutional one, important for the conduct of national affairs. On the other hand the act created new unrest and criticism among the Labourites. "Now Clem's job is worth having!" was a poisonous phrase that went the rounds. Why should, as was officially stated, "lack of funds embarrass the alternative Prime Minister"? The Leader of the Opposition has no more expenses than an ordinary M.P. The truth was, they said, that Clem was now the prisoner of his opponents.

To demonstrate that this was by no means the case, Attlee —probably without relish—had to stiffen his opposition. He showed that when in form, he can be magnificently offensive. The House listened to carefully worked-out epigrams, sarcasms, gems of eloquence. Perhaps his rhetoric was a trifle too elaborate, too literary. It did not ring quite true in a voice that was as thin as the speaker's personality. When he rose from his opposition seat, his lean figure nervous and highly strung, with a manuscript in shaky hands, he looked more pathetic than dangerous. He was a little too anxious to succeed. His educated intelligence seldom missed the mark. He was a clever critic. A leader he was not. He remained a gentleman, torn by scruples.

He needed the relaxation of home life. In his house in Stamford he could be himself—a country squire who happens to be the Socialist leader to boot. He is an excellent bridge player, altogether a model husband, and a tender father. He is the favorite companion of his four children, Janet, Felicity, Martin and Alison, today aged between twelve and nineteen. He is perfectly happy when, with his pipe drawing well, he can revel in a bit of carpentry. His three daughters used to keep rabbits as pets. He knocked together a new hutch, thoroughly enjoying the sawing and hammering. He was very proud of having helped his children. Perhaps they could have made it better themselves, but they wanted to give their father the pleasure of being pestered for his help.

Besides the delights of carpentering Clem Attlee enjoys an occasional glass of sherry, and even more his garden and his library. He is pleased that he could manage a housemaid for his wife after the Minister of the Crown Act became law. He is a thoroughly peaceful man.

But he despises appeasement. When Sir Samuel Hoare resigned in tears after the failure of the shameful Hoare-Laval pact, and Baldwin, who first ratified and then repudiated the pact, stayed on, Attlee even rose against his old friend and idol. "There is the question of the honor of the Prime Minister!" he yelled. He had to yell. The words would have stuck in his throat if he had tried to attack Baldwin personally in his habitual considerate fashion. His attack, incidentally, backfired. Sir Austen Chamberlain, already an

elder statesman, loathed the Hoare-Laval pact as vehemently
as did the Opposition. But it now proved that Attlee had
overshot the mark. "The Leader of the Opposition, by pointing to the Prime Minister and saying that his honor is at
stake, has made it certain that no government supporter
will abstain in the division," Sir Austen decreed. Baldwin
was rescued. In fact, Attlee, the Leader of the Opposition,
had saved the Prime Minister's political life.

Attlee's attitude remained contradictory. Early in 1938,
he asked for the establishment of a Ministry of Supply for
the fighting services, which was, indeed, established in the
spring of 1939. But he opposed peacetime conscription. It
would not remain military conscription. It would develop
into industrial conscription, he argued, and British Labour
was unwilling to give up its hard-won rights. Perhaps he
could not forget that he had once headed a "No More War!"
committee until Munich made him forget it. "Chamberlain's
policy is not a policy at all, it is only an attitude—an attitude
of deference!" he said after Munich. He appeared to be the
wild man of the House. But in his heart he was certainly
longing for coöperation and coalition.

To many Englishmen the outbreak of the war brought
inner peace. Clem Attlee is one of these. He buried the
hatchet with the words: "We disagree profoundly with the
government. But we support the war because everything
we stand for is attacked by evil forces!" Never has a warlike
declaration sounded so utterly ready for compromise.

Of course no compromise with Hitler was to be thought
of. It was as in the days of his youth when Attlee first heard
the voice calling. Again the gentleman, the defender of the
weak, was aroused. "We reject the conception of power,
and repudiate Imperialism," the British Labour leader stated

soon after the outbreak of war. "We believe that all people of whatever race and color have an equal right to freedom and to an equitable share in the good things of the world." The issue with Hitler had to be fought out.

During the first months of the war Attlee exercised all his influence as Leader of the Opposition to avoid disturbances of domestic unity. Although Mr. Chamberlain's conduct of the war neither gave nor deserved encouragement, both patriotism and natural inclination kept Attlee silent. The two speeches he delivered in the House were, characteristically, devoted to the two little nations whose rebirth he proclaimed a British war aim. On October 3, 1939, he pledged the Labour Party's fidelity to Poland; on March 13, 1940, he demanded greater assistance for Finland.

Six days later, however, Finland was already a fading memory. On March 19, 1940, Attlee could no longer be silent. He exposed Chamberlain's conduct of the war in a penetrating analysis. He attacked the policy of wait and see and the half-heartedness in which the government indulged. He referred to the idle mines and idle ships that stultified the war effort after six months of fighting. Infuriated, he read to the House a letter that a movie magnate had written to him. The good man boasted of having just completed his newest theater, a building which consumed quantities of steel. "Have we nothing better to do with English steel?" Attlee asked. The gentleman's contempt for business-as-usual exploded.

On April 2, 1940, before France fell, Attlee pointed out the "danger from Paris." A few days later Norway and Denmark were invaded. In the debate on this disaster, on May 7, 1940, Attlee called a spade a spade: "This government," he declared, "has no plan, no intelligence, no concentration on essential objectives. It does not even understand the importance of the air in this war. Mr. Chamberlain has missed all the busses since 1931. Men who need a rest should have a rest. We will win this war, but we need different people to win it!"

Three days later the Churchill government was formed. Attlee himself now belonged with those men who had to pull England through the war. He was appointed Lord Privy Seal. His great hour came when Churchill flew to Paris. Winston knows when he should fly abroad. When, for instance, he wants to let another fellow speak in his stead. War dictatorship was to be introduced. Better not by the war lord himself, but by the Socialist leader.

Attlee knew that he acted as front-man. Loyally he was willing to do it. He introduced the Emergency Powers Defense Bill to the House. A hundred and sixty-three minutes after he began to speak the Act was signed by King George VI, and promulgated. For the duration, England's liberties —the true prize of this war—are in pawn.

The Lord Privy Seal, a very British institution, almost unknown and little understood abroad, is, in fact, the government's handyman. If the office did not carry a glorious, centuries-old tradition, it might have been invented on purpose to give Clement Attlee the job of his life. His main concern is to straighten out such differences as must necessarily arise between the various governmental departments. His patience in managing difficult matters and conflicting temperaments is unfaltering. So is his working capacity. Attlee was always a hard worker. Even before the war he used to work from 8 A.M. to midnight. Now he merely snatches four or five hours' sleep on the cot in his office. He has his breakfast in the entirely un-proletarian "Oxford and Cambridge Club," where he has had a telephone installed at his bedside. He usually has for lunch guests whom he calls, with a certain naïveté, "important people." His frugal dinner he takes alone in the canteen of his Ministry. Air raids cause the only break in his routine. Not that he takes to the shelter. He is incorrigible in never losing the gentleman's poise when his staff rushes downstairs as prescribed. For him every raid is an incitement to visit his crowded constituency and personally to take care of the needs of the people there who trust in him.

His staff adore him. He is amenable to all suggestions. He always asks courteously, never barks his orders. When a more outspoken cabinet colleague once asked him how he manages to keep his even temper with "some fools," he asked in return: "Why, is not a Lord Privy Seal allowed to be a gentleman?"

Perhaps Mr. Attlee might not like this retort of his to be published. In his high office he has retained his old shyness. He shuns publicity and does not like being mentioned in the papers. He has no longer any personal ambitions. He lets the other fellow do the talking. For himself, he prefers to listen attentively, crouching in a large leather armchair. Sometimes he jumps up rather abruptly and paces the room as he talks. There is still quite a lot of fight left in him.

He will need it. He has not always easy times in what he calls the "war cabinet's clearing-house." As deputy leader of the House, in addition, he acts as the link between Parliament and government, always on call when the House is sitting. He does the dirty work for Winston Churchill. But no man in Great Britain has cleaner hands and a purer heart than the immortal gentleman.

A Lord Who Rules the Water

ALBERT VICTOR ALEXANDER

WITH A THIN SMILE ILLUMINATING HIS THOUGHTFUL prophet's face Abraham Lincoln looks down. He blesses a good fight. His picture hangs above a high table behind the First Lord's desk. It arrived, a few months ago, from America—a gift from Mr. Knox, our Secretary of the Navy, to his British opposite number, the First Lord of the Admiralty. "Surely in a war being fought for the preservation of human liberty no more significant name could be remembered," Mr. Knox wrote in sending the picture. "Bert" acknowledged it gratefully: "The gift of this picture expresses sympathy in the battle for human freedom, the thing to which Lincoln dedicated his life. No gift from you could have been more happily chosen to express the struggle in the same cause to which Lincoln was devoted."

"Bert," of course, is the Right Honorable Albert Victor Alexander, Winston Churchill's personal choice as his successor in the Admiralty. To many people it was a rather surprising choice. Outside England Mr. Alexander's name does not awake many associations. Inside his country every child, of course, knows Bert. But they know him rather as a voluble Baptist lay preacher, as the indefatigable promoter of

184

ALBERT VICTOR ALEXANDER

the co-operative movement, and, among his friends, as the owner of a loud and cheerful bass. His first term as First Lord—in MacDonald's Labour government, from 1929 to 1931—has been forgotten by many people. Bert was never a great one for parades and flag-waving. He was an unassuming ruler of the waves, but he is, according to Churchill's description, "the best naval expert to be found." No office is nearer and dearer to Churchill's heart than the house next to the Admiralty Arch. From its rooftop, where wireless messages from the seven seas are picked up, down to the air-raid shelter, the whole building is permeated with Winston's personal atmosphere. Churchill would never accord the run of this house to a man in whom he had not unlimited confidence.

When Mr. Alexander stepped into the First Lord's shoes, he did not alter much in his surroundings. True, the walls of the First Lord's room, which overlooks the Horse Guards, are now plastered with maps and charts, which might indicate the new landlord's sense for detail. An oil-painting of the battle of Trafalgar adds new color to the venerable hall. The globe in the corner and the pictures of Nelson and Pepys, which Churchill treasured, have not been moved. An innovation, however, is the high table behind the desk, the same table above which Lincoln's portrait now hangs. Mr. Alexander uses this table to continue his work standing when he feels tired from many hours at his desk, which, incidentally, is adorned with five telephones and the photographs of his daughter and his grandchild. He has his predecessor's indefatigability. Like Churchill he sleeps in his office. Breakfast is over at 8 A.M. After a rapid glance at the morning papers the First Lord goes to his desk and remains there—only interrupting his work to attend cabinet meetings or to go to the House of Commons—until 3 A.M.

If an important message comes through any later, he is to be informed immediately. In the Cabinet and in the House he is the spokesman of the navy. For the rest, his job consists in supervising the movements of every single British naval vessel. Most of the cables he sends across the world are orders to commanders to proceed to a certain destination. He is, incidentally, quite well informed about the movements of enemy vessels.

It is not quite as simple as it sounds. In fact, Albert Victor Alexander holds one of the key-positions in this war. The fate of the British Empire and of democracy all over the world depends largely on the ability of the Royal navy to keep open the sea lanes, to reassert Britain's traditional supremacy at sea, and, first and foremost, to prevent Hitler from cutting the artery of civilization—the connection between America and the British Isles.

In this terrific struggle, the British navy and her First Lord fight against tremendous odds. In the last war four powerful fleets—the American and the French, the Italian and the Japanese—helped the Royal navy to do the job which, today, she must carry out singlehanded, with the Italians lined up against her, and the French and Japanese fleets potential enemies. The Kaiser's U-boats were practically bottled up in German waters. Every raid involved the danger of crossing the heavily mined outlets through the Channel and the North Sea. Today Hitler has his U-boat bases along two thousand miles of Atlantic coast line, from the Norwegian North Cape to Bordeaux. The outlook seems heavy with dark foreboding.

But Mr. Alexander is undaunted. He carries on his job in the Churchill tradition. He, too, belongs to this bulldog breed of blunt and bluff, breezy and determined Englishmen, who make the best of the worst. Two thousand miles of German-dominated coastline are just two thousand miles of target to him. Hitler had better watch out. "Amphibian actions," like the raid on the Lofotens in the spring of 1941, may easily disrupt his coastal defenses and communications on a larger scale. The first full-sized amphibian action was Churchill's attack on Gallipoli in the last war. Military history has long recognized it as a master stroke, the failure of which was only due to the bungling, the half-heartedness and the insufficient support at home, which doomed the action. Today the home front, Downing Street and Whitehall, are in the firm grip of Britain's toughest pair of fists. Audacious attacks no longer backfire.

The British navy is ready for the showdown. Mr. Alexander likes to point out that the number of ships in most classes—"and especially in the destroyer classes"—is greater than at any time since the war began. True, the task itself is infinitely greater. All the calculations of the Admiralty at the outset of the war, when it was planned to fight as the ally of France, then the second strongest naval power in Europe, have been upset by her collapse. England expected an immediate invasion attempt by Germany. "They may land," says Mr. Alexander, "but they will never get home again. The navy," he insists, "charts the course to victory. And the merchant fleet," he adds, with strong conviction, "is the cornerstone of our national defense."

It sounds like the bark of naval guns to hear this man speak of the King's ships. He by no means minimizes the dangers of German raiding on the seas, but he is unafraid of the ultimate outcome. He gives every credit to the rapid changes in German naval tactics—but British tactics change just as rapidly to meet new dangers. "As our resources grow, so will the raider's opportunities become fewer," he predicts, and thoughtfully adds that "not every raider lives to raid another day." Acknowledging that German raiders have a few times attacked "convoys with inferior protection" and inflicted a relatively heavy loss, he points out the fact that for every convoy thus attacked, scores have come through without molestation, and that great armies with their full equipment have been successfully shepherded all over the oceans by the navy, without the loss of a single ship. He speaks with unconcealed delight about ships and oceans. He loves them. Before the war, he twice sailed around the world. His nostrils quiver with keen enjoyment as if they inhaled a salty breeze in the stuffy office.

The Right Honorable Albert Victor Alexander, however, was not baptized with salt water. He is a landlubber by descent and birth. He was born in Weston-Super-Mare, in the West of England, fifty-six years ago, the son of a modest artisan-engineer, without any great expectation of an adventurous life. What formal education he had, the Barton Hill School and later the St. George Technical Classes—both in Bristol—provided. His schooling ended in his thirteenth year. Then he got his first job as an errand boy. The date was January 23, 1898. This date is important since Mr. Alexander believes that 23 is his lucky number. His voice, whose trumpet tone has more than once aroused House and country, is subdued, and almost awe-stricken, as he confesses: "I began my work on January 23. I took my oath in the Commons on November 23. I was assigned seat 23 in the House. On July 23, 1924, I was gazetted as Parliamentary Secretary to the Board of Trade, my first government office. On July 23, 1929, I was appointed First Lord of the Admiralty in the Labour Administration. But most important and luckiest of all—I was married at 23, earning, incidentally, less than two pounds a week." No common sailor can be more superstitious than this highly uncommon First Lord.

The "uncommonness" of Alexander's career is typical of the great, if silent, transformation that England has undergone within the lifetime of this generation. The possibility that an artisan's son, minus the old school tie, without "pull" or connections, might preside over the truest and bluest of His Majesty's fighting services—and this at the Empire's crucial hour—would have dumbfounded an earlier age. Young Alexander himself had certainly not the faintest notion of his promising predestination, when he first entered public life. He did not make his debut in politics, but in religion. To rise from the humbleness of an office boy to the dignity of a shop clerk, a fortuitous change which occurred when he was twenty, did not satisfy his ambition. Probably it was more than ambition. The young man hearkened to the voice. The urge to do great things spurred him on. Perhaps visionary shop clerks are not really so rare. In America they dream of owning a mighty chain of stores. In the old country—in the times, at least, in which Mr. Alexander was young—they embraced religion.

The voice from within demanded an outlet. One day, much to his own surprise, young Alexander heard his inner voice rolling, thundering, fairly swamping a Baptist meeting. He spoke of the brotherhood of man. Since that remarkable Sunday he has spoken a few thousand times about the brotherhood of man. He became one of the most popular Baptist lay-preachers in England. Even today, as First Lord of the Admiralty, waging a merciless war at sea, the brotherhood of man is his favorite topic and the pulpit of the lay-preacher his preferred platform.

The brotherhood of man is no illusion to him, but an eminently practical reality. Albert Victor Alexander is a matter-of-fact idealist. He has not forgotten his grooming as an office boy and shop clerk. The Co-operative Marketing Movement, which he helped to create in England, and the leading representative of which he soon became, expressed his "practical Christianity." As the organizer, the spokesman, the secretary-general of the Co-operative Movement, he established a nation-wide reputation. When he first entered Parliament, in 1922, as Member for the Hillsborough Division of Sheffield, he was careful to call himself: representative of the Co-operative Society, affiliated with the Labour Party. And his first success in politics was to have a Parliamentary Commission of the Co-operative Congress instituted, with himself, of course, as secretary-general.

He fought for his co-operative movement with truly religious zeal. He attracted hundreds of thousands of followers, and, inevitably, he antagonized business. His most determined antagonist was Lord Beaverbrook, publisher of the *Daily Express,* the voice of the large, shop-keeping middle class. Beaverbrook always liked a good fight. So did Alexander. His career as a street preacher had made him a fluent debater. He preferred the sharper note: "Until Beaverbrook is willing to come out into the open where he can be met, and not shout from a coward's castle, the public will not be able to judge the sincerity of his campaign against us." Beaverbrook was outraged. In return, his editorials did not mince words.

But it would be all wrong to see Alexander in his formative years as a trouble-maker and rabble-rouser, in spite of his heavy broadsides of argument and dialectics. Quite the contrary. Like most British Labour leaders, he soon acquired respectability. He did not, however, follow the personal example of Ramsay MacDonald, who, starting his life as a revolutionary, almost an outcast, ended it with the appear-

ance, the tastes, the predilections of a quasi-Tory and country squire. Alexander, born in poverty and educated in pen-
ury, had but one social aim: to become one of the dull,
patient, invincible, immortal English middle class. He succeeded. Soon he was not only a leader of men, but a favorite
in his own neighborhood. His voice, sharp and slashing in
the House, had an agreeable, warm quality in conversation.
He cultivated his voice, joining several men's choirs—an
English institution, which takes the place of our barber-
shop quartets. He taught himself to play the piano. Today
he is famous for his perfect command of all the popular
ditties of the last forty years. He did not play golf; bowling
was his game. As his hair greyed, he combed it neatly; he is
a neat man. He is clean-shaven; unassumingly, but impec-
cably dressed. He was perfect ministerial raw material, when
MacDonald, in 1929, built his cabinet and had to find suit-
able colleagues, who would not compromise him.

Alexander's appointment as First Lord in the Labour
government was a thunderbolt to the navy. Of course he
had had no naval experience whatsoever. In the last war
he had served as a buck private, but he was gazetted out
of the army with the rank of Honorary Captain, and his reputation as a fighter had been established. "Alexander is the
right bulldog breed," an Opposition member admitted, who,
for the rest, regarded the Socialist government with appre-
hension and misgiving. This critic was Winston Churchill.
The naval officers, among whom Winston's prestige always
remained almost legendary, took comfort from this opinion.
They agreed on the bitter-sweet formula: "At least he will
be the first co-operator, and the first Baptist lay-preacher
to be the ruler of the King's navy." He would, they imag-
ined, prove a mild ruler. The service-men have, fortunately,
a way with their civilian chiefs.

Their technique failed with Albert Victor Alexander. The First Lord did not confine himself to ruling the waves—he waived the rules. In his two years in office he became a great reformer of the navy. These years were not spectacular, but they were utterly successful.

His first innovation was the reform of Dartmouth Training College, the English Annapolis. Until his time Dartmouth had been entirely a rich boys' school. A system of scholarships, established by Alexander, now enabled gifted boys from poor families to embark upon naval careers. Undoubtedly, the large group of brilliantly trained naval officers that this war demands would never have been available if Alexander had not thrown open the doors of Dartmouth. With the same sense of social obligation, the Labour First Lord inquired into the living conditions of the ratings and actually did much to improve the lot of the sailors on British warships.

But some experts and technicians were shocked when their "civilian" First Lord launched his expanded cruiser program. They approved of the expansion. It was the answer to the threat of the new German pocket-battleships. Alexander was one of the first political leaders in England who understood the deeper meaning of the German rearmament, long before Hitler had even appeared on the scene. But his answer to the pocket-battleship seemed unorthodox. The "Alexander cruisers" were smaller than their predecessors, and they carried only 6-inch guns, instead of the traditional 8-inch. These shortcomings, the civilian First Lord assured his experts, would be more than offset by the double rate of fire power and the speedier maneuverability of the new cruiser type. It did not sound at all reassuring. But eight years later, two of the "Alexander cruisers"—the *Ajax* and the *Achilles*—met the *Graf Spee* off the mouth of the Rio

Plata, and gave the German pocket-battleship the answer that Albert Victor Alexander had planned.

He was forty-four years old when he went to the Admiralty for the first time. A lifetime of labor, struggle and success already lay behind him. But it was then that life really began. Sooner or later the Englishman must smell the sea. Accustomed to hard work and relentless striving, Alexander plunged headlong into the waves that were to carry him to the peak of his life. His job became his passion. No technical detail was too complicated for this earnest, if untrained, man. He terminated an endless discussion by authorizing the general equipment of British submarines with the Davis escape apparatus. Again he was accused of being unorthodox. But again British sailors, the tough, hard-pressed submarine crews of this war, can sing his praises, when they return to the safety of the harbor.

Alexander did not dissociate himself from the navy, when he had to relinquish his job with the fall of the Labour government. He was recognized as the leading authority of his party, every year when the Naval Estimates came up for discussion. He found himself in a difficult position. For political reasons—and by honest conviction—he had to criticize the Tory government. But the urge of his heart was not for cutting, cutting, cutting down naval expenditure, as the pacifist trend in the Labour Party demanded, but for an increased strengthening of the fleet. He regarded the supremacy of the British fleet as the strongest assurance of peace. He would, at that time of party strife, never have publicly agreed with Winston Churchill, then famous as a "red-baiter." But friends surprised him in possession of a copy of Churchill's *World Crisis,* in which the words were underlined in pencil: "Open the seacocks and let our ships sink. In a few minutes, half an hour at most, the whole outlook of the world would have been changed. The Empire would dissolve like a dream . . ."

Like hostile watchdogs, Churchill and Alexander, the Conservative naval expert and his Labour counterpart, showed their teeth from opposite benches. Both are the bulldog type. Both have a dangerous growl. They seldom exchanged words—but less infrequently, a smile.

Alexander was one of the first parliamentary admirers of Churchill, when the latter opened his one-man crusade against Neville Chamberlain's policy of appeasement. It is well known that Churchill restrained his language, never lowering his level of speech to a personal attack. Mr. Alexander does not suffer from similar inhibitions. He is, after all, no scion of the Duke of Marlborough, but a political product of street speaking. As a deeply religious man he knows that our Good Lord does not want us to whisper in castigating sin. So he interfered in one of the habitual, polite brushes between Mr. Chamberlain and Mr. Churchill, shouting at the Prime Minister: "You were elected on a lie, and now you desire to stay in office by fraud!" A veritable sea breeze swept through the House of Commons. The House was embarrassed. Afterwards, in the lobbies, there was much talk of the possibility of a Churchill government with Labour support.

It is doubtful whether Mr. Alexander, in this great moment, was a conscious coalition-maker. Once again he waived the rules, because he was heartily sick of the appeasement claptrap. He knew that you cannot appease the devil. And Hitler, the enemy of that democracy, for which a fiery passion lives in Alexander's big head and broad chest, is the arch-devil in person to him.

His hatred of dictatorship sees no difference in colors. He despises Red and Brown with equal vehemence. Alexander belonged to the most energetic Labour leaders, like Bevin, who ousted fellow-travelers from the Party, and stopped all the talk of a "Popular Front," a transmission-belt for Moscow.

The tragic May of 1940 came. Norway fell; Belgium and the Netherlands followed. France was on the brink of the abyss. Panic-stricken, England turned to Churchill for guidance and protection. Within three hours a new cabinet had to be formed. It is related that Lord Beaverbrook had a big hand in helping to form the Churchill government. When it came to making a choice for the Admiralty, Beaverbrook said: "Why, Alexander, of course!"

Then the two former arch-enemies met. They shook hands, each sporting a determined grin. Lord Beaverbrook opened the friendly hostilities: "My finest political Aunt Sally!" he said. "For years the controversy about you has increased my newspaper sales!"

"My best commercial traveler!" Alexander retorted. "Every time you attacked me, you brought new customers to the Co-operative!"

So English feuds end. But the war was on in full fury, and there was not a second to lose. Alexander did an unprecedented thing. For years he has been an enemy of the airplane. He has never given his reasons. Perhaps he felt too deeply committed to the old-fashioned navy to relish the new air competition. Progressive, liberal, a reformer as he may be—in his heart of hearts this Labour leader is an old-fashioned man, who does not want to offend God by intruding in his skies. But he now committed the offense. For the first, and so far the last time in his life he took an airplane and flew to Bordeaux. The brand new First Lord felt it his duty to speak with the French authorities about the future of the French fleet. He calls his flight to Bordeaux "memorable." But he still refuses to divulge the outcome of the conversation.

One can guess at this outcome. The action at Oran is a perfect explanation. Mr. Alexander regrets that the action had to take place. He sympathizes with the French in their plight, for which they are themselves responsible, but he could not have assumed the responsibility of letting the most important French units fall into Nazi hands. Admiral Darlan's threat that his remaining ships would co-operate with Hitler's fleet in breaking the British blockade, has, many months later, again vindicated Oran.

"I can't tell you how deeply I regretted the necessity of the action," he has explained. "But what could we do? We possessed fourteen capital ships, Germany two or three, Italy six. The French had nine. Add three and six and nine together. If we'd let the French ships fall into enemy hands, the balance in heavy ships would have been against us and our ocean convoys would have been liable to destruction by hostile surface forces. We had to do it. We couldn't help ourselves. What security would there have been for the commerce of America, if the power of our main fleet had been outweighed? Why, even American territory would not have been safe!"

The thought of America is ever-present in Alexander's mind. Here too, he is true to Churchill's type. "Britain is building escort vessels so rapidly," he recently stated, "that American help cannot be prevented by enemy action from arriving. Britain will take full advantage of what the U. S. A., and the Dominions, can do in regard to construction of shipping. True, the main clash with Germany has still to come. But with the aid of American shipping, I can see no reason to expect anything but that we shall win through."

Alexander does his "bit" for victory. He is anything but

a desk-admiral. As often as his office duties allow him, he mingles with the people of his own navy. "I can't get enough," he admits. "I want to talk to captains and commanders as much as possible. It is from them, and from the men on the drifters, mine-sweepers and little corvettes that we learn a lot. It is from these frank tales that we get new experience and learn new tactics."

His insatiable curiosity brought him recently into a rather difficult situation. He was inspecting a naval yard. In mufti, as always, he started interviewing a workman. He asked about the hours and conditions of work. He wanted to know about the latest mechanical devices. Patiently, the workman answered. But suddenly a glance of suspicion flashed across his heavy face. "Who is the bloke who asks so many questions?" he quick-fired, and his calloused hand rose in an unmistakable gesture, a danger signal.

"Of course," laughed his interviewer, "I have forgotten to introduce myself." He stretched out his hand. "I am Albert Alexander, the First Lord."

For a moment the workman stuck to his suspicions. Then a broad grin illuminated his honest face. He had recognized the much-publicized physiognomy.

Two hands clasped in a firm grip. "Hello, Bert!" the workman said. And then, to a group of his pals, who were attracted to the little scene: "That chap is all right! He belongs to us!"

Empire Builder, New Style

ARTHUR GREENWOOD

RTHUR GREENWOOD IS ENGLAND'S WHITE-HAIRED BOY. FOR
many years he enjoyed the reputation of being his country's most hilarious politician. Everyone believed in his tal-
ents, most succumbed to his charm, but the whole country
refused to take him seriously. "A good mind is allowed to
go to pieces through lack of intellectual self-discipline!" expressed a common opinion. He was widely criticized as "un-
worthy of his good equipment." He made up for the worst
setback in his political career, the loss of his parliamentary
seat, by advocating a reduction in the beer-tax. This popular crusade brought him back to the House. A choir of fellow M.P.'s, party friends and opponents alike, received the
prodigal son with the cheerful welcome: "You swam in on
a wave of beer." When he was already in his middle fifties,
a high-priest of his own Labour Party shook his wise head.
"With a little more serious effort A.G. would have lifted
himself to the front rank." Even the high-priest called him
by his popular initials. Much as they disapproved of his
frivolities—or rather of what is the English conception of
frivolity—few Englishmen would have questioned the identity of the man behind the initials A.G. In the West Riding

ARTHUR GREENWOOD

of Yorkshire no one at all asked such a foolish question. There he was the personification of themselves.

Five years have passed since the last wave of head-shaking engulfed him. Past sixty, Arthur Greenwood stands in the front rank. He is a member of Churchill's inner war cabinet. As Minister without Portfolio—the only one besides Beaverbrook—he is relieved of departmental duties. His advice, the sum of his experience, his unrivaled knowledge of men and things, belong to all who strive and toil and sweat. He is his party's elder statesman, and his country's counsellor number one. After having, as many believed, squandered a brilliant past, he stands on the threshold of a greater future. His personal job is to blue-print the Empire that shall emerge from the war. Close to the patriarch's age, he points the way to the future. He is a prophet minus a beard.

In his flippant fashion, which has antagonized viscountesses and trades-union bosses alike, he likes to recall that it was nothing but his darned carelessness that made him stumble into politics. It happened at an age when he should have long since relinquished mundane ambitions and devoted himself to watching the antics of his grandchildren. Indeed, he was past forty when the political bug bit him.

His youth was devoted to study, his early middle age to a brilliant career in the civil service. He was born in Leeds, of a respected middle-class family. He received a scholarship to Manchester University, studied history and economics, became head of the Department of Economics at Huddersfield Technical College and lecturer on economics at Leeds University. He would certainly have become an important government adviser on economic affairs had he not constantly flouted convention. He could not accustom himself to disciplined obedience, nor would he kowtow to anyone.

Among his wide circle of friends his reputation for loyalty, for courage and comradeship rose steadily. He stood by a friend even if the fellow was wrong. Personal ethics, he called it. The necessary restraint and routine of the civil service were not to his taste. Although a tireless worker, he was unwilling to do things in which he did not believe. Under the English stiff-shirt he was the revolutionary type. By choice he avoided highly colored phrases. But sometimes he referred to the "inner flame," which urged him to "go at it." Occasionally his consuming enthusiasm frightened his friends more than his critics.

The khaki-elections of 1918 had given the pre-war generation a short new lease on life. Not before the General Election of 1922 did the new generation come to the foreground. In the fifth decade of his life Arthur Greenwood still felt very much of the new generation. Against all family tradition he contested the constituency of Nelson and Colne for Labour. Although his life thus far had been lived primarily in science, the debutant with the greying temples demonstrated a surprising knack for the game of politics. He spoke to his constituents with the strong emphases of Sheffield and Leeds. The people there pride themselves on their bluntness of speech. This native outspokenness became both an asset and a liability in Arthur Greenwood's political career. His Yorkshire people idolized him; he swept his audiences off their feet. They loved their "grand fighter." Even more they enjoyed his provincialism. They discovered in him what the English masses like best of all—a learned man of spontaneous democratic bearing. Southerners, and even the people of London, on the other hand, were less trustful of A.G. For many years they called him rude and even insincere. Indeed, in his formative years, he used to pour torrents of abuse out on his opponents. Besides, they harbored a certain suspicion of his obvious delight in the good things of life. As in many another case, Winston Churchill found the definite formula to save an adversary's soul. He said of A.G.: "There has always been, and still is, too great a flame in him for the pleasant things to count just because they are pleasant."

Greenwood's reputation in such matters as relations between employers and workers, adult education, trusts and trust-busting, public health, rapidly won him the respect of the House. He was an important expert in the period of reconstruction that followed the first war. MacDonald made him Parliamentary Secretary to the Ministry of Health in his first administration. There was general surprise that Greenwood had not received a Ministry of his own. A little later the fact was revealed that he himself had preferred the minor vacancy in the Ministry of Health to an independent position, in which he could not have contributed so much to relieving the sufferings of many thousands of his fellow men.

Five years later, in 1929, MacDonald was again at the helm. In the second Labour administration Greenwood, indeed, was made Minister of Health. Now he was riding the crest. In 1930 he received an honorary LL.D. from Leeds University and became Honorary Freeman of the City of Leeds. His seat in the House was considered the safest on the Labour benches. But MacDonald's administration failed ingloriously. Greenwood's conduct of his office was singled out as the main target for all the attacks on the Labour government. Left-wingers criticized the Anomalies Act; Conservatives stormed against the mounting insolvency of the Unemployment Fund. The bulk of his own party made Greenwood responsible for the failure of his Housing Act. It took them some time to understand that this Act provided the machinery for the fight against slums which was carried on further by the National government that followed. At the elections in 1931, Labour was completely routed. Even Greenwood's supposedly safe seat was lost.

A lesser man would have lost heart. A.G. remained undaunted and undismayed. A year after his defeat a by-election furnished the opportunity to renew the fight. He contested Wakefield. He had learned the lesson of his failure and now he abandoned a certain radicalism that, indeed, had never rung true with him. He learned to call every Wakefield voter by his Christian name; soon he was on personal terms with everyone. Campaigning, he studiously avoided all semblance of personal ambition. Rather, he showed his talent for getting straight to the basic things. This method came natural to him. He felt at ease. The electorate was impressed by his grasp of essentials and by his uncanny accumulation of information. A local bigwig admitted: "His memory is his library." Then the good burgess thought a while. Finally he grumbled: "I don't care for him. But I shall vote for him." Undoubtedly, Greenwood had considerably bettered his style, which, in England, pays dividends.

His return to the House was happy. Members of all parties visited his friendly Essex cottage, where the hospitality was entirely informal. A.G. wore flannel slacks, a disreputable old jersey, and sandshoes. He is tall, thin and long-legged. He has a winning face and a hearty laugh; his smile is reassuring. As with many an Englishman, increasing age suits him well. His sandy hair has turned white, giving him an additional air of respectability. His wife, incidentally, urges him to go to the barber more often than he likes. He protests that he has no time for such nonsense. He has serious business on hand—for instance, to watch his grandchildren, Michael and a little girl he calls Tillikens, at play. He used to play with them a good deal. One of his favorite ruses was to give them a wrong answer to a crossword puzzle, pretending not to understand the clue. Then the children could laugh at the old man. His guests smiled. However busy A.G. was, he never let a petitioner for his advice go, without having listened patiently and racked his brain for the right solution.

In 1935, the Labour Party elected him deputy leader. The dignity of his new office mellowed the old fighter still further. He carried out his increased responsibilities with a deeply serious sense of duty. His speech supporting the address of welcome on the King's return from Canada won him high praise from the Conservative benches. The workers he represented also liked the new tune. When it is a question of the King, duke and ditch-digger are equally enthusiastic. The same enthusiasm, however, did not apply to Mr. Neville Chamberlain. Greenwood went a little out of his way, it was felt, in saying to him: "If the Prime Minister succeeds, he will wear the laurels of victory on his brow. We on these benches shall not complain."

"How generous . . . How statesmanlike! . . ." the Tories murmured. But from the Labour benches the applause was weak. When Mr. Chamberlain, in turn, complimented Greenwood for maintaining the debate on a high level, some uncomfortable questions arose among the Labour supporters. Had they nursed another MacDonald in their bosom? Did A.G. fancy a new coalition? Was another party schism inevitable?

Once more they misunderstood him. Greenwood was a jolly good fellow, ready even to humor Mr. Chamberlain's inflated ego. But he was no softy. He gave Hitler a lesson in

English psychology, when Europe's tragedy was rapidly nearing its climax.

Clement Attlee, the Labour leader, was suffering from the consequences of a grave illness that had stricken him in the summer of 1939. The task of speaking for Labour in the days of worst crises went to his deputy. Greenwood rose to his full stature. The easy smile on his clean-shaven face faded. His voice no longer sounded under perfect control. It rang with the heavy accents of an aroused Yorkshireman. He spoke almost every day, pledging British Labour's full support for the war effort and leaving not the faintest doubt as to the workers' final determination to do away with Hitler, whatever the price might be. In fact, in those days of terrible tension, Greenwood did more than any other man to rally Labour to the Empire's cause, which, in this war, is the cause of mankind.

On August 29, 1939, in the first of his string of stirring speeches, he was still willing to give Chamberlain a chance. "The Prime Minister says that the door is still ajar," he declared. "I hope the door will remain ajar until it closes with the angel of death and the monster of aggression outside the threshold forever. But aggression must cease now." On September 1, he stated: "This is the turning point in human history. Hitler is the arch-enemy of mankind. But after his fall a new order of society will arise."

Another twenty-four hours later, while Hitler's legions were already raping Poland, Mr. Chamberlain still pleaded that England must wait for her allies. "There shall be no more devices for dragging out what has been dragged out too long," Greenwood retorted. "The moment we look like weakening Dictatorship knows that we are beaten. We are not beaten. We cannot be beaten. But delay is dangerous.

I cannot see Herr Hitler, in honesty, making any deal which he will not be prepared to betray."

The next morning war was declared. To Greenwood, as to the country as a whole, the declaration came as a relief. "This morning we meet in an entirely different atmosphere —one of relief, of composure and resolution," he stated. And it was he, the spokesman of the masses, who coined the British war aim: "In this titanic struggle, unparalleled I believe in the history of the world, Nazism must be finally overthrown."

For almost five months he waited and watched Mr. Chamberlain and his band's timorous efforts to overthrow Nazism decisively. The self-restraint British Labour showed during this time of grave testing and of nervous strain will be recorded, when the history of the war comes to be written, as high proof of the poor man's patriotism. Greenwood had a big share in keeping a deeply dissatisfied nation under control. But things went from bad to worse. It would have been unpatriotic to remain loyal any longer to an inefficient government. The old fighter awoke. He was, he felt, quite particularly called to attack the enemy that had frustrated all the efforts of his own early life, the old enemy and seemingly inseparable companion of the English—bureaucracy. "If I understand it aright," he said in the House, "the dead hand of officialism is throttling the national effort. I have never heard anything so bureaucratic as the machinery which the right honorable gentleman [Mr. Burgin, then Minister of Supply, who had just spoken] has outlined to us for discussion. An ounce of experience is worth a load of theory." It sounded odd from the lips of a well-known theoretician; it was the lesson of a lifetime. There was a touch of humbleness to it, a new achievement in the old man's reform. "Young men should have been called in," he continued, "acquainted with modern requirements and understanding modern developments to mobilize every atom of industrial energy that this country possesses. The bureaucratic system will not work. But the country will not permit a repetition of the bloody shambles of the last war through lack of supplies. Britain will not send her sons to suicide clubs to be mown down by the greater weight of metal. But she will send her sons to fight and to sacrifice if they go with the implements in their hands and their reserves and supplies behind them."

This speech preceded the Blitzkrieg. Prophetically it pointed out its dangers and horrors. The impact on the House was terrific. Both government and opposition members were stunned. From the Conservative back-benches one pair of hands was heard applauding wildly. Winston Churchill has an unmistakable way of registering approval.

Churchill did not hesitate over whom he would make his number two man. The position of Minister without Portfolio, free from departmental cares, joined with the Chairmanship of the Imperial Reconstruction Committee, which Arthur Greenwood has held since May 11, 1940, gives him tremendous influence. He supervises England's armament and the economic conduct of the war. Besides, and perhaps still more important, he is in charge of rebuilding the country when it emerges from Armageddon.

His first duty was the co-ordination of Britain's economic system with the necessities of warfare. He gave a hint of the difficulties he had to surmount in explaining to the House on August 7, 1940: "We were not fully mobilized when war was forced upon us. It is no simple thing, except perhaps in a totalitarian state, to switch over from peacetime production to war work." America, today, should understand this problem.

Greenwood is a firm believer in centralization of the war effort. The committee he directs corresponds in some measure to America's O.P.M. But its scope is infinitely wider. It is not only concerned with production, but with all the economic aspects of the war conduct. The Foreign Office, the Treasury, the three service departments, the Ministry of Shipping and the Ministry of Economic Warfare are represented in and co-ordinated with the central commission, which, in turn, is divided into groups dealing with particular problems. Everything is Greenwood's concern—from the rationing of exports to the regulation of working hours. Of course the eight-hour day had to be abolished. For his own work Greenwood decreed a twenty-four hour day.

His friends believe that he must have a twenty-fifth hour somewhere up his sleeve. How otherwise could he work day and night and still find time for what he calls his hour of dreams? This most precious hour is devoted to a vision which shall become a reality after the war. The vision carries a very sober, a very English name. It is called the Central Planning Authority. It works out plans for what is officially termed "the physical reconstruction of town and country." The name does not divulge much. The shy, somewhat evasive smile with which Arthur Greenwood, rarely enough, speaks about his supreme task, divulges a little more. He is blue-printing the dream of a better England in a better Empire in a better world.

PART THREE

Soldiers

The King's First Soldier

SIR JOHN GREER DILL

HIGH ALTITUDES ARE COLD. THE MAN AT THE HEAD OF Britain's fighting services has reached the pinnacle of life. If he grows further he can only grow into history. This side of heaven the King's first soldier is lonely. In Whitehall passers-by doff their hats with a certain shyness when they see a tall, carefully dressed, grey-moustached gentleman, aged sixty but looking fifty, walking with rapid, determined strides to or from the War Office. Since he is in his office before 8 A.M. and never leaves it until after midnight, he is a familiar figure in the night life of London's streets. But there is no atmosphere of dusk and dawn and twilight about him. If you try to sum up Lieutenant-General Sir John Greer Dill, K.C.B., C.M.G., D.S.O., Chief of the Imperial General Staff, with a single word, the word is: straight.

He carries a finely modeled head on a lean, erect body. His face is impassive. His thinning hair is cut short and carefully brushed back. His forehead protrudes a little. His eyebrows are sharply drawn. His eyes, at the first glance, gaze without expression. To a second glance they show their restless alertness. His pugnacious nose and his firm chin reveal a fighter. But his mouth, it seems, belies the stubbornness

211

of nose and chin. His lips are slightly curled, playful, indicating the hard-riding, soft-spoken Irishman's sense of humor. In speaking he divulges an uncanny flexibility of mind.

But he speaks rarely, and he divulges nothing. Every bit
of information he has amassed behind his high forehead is
a precious state secret. Every innocent joke, if indulged in,
would be analyzed, interpreted, discussed by a crowd of
friends and legions of enemies. His solitude is self-defense.
His life is defense of the Empire. His style is silence. His-
tory-making is a silent business. That is, incidentally, one
of the reasons why verbose Adolf will never make history,
but remain a nuisance of world-shaking dimensions.

Compared with the task of saving Britain and all the human values it stands for, even personal tragedy is submerged
into unimportance. Sir John Greer Dill never betrayed the
agony he felt in watching his beloved wife, the former Ada
Maud Le Motte, die, after a long and painful illness, on
Christmas Eve, 1940, while Hitler was snuffing out the
world's candles. Has the General no heart?

His silent heart is full of love for his two sons. One of
them, a junior officer, fights, at present, somewhere in the
East. The other fights everywhere where the banner of freedom waves. His name is Tommy Atkins.

Christmas has another significance not to be overlooked
in his life. On December 25, Mrs. Jane Dill, a native of Lur-
gan, Ireland, bore her husband, John Dill, of Belfast, a little fighting Irishman who was baptized John after his father,
and Greer after his mother's maiden name. Being an Ulster
boy, he was, of course, destined for the King's army before
he could walk. He studied at Cheltenham College and at
Sandhurst, the British West Point, and entered the service
in 1901. He was gazetted to the Prince of Wales's Leinster

LIEUTENANT-GENERAL SIR JOHN GREER DILL

Regiment, with which he remained until it was—with several other South Irish units—disbanded in 1922.

Neutrality was not yet the fashion in Ireland when Lieutenant John Greer Dill joined the forces. The Leinster Regiment was dispatched to South Africa. In five major engagements during the Boer War Lieutenant Dill won the Queen's Medal with five clasps, for gallantry in action. He did not return home a spectacular war hero as did another junior officer, whose first name was Winston, but he had established a solid reputation as one of the fightingest men who ever came out of Ulster. In 1911, he was promoted to Captain. At the outbreak of the first World War he became a Major. A year later he won the Distinguished Service Order. He does not remember for which particular feat. Those were busy days on the Western Front.

Major Dill was a favorite with the French. Messrs. Pétain and Weygand are apt to forget it. But it is a fact that the now Chief of the Imperial General Staff was decorated with the Légion d'Honneur, the Croix de Guerre, and the Croix de la Couronne, for his service in the defense of France. The King of the Belgians, father of Leopold of second World War shame, conferred the Belgian Croix de Guerre upon him.

When the first war ended, Dill was thirty-seven, and serving as a brigadier-colonel on the General Staff. Already, almost twenty-five years ago, experts regarded Dill as one of the most able men in the British army. He was known as an exponent of tank and bomber warfare. Colleagues called him a brain soldier, a twentieth-century officer, a scientific fighter. Such flattery is not usual in the service. It did not affect Sir John. He remained a man of quiet tastes, indifferent to social prominence, rather reluctant in manner and speech. He carried the marshal's baton in his kit, but he retained his serenity and courtesy, avoiding hasty judgments or dramatically quick decisions, a confirmed believer in the strategy of exact knowledge and careful consideration as a prelude to vigorous action.

Perhaps his career developed a little too rapidly for his own taste. He was singled out for the most promising commands. Every British colonel dreams of commanding a brigade at Aldershot, regarded as the most distinguished garrison in the tight little island. Colonel Dill got his brigade at Aldershot. As a brigadier he was dispatched to India, where he served for a year as principal staff officer at Quetta. Subsequently he was shifted to the newly established Imperial Defense College, and finally appointed Commander of the Staff College at Camberley. He knew by heart, his disciples insisted, every line ever written on strategic and economic warfare. He was made Major-General in 1930, but this title did not fully convey his importance. In fact he was the ranking authority in Britain on the science of war.

It is a practical science. Its adepts must keep themselves informed on events and innovations in every army. There was only one foreign army really worth watching. A year after Hitler had usurped power in Germany, Sir John Dill became director general of military operations. His appointment was explained as "mobilization of British brains." Unfortunately London countered the establishment of the Nazi regime only with this partial mobilization.

In his new position Sir John was where he had belonged throughout his career. He now held a key position in what Colonel Blimp, in a somewhat derogatory fashion, used to call the "thinking department." The Imperial General Staff had been created in 1909, and since then remained the army's heart and nerve-center. The director general of military operations has to keep in the closest touch with problems affecting possible operations in every country in the world. This, at least, is the official version of his task. In fact, he directs the military intelligence. In taking over his new office Sir John Dill demonstrated that the right man had found the right job. He did not hesitate courteously to notify the German General Staff of his appointment. In that year, 1934, the German army, of course, was still forbidden to have a General Staff. On paper, at least, the military clauses of Versailles were still valid.

The German comrades were not to be outdone in courtesy. The following year they invited Sir John to attend their maneuvers in Tannenberg, East Prussia, the first Nazi maneuvers on a war scale. They knew that they were inviting the spy-master of their potential arch-enemy. Hitler had not yet arbitrarily cancelled Versailles. He should have hidden what he showed. He preferred an impertinent bluff.

If the Reichswehr did not succeed in bluffing Sir John, still, the might of the German military machine deeply impressed him. On his return to London he wrote a substantial and well-documented report, advising immediate measures of British military counter-preparation. Had his advice been heeded, history would, without doubt, have taken a different turn. The remilitarization of the Rhineland could never have been carried out. The rape of Austria, the tragic dilemma of Munich, the assault on Poland would never have materialized. There would have been no second World War. In London, blundering politicians would probably still enjoy the confidence of a party-ridden House and the support of a great nation, stricken with sleeping-sickness. And Hitler would once more peddle his daubs.

But the powers that were did not listen to Dill. The mighties of 1935 did not welcome the dabbling in politics of a simple major-general. Dill discovered for the first time what it means to stick out one's neck too far. He was neither snubbed nor reprimanded. He was simply forgotten, which is a great deal worse than either. He still represented the British in the general staff talks with France and Belgium after Hitler's remilitarization of the Rhineland. But again he was only asked for his technical opinion without being in a position to influence political decisions.

The first Blitzkrieg brought him back to the foreground. The Blitzkrieg, it must be remembered, is not of Hitler's devising. In Norway, in the Lowlands, in France and in the Balkans, the Führer, endowed with the German genius for copying, simply applied an invention of Sir John Dill's. He is the real father of the Blitzkrieg, the high-powered, lightning-swift, mechanical assault. He had spent many years thinking about and planning for it. When the Jewish-Arab fighting in Palestine assumed the dimensions of a colonial war, he had his opportunity to test his streamlined strategy. For the first time in modern military history other considerations were secondary to that of speed. Small mechanized units proved superior to large masses of old-style infantry. The machine knocked out the man.

The bigwigs had not liked his dabbling in politics, but they knew that they had no better man to fight a war. In April, 1936, Dill was promoted Lieutenant-General and dispatched to the Near East. His force was small, no more than 15,000 men, but they were equipped with all the devices and weapons of modern warfare—above all, tanks and airplanes.

Dill knew that he would meet a formidable adversary. The rebel Arab chieftain, Fanzi Kawkajii, is a product of Islamic fanaticism and Oxford education. He had had experience with the Turkish and French armies and had served as military adviser to King Ibn Saud, the desert-Napoleon. Besides, he spoke fluent English and could well pass for a white man. He put up a valiant show of resistance. For the first time in military history, the mobile and military tactics which have served Hitler so considerably in the first part of this war, and are just about to be reappropriated by Dill for its second decisive phase, came into play. Fanzi Kawkajii fled into Northern Iraq. Even as a refugee he did not give up. On the contrary. He offered a prize of £2,500 for "the British devil Dill's head." The prize was to be raised to £3,000, if the head was served to him on a silver platter.

Calmly Sir John stroked his neck. When he had made sure that his head was still sitting firmly, he decided to fight it out. He assembled a group of officers from the Dorsetshire Regiment. The gentlemen were thrilled at having just met a charming English professor at the house of an Arab sheik. He had been so witty, and so familiar with the country. For half an hour he had entertained them with his oriental gossip. Sir John drew a photograph from his breast-pocket. "Is this your professor?" he asked. What a strange coincidence, the officers observed. Their chief really was a British devil. Did he not carry in his pocket the picture of a wandering scientist?

It was, of course, a photograph of Fanzi Kawkajii. It was copied, and every officer of the Transjordanian forces was supplied with a print. The rebel was cunning enough not to show himself again. So Sir John decided to visit him in his lair. A small "unprotected British force," led by the commander-in-chief, paid a courtesy call in Northern Iraq. When the refugee rebels had safely trapped them, it is true, the "unprotected" force produced machine-guns and all sorts of true American gangster equipment. The rebels were annihilated. Only one among them escaped. The recent revolution in Iraq proves that Fanzi Kawkajii managed to save his life to fight another day.

In the summer of 1937, after his brilliant success in Palestine, Sir John Dill returned to Aldershot, this time as chief, holding the most important executive command in the army at home. He did not forget his Near Eastern experience on the parade grounds at Aldershot.

Already, in 1937, the decisive showdown appeared inevitable. Dill was the great hope. Under Defense Minister Sir Thomas Inskip he drew up plans for Britain's accelerated rearmament. The English army regarded him as their number one choice, if and when war should break out. But at the end of the year, to universal surprise, old Ironside—Sir Edmund Ironside, now Viscount Ironside of Archangel— was chosen instead, although the aged veteran of the last war was much less popular with the army and people than was the hero of Palestine. Obviously to counteract the unfavorable impression made by promotion accorded solely by reason of seniority, Leslie Hore-Belisha, then War Minister, reduced drastically the upper age limit for the High Command. A general officer younger than and junior to Dill became Assistant Chief of the Imperial General Staff. Dill got only the command of the First Army Corps. When the hour struck, he took it to France.

In the first days of the second World War, unwarranted optimism prevailed among the Allied leadership. Winter was ahead. The Maginot Line, armchair strategists were convinced, was impregnable. Dill was the only responsible general openly to dissent. In the first days of September, 1939, he warned Le Mans, which was the seat of a part of General Headquarters, against over-optimism. "It is only a question of whether Hitler launches a full scale attack with one hundred divisions this autumn," he predicted, "or waits for the spring to do it with two hundred."

Such a prophecy was unpopular. At least with the big-wigs. His own soldiers listened attentively. They trusted "father John." The strong attachment of his troops finally impressed the authorities. In April, 1940, Dill was trans-ferred from the command of the First Corps and made vice-chief of the General Staff, in London, "to put the British war effort on a twenty-four hour basis and to relieve the strain on Ironside." He received the news of his appoint-ment one evening at ten-thirty. He was to leave Douai the following morning at eleven to be at General Headquarters at noon. It was impossible to organize a farewell in so short a time. Yet the news that "father John" was leaving his sol-diers spread like wildfire. All the way from Douai to Arras— some twenty miles—the roadside was lined by the men under his command. He was cheered in every village. It was an absolutely spontaneous demonstration.

He had left France to organize the defense from his new central position before the Blitzkrieg started. The German attack swept away not only the Chamberlain government, but also the Chamberlainites in the High Command. On May 26, 1940, Sir John Greer Dill became Chief of the Im-perial General Staff, England's first soldier. "Fate has given the wheel a twist," he said of his belated appointment. He proved to be utterly disinterested now that his life's dream had come true in the midst of turmoil and tragedy. In fact, fate had the rubicund face and the energetic hands of Win-ston Churchill.

The situation on this 26th of May was desperate. The Brit-ish expedition in France had come to a sad end. Boulogne had fallen three days earlier, Calais was about to fall. The

B.E.F., battered but not bettered, was slowly struggling back to the beaches of Dunkerque. The 51st Highland Division went down fighting at St. Valery. A few days later France abandoned her British ally. The nerve strain was terrible.

The miracle of Dunkerque saved seven-eighths of the B.E.F. But all its equipment was gone. Dill knew where his next task lay. The inside story of his work in the following seven months cannot be told before the end of the war. But when the seven months were over he had raised the army "from a state of comparative nakedness and doubt" to a position of readiness and renewed confidence. The British people, he said, would need all their confidence. Calmly Dill warned them of the impending invasion.

He had not one idle moment. Yet the necessities of the days did not blind him to the possibilities of the future. In July, 1940, the first shipments of guns and munitions sailed around Cape Horn to prepare General Wavell's winter offensive. The former chief of Britain's military intelligence knew how to preserve the secret of these shipments. Gestapo and German High Command rubbed their eyes when the guns barked at Sidi Barrani. The German Intelligence had not even known that they were being produced in such numbers and quality.

In the Mediterranean, as well as everywhere else, the British Imperial General Staff is up against tremendous superiority in men and machines. Early in the spring of 1941, reports came that Hitler was about to launch his Balkan campaign, with the ultimate aim of Suez, India, and probably the moon. Dill embraced the hope of co-ordinating resistance among the next victims of the Axis drive. He accompanied the Foreign Secretary, Anthony Eden, to Cairo, Ankara, and Athens. In Belgrade he was not admitted. The rapid defection of Jugoslavia a few days after her gallant people had again found their soul, astonished all military experts. Dill was not astonished. He knew that no one goes unpunished who for seven years picks up the crumbs from the Axis table.

He knows that only cleanliness and purity pay. Nazism does not know it. That is the little difference that this war is all about. God willing, and neither Britain nor America faltering, Sir John Greer Dill will emerge from the struggle as the next Kitchener.

The General and the Desert

GENERAL SIR ARCHIBALD WAVELL

WAS IT A DREAM? THE GENERAL ROSE AT DAWN. THE mocking stars still glittered overhead in the Egyptian winter night as he pressed the button. The desert ghosts awoke. Shadowy black lines formed. Tanks, trucks and ammunition dumps came suddenly alive. Pandemonium broke the majestic silence of the infinity of sand.

That same forenoon—at 10.15, to be precise—the General assembled the war correspondents at his headquarters, which are installed in a modest room on the third floor of a Cairo hotel. Nothing in this small, almost empty room indicates that this is the neuralgic spot of World War number two. "The reconnaissance in force has started!" the General announced.

The correspondents feigned polite surprise. Had they not all heard the hellish racket coming from the British camp out on the road to Sidi Barrani, the Italian spearhead? Even those who by long experience were oblivious of the noisiest air raids were in the know. Desert gossip travels faster than lightning. And Cairo is the world capital of gossip and rumor. There are more Italian spies at large than the sum total of all the barkeepers, streetbeggars and neutral military attachés.

GENERAL SIR ARCHIBALD WAVELL

In fact, barkeepers, streetbeggars and military attachés were just as ignorant as was the correspondent Mr. Ever-Scope. Not until this morning of December 9, 1940, was the fact revealed to them that the tanks, trucks and ammunition dumps on the road to Sidi Barrani were wooden constructions. The lines of cars that had supplied them in endless nightly caravans, well within sight of Italian reconnaissance fliers, drove empty, simply wasting their gasoline to fool the observers. The big British camp was a dummy.

The real base for the attack, much smaller in size, and perfectly inconspicuous, was set up somewhere to the south. It was just too bad for Marshal Graziani, the desert-Caesar,— he does not object, either, to the proud title "nigger-slayer," commemorating his faded triumphs in Abyssinia—that he only learned it two days later: on December 11, when Sidi Barrani was captured and 25,000 Italian prisoners were taken.

On December 16, the Solum-Fort Capuzzo area with 18,000 prisoners fell to the British. On Christmas the General threw a party at swanky Mena House in Cairo for the Egyptian government and the diplomatic corps. Spirits were high, but the consumption of spirits was modest. Three days later he went hunting with youthful King Farouk. He does not distrust the boy-King, but one had better keep a young man with a marked sense of independence under friendly surveillance. Forty-eight hours afterward, Bardia fell and 45,000 Italians surrendered. On January 22, Tobruk, an excellent harbor, with its last 20,000 defenders, was captured. On January 30, Derna submitted to the British. On February 6, Bengazi fell. This was, it seemed, the end of Italy's Empire. Tripoli, the capital and last port of call, although protected by a stretch of a few hundred miles of desert sand, would be the General's for the asking.

He could not ask at the moment because the German

onslaught on Greece was in the making, and he had to dispatch the bulk of his troops to Hellas. All right, Tripoli should enjoy a breathing spell. Anyway, it was a good job done. Between the fateful 9th of December and February 6, in less than two months, the whole Italian army in East Libya was destroyed. More than 150,000 men were killed or captured, as compared with 438 killed, 87 missing, and 1,249 wounded among the British. The mothers of the 438 killed will perhaps not believe it, but it was an almost bloodless victory, such as Hitler has never scored. The General had outblitzed the Blitzkriegers. Admitting it, Marshal Keitel, Supreme Chief of the German Army Command, said: "Wavell is the best general the British have, and he is very good."

Was it a dream? While the General's attention, his men and his equipment, were deflected to the Balkans, huge German transports, aided and abetted by Messrs. Pétain and Weygand, hugged the French coast, landed at Tripoli, and probably in French Morocco, carrying a new Axis Expeditionary Force. There was but one armored brigade left on the British side. It retired to Tobruk, and still holds that formidable sea-fortress as this is written. The Germans, it is estimated, succeeded in landing 200,000 mechanized troops on the North African coast. Outnumbering the last British defenders twenty to one, they recaptured thousands of square miles of desert sand. Their gain is impressive; their victory, as related to their task, is not. General Sir Archibald Percival Wavell still commands two million square miles in the Middle East, probably the largest area ever under a single general. His military realm includes Egypt, the Sudan, Kenya, Somaliland, Palestine, Trans-Jordania and Cyprus. More important, he commands unbreakable faith.

A scholarly soldier, who reads Browning and his pocket Shakespeare, occasionally also P. G. Wodehouse, while flying to inspect his troops at the front line, he quotes Voltaire's appraisal of Marlborough's "calm courage in the midst of tumult and serenity of soul in danger, which is the greatest gift of nature in command." It is probably his Scottish heritage that makes him feel that the quality of robustness —to quote his own words—the ability to stand the shocks of war, is the first essential of a general. He demonstrates this quality. For him, the war has just begun. The lightning speed with which he shattered the Italian Empire, was not a dream. It was a prelude. He had no more than 30,000 men, as Churchill testified, when he smashed five times as many Italians so thoroughly that not one of them escaped. He had to surrender Libya in a moment of direst plight. But meanwhile he has gained enormously in strength and stature. His tasks have multiplied. But today, again according to Churchill, 500,000 British soldiers are at the General's beck and call. He views the fortunes of war with equanimity. Whatever comes to pass, General Sir Archibald Percival Wavell has already emerged as the first spectacular soldier of this war. He has inscribed his name in the books of history. The desert march of the thirty-thousand is written in the same pages in which Xenophon reports the Anabasis, the march of the ten-thousand.

In Crete the General's men fought German parachutists who descended in Anzac uniforms, savage and cowardly as jungle beasts. In Syria they fought honey-tongued, poison-minded French turncoats. In Iraq they combated the fanatic hordes following a phony green banner of the Prophet—a rag of synthetic silk, manufactured in Hoechst am Rhein, by the German I. G. Farben Industrie. In Abyssinia they have routed the blood-crazed Italian Empire builders. But in Libya they are engaging an enemy more formidable than any. In Libya the General fights the desert.

Wavell has wooed the desert for the six or seven years he has held his Middle East command. He knows more about the mystery of sand than any man alive, with the possible exception of Major Ralph Alger Bagnold, believed to be his geologic chief adviser. Personally he has made innumerable expeditions to the most dangerous and treacherous places to wrestle with the desert and steal her secret. Once—on the march of his thirty-thousand—he conquered her. Another time she aided him by slowing up the counter-advance of the mechanized barbarians until their tanks were stalled before they could cross the Egyptian border by a sun burning at 130 degrees. But on the whole, the desert is a neutral. She defends her independence with terrific heat spells, sometimes, by night, interrupted by equally unbearable cold waves; with lack of water and shade; with murderous sun rays that make the water evaporate in the canisters; occasionally with torrential downpours of rain. Her sharpest weapon is the wind. The *khamsin* carries sand from the equatorial regions. It fills the air with a thick smoke, reducing visibility to ten feet. The skies are blotted out. All landmarks disappear. The *khamsin* penetrates all but the finest gas masks. It roars, blowing heavy trucks from their wretched tracks. In winter the *khamsin* is ice-cold. It cuts the men it attacks with a thousand knives. It is the scourge of the desert.

Then there is the poison that fills the desert. The slightest wound, a mere scratch on the skin, attracts some deadly virus. In its wake follow the flies, the most ferocious of desert fighters. It does no good to apply lotions or ointments against them. It only invites more poisonous flies.

Tornados and torrents, heat, poison, flies are hostile elements man has learned to cope with in one way or another. There is no way of coping with the sand. As far as human knowledge goes, the General is possessed of it. On his staff are three young officers—it is not permitted to divulge their names—who have "just for fun" devoted the last ten years to crossing the desert and studying the phenomenon of sand. There is no definite solution to the riddle. There is no way of foretelling where dunes will grow—new ones, incidentally, grow from the fusion of two old ones—and how they will affect the topography of the embattled desert. Yet success or failure of an expedition can easily depend on the behavior of sand. As far as is humanly possible, Wavell and his small band of experts are familiar with the sand's habits. They guess when and where it is pretty safe to bury huge dumps of weapons, munitions and any commodity that attacking troops might require, and they rely on the assistance of the dunes to conceal their marching lines.

Trusting in God and their experience, Wavell's mechanized forces have covered 500,000 miles of desert in harrying the Italians in Libya. The first raiding column, led by men who have made a hobby of desert exploration, traversed the great sand sea of inner Libya for many months, attacking Italian forts and communication lines. After having driven 1,200 miles across the dune-ridged desert, always careful to avoid wells where they might have been caught by Italian outposts, they joined the Free French Forces under Colonel Dornano. The Colonel, with his French and Senegalese troops, emerged from an area of 10,000-foot high volcanic peaks. Combined, the forces proceeded to the Italian stronghold of Murzuk and annihilated it. Colonel Dornano fell, killed by the Italian machine-gun barrage, within twenty yards of his goal. One of his aides was wounded. He was taken 790 miles to the nearest airfield, and from there flown to Cairo. The General watches over every one of the lives entrusted to him.

His soldiers adore him, although they are no great respecters of dignity. Wavell's army in the Middle East is probably the world's toughest soldiery. The bulk comes from the British Isles. But since the Anzacs were the first troops in this war to attack with a song on their lips—they stormed Italian strongholds singing, whistling, yelling, "We're off to see the Wizard, the wonderful Wizard of Oz"—they have become the undisputed favorites. They rub shoulders with Free French and Indian tribesmen, with Arabs, Hindus, Czechs, Poles, Maoris and Bedouins. Each group retains its racial individuality which is best illustrated by the food they are served. The Free Frenchmen need not go without their accustomed bread and red wine. The Asiatics get their rice, the English and the Anzacs their beef, and in the special case of the New Zealanders, vegetables are plentiful. The trouble they share in common is the difficulty of obtaining a sufficient water supply. The British desert fighter consumes about half a gallon of water daily, considerably more than his Italian counterpart. It is almost impossible to describe the lengths to which Wavell sometimes goes in order to assure the supply of water for his boys. During last winter's rapid advance across Libya, he discovered that desert oases could not furnish enough water for large forces, so he asked for fifty commercial planes for conversion into water-carriers. The army had no commercial planes. But President Roosevelt heard of the plight of the thirsty desert fighters. He immediately ordered Federal Loan Administrator Jesse Jones to buy a sufficient number of planes from private owners and airlines for transfer to Britain. They were flown to South America and across the Atlantic to Freetown, Sierra

Leone, a British colony 500 miles southeast of Dakar. From there they flew to General Wavell's army, where they are now serving as flying water tanks. No toast to the President has ever been drunk more jubilantly than by the desert fighters who drink his health as they raise their water-filled cups to their lips. General Wavell, incidentally, drank the first glass of water to arrive by an American water tank. He smiled. To keep off famine and thirst, he firmly believes, is the first duty of a good general.

It is not a theory of his own invention. Surprisingly—at least surprisingly to those who don't know him intimately— the General falls back on a doctrine expressed almost two and a half thousand years ago by Socrates, whom Wavell counts among the master strategists of all time, although the sage of Athens, it is well known, never led a battle or a campaign, but only served as a humble soldier in three skirmishes. "The General must know how to get his men their rations," Wavell quotes Socrates, "and every other kind of stores needed for war." Ninety-nine out of a hundred of Wavell's soldiers have never heard of Socrates. Yet it is their good luck that their general has studiously read the dialogues. True, General Wavell also derives less agreeable advice from Socrates, whose words, "A disorderly mob is no more an army than a heap of building material is a house," he frequently quotes.

Discipline under the General is strict. Tradition and discipline, he affirms, are the essentials of an army, "anyway, as far as the British are concerned." The General's business, in turn, is to see that justice is done. The soldier, Wavell is sure, does not mind a severe code provided that it is administered fairly and reasonably. The chief, for his part, is in charge of the soldier's personal comfort—regular rations, proper clothing, good billets, hospital arrangements—and of his personal safety; this means that a man must go into the fight with as good a chance as possible of victory and survival.

Fat, bulky Marshal Goering coined the slogan: guns instead of butter. Spare, lean General Wavell decided for butter and guns. Their outward appearance belies them both.

Lieutenant-General Sir Archibald Percival Wavell is a medium-sized, bony Scotsman with a sharply-cut face, in which an almost incredible sum of adventures and experience have left an expression of hard-boiled energy, diluted with a touch of smiling understanding. His receding hair is grey, his moustache close-cropped. He wears a monocle in his left eye, which was shot out during the first World War, at Le Cateau. He looks like a horseman, indeed he is a keen rider to hounds, but professionally he prefers to be regarded as an infantryman, still devoted to the "queen of the fighting services," although, nowadays, foot-soldiers are largely motorized.

He comes from an old military family. His father, Major-General Archibald Graham Wavell, fought in the Boer War and was later chief of staff in Ireland. His grandfather, Major-General Arthur Goodall Wavell, had, it seems, a touch of the adventurer. He served Spain and Venezuela as a soldier of fortune. Still worse, his great-grandfather was a scientist, a physician, and the discoverer of the mineral, Wavellite. Archibald Percival, born in May, 1883, in Essex, has inherited his father's fighting forthrightness, as well as his grandfather's inclination for adventure and his great-grandfather's scientific interest into the bargain. Today still, a man of fifty-eight, he insists that a good general must have the touch of a gambler and an adventurer. As to his scientific interests, he has twelve articles in the Encyclopædia Britannica, he has a perfect command of the classics and of practically the whole of world literature. He has written three books, one a military manual, and two volumes which are widely regarded as masterworks not alone of strategy but of literature.

He was a "bookish boy," not entirely to his father's relish, and consequently was sent to Winchester College, Britain's most academic "public" school, which grooms the élite among the prospective holders of great positions in the civil service. Somehow, however, the family's military blood awoke in the boy. He asked to be transferred to the Royal Military College, Sandhurst, and later studied at the Staff College. His career in active service began in 1901, when he was appointed to the Royal Highlanders, the famous Black Watch. He served throughout the Boer War, at the close of which he had won the South African Medal with four clasps. In 1908, he was transferred to the Indian Frontier, where he achieved a reputation as a reliable officer.

So far his career was gallant, if by no means startling. It was about the same career that hundreds of promising young men in the King's forces were making. In 1910, however, Captain Wavell startled his superiors by asking for a year's leave. He wanted to go to Russia to familiarize himself with that strange country. The leave of absence was granted. Wavell donned civilian clothes, which, he admits, don't suit him particularly well, and lived for twelve months with a Russian professor's family, learning their language and acquainting himself with the Russian enigma. Young Englishmen are odd creatures. One spends his vacation in the eternal winter of Moscow, another in the eternal blinding glare of the African desert. It is all "for the fun of it."

The first two years of the first World War Wavell served in France and Belgium. He was awarded the C.M.G. and the

M.C., he received the brevet of Lieutenant-Colonel and was three times mentioned in dispatches for gallantry. The wound he received at Le Cateau ended his front-line service in 1916. On his recovery he was sent to Russia in the capacity of military attaché to the Caucasus army. He used the brief space of time between his service on the Western Front and his assignment in Russia not only to recover, but also to marry Miss Eugenie Quirk, daughter of the late Colonel Owen Quirk. He remained with the army of the Caucasus until hostilities ceased on that front. A little incident occurred while he was serving in Russia. Wavell had received his instructions from the War Office in London in the Russian language; they were marked with the word: secret. How it came about that they fell into the hands of the allied Russian military intelligence, the General is much too polite to understand. He simply recalls being summoned to the Intelligence Officer and questioned as a spy. Obviously, the Russian Intelligence Officer was not very intelligent. He did not understand that he was dealing with British documents in the Russian language. The High Command of the army of the Caucasus had to intervene. Wavell received profuse apologies, and a gold watch which he carries today as a souvenir. But he had now his own opinion of Russian military efficiency. To be sure, a few months later, in the autumn of 1917, Russia collapsed.

The collapse of Russia was Wavell's great opportunity. He was shifted to the staff of General Allenby and met, in the person of his new chief, his man of destiny.

On the surface there could hardly be two men more different than Allenby and Wavell. Field-Marshal Viscount Allenby of Megiddo and Felixstowe looked as impressive as his titles sounded. He was the perfect specimen of handsome virility, even in his advanced years resembling suspiciously the statue of a Greek god, plus a Guardee moustache. His majestic bearing, his dominating personality and his resounding voice contributed to make the absolute superman. He liked to raise his voice until it thundered. A few words were enough to shatter and smash completely a subordinate who had aroused his wrath. Wavell, on the other hand, liked to call himself a "chunky Scot." A truly Socratic self-teaser, he coined the phrase "good generals like good race-horses run in all shapes," as if to excuse his own shortcoming. No one has ever heard him speaking louder than *parlando*, least of all his subordinates, and even these quiet utterances are rare. As the years go on he has eased up—a little late, in true British fashion. He is no longer quite as taciturn as he was. In fact, his sharp and witty remarks, always to the point, have won him, among the French allies of yore, the reputation of possessing "Gallic spirit." But in his formative stage, when he joined Allenby, his nickname was "guinea-a-word Archie." Together they looked like a glorified edition of Don Quixote and Sancho Panza. This strange team, observers were convinced, would not work.

It did work beyond all expectation. Observers, it seemed, had overlooked an admittedly invisible bond that held the two together—their genius. Each understood the other. Allenby soon promoted the newcomer to the position of his chief of staff. When he dealt the Turks the death blow, Wavell executed it as Brigadier-General to General Chetwode's Corps.

Wavell, for his part, idolized his chief with an exuberance that accorded strangely with his customary reserve. He frankly adopted the attitude of the pupil before the master. He was, to be sure, a quick and thorough pupil. In his own Libyan campaign during the second World War he used all the tricks of desert fighting which Allenby had taught him.

The attack on Sidi Barrani is exactly modeled after Allenby's brilliant ruse in the Giza battle. Allenby's plan for successfully starting his campaign hinged on taking Beersheba with the greatest possible speed. In the second war Wavell's plan depended on the taking of Nibeiwa, an Italian stronghold fifteen miles south of Sidi Barrani, in the same way. Allenby moved troops by night and had them hide in dried-up river beds by day. Then he flung a brigade of Australian light horse at Beersheba with such speed that the Turks were prevented from destroying wells or escaping. Similarly, Wavell moved troops across the desert by night and had them hide as best they could in the daytime. Then he hurled tanks, followed by infantry, at Nibeiwa, seizing all supplies and immediately turning them against the Italians. As in Allenby's Palestine campaign Wavell followed up the first thrust with swift crescendo blows, continuing to surprise the enemy after the assault began. Allenby's preferred use of cavalry to speed up the mobility of his actions was copied by Wavell in his use of mechanized units. Allenby's rapid exploitation of the Turks' first retreat, pushing on and on, inspired Wavell to chase the Italians through the greater part of Libya without allowing them a breathing spell. He has followed his own example in mopping up the enemy in Abyssinia. The Duke of Aosta was constantly on the run, and finally surrendered, while the British soldiers were footsore from chasing their prey.

Wavell did not forget how deeply he was indebted to Allenby's example. He called the Field Marshal "England's greatest soldier since Wellington" and wrote two books commemorating him, which, perhaps more characteristic of the author than of his hero, listed over two hundred personal qualities of the man he described.

Incidentally, he made another friend during the Palestine

campaign. He met, and liked at first glance, Lawrence of
Arabia. From him he learned that no one can fight in the
desert without loving the desert. From him he gained the
deep understanding of the desert people that, almost a
quarter of a century later, stultified all the efforts of Axis
agents to drive the Arabs into revolution. The vast realm
under Wavell's military command, where the world's most
restive tribes dwell, is traditionally hot soil. But in this war
perfect calm reigns in the desert. There are two reasons.
The Arabs laugh at a Mussolini who proclaims himself Pro-
tector of Islam; and they smile at their "great Sheik Archie."

A pastel portrait of Lawrence still hangs in Wavell's study.
It is one of the few pictures that Lawrence presented to his
most intimate friends. The colors are a little damaged.
Lawrence of Arabia, Wavell recalls, found them too gentle
and too flattering. So he rubbed and rubbed the picture and
finally trod on it with his bare feet, executing a sort of
Dervish dance, to give it the touch of shabbiness that the
mystery man sought in his likeness.

After the first World War Wavell was on regimental duty
in the Rhineland. He acquired considerable insight into
what is called the "German soul," and today still speaks of
the phenomenon with some amusement. He wonders that
his German opposite numbers don't address their soldiers
as "fellow-Aryans." "We British generals call our men simply
—men!" he adds. It makes a world of difference.

His career was now assured. Everyone predicted a brilliant future for Allenby's brain truster. With clockwork precision he rose. He served as a General Staff Officer, Grade 1,
at the War Office from July 1, 1923, to January 11, 1926,
and then in the Southern Command until June, 1930. From
the following day to January 15, 1934, he commanded a Bri-

gade at Aldershot, and a Division in the same Command from March 11, 1935, to August 18, 1937. Meanwhile, from March 1, 1932, to October 15, 1938, when he was promoted Major-General, he was an Aide-de-Camp to the King.

Buckingham Palace liked him, although he sometimes looked like a stranger in the surrounding of dress uniforms and courtiers. However, he did his best to fit into the picture. With Lady Wavell he accompanied his eldest daughter, a debutante of the season, to all the prescribed balls and parties. He took time off for his favorite sports and hobbies; riding, shooting, skiing, and now and then a round of golf. Nothing seemed to disturb his peace of mind. Occasionally, it is true, he exploded.

Sir Archibald Wavell was never a desk general, and much of his life has been a struggle against obsolete regulations. As a Commander at Aldershot he once paraded his division complete with all the equipment the regulations called for. This prescribed equipment included mule-carts as well as mosquito-nets. The soldiers panted under their loads. After a fifteen-mile march the road was completely jammed. The regulations were re-formed, but Wavell was marked as a dangerous revolutionary.

In the same year, 1936, he proved his inclination toward innovation on another occasion. The Red army invited foreign military observers, among them Wavell, the old Russian hand, to maneuvers which for the first time displayed the use of parachute troops. Most of Britain's military experts had their biggest laugh in years when Wavell returned to London—after having stated to the Russian press how greatly he admired the work of the parachutists—and insisted that he had just seen "a brilliant spectacle of courage and good training." Certainly, the experts said, it is all very well as a stunt, but fancy trying to do such a thing under real war conditions! Unfortunately, Herr Hitler fancied it "under real war conditions," as every peasant and fisherman in Crete can bear witness.

Wavell's was a hopeless case; he was a reformer. But even the experts knew that he was also a man of action. In 1937, when the Jewish-Arab fighting in Palestine had reached its height, he was dispatched to succeed Sir John Dill, and to break the terror with an iron fist. He did not relish the job. But he executed it to perfection. He instituted the system of "flying columns" which suppressed the Arab bands in short order and in the nick of time. There were many death sentences and long prison terms to be dealt out. In revolutionary hangouts Wavell acquired the nickname "big bloodhound." But order was restored. The revolution, smoldering for many years with occasional flare-ups, was definitely broken. Palestine, a key position in the battle of the Mediterranean, was ready when the test of the second war came.

So was Wavell. After his return from Palestine, in recognition of the good job he had done there, he was appointed to the Southern Command, England, and early in 1939, to the command of Aldershot, the highest appointment a serving soldier in the British army can hold. But he did not bask long in the glory that was Aldershot. The War Office realized the fatal blunder of Munich. The signatures on the document that was supposed to ensure "peace in our time" were not yet dry when, as a measure of preparedness, Wavell was dispatched back to the Middle East where he had built his reputation, this time as Commander-in-Chief. A dream came true. He stepped into Allenby's shoes.

Sir Archibald Percival Wavell is a realistic dreamer. He was fooled neither by Mussolini's play for time nor by the professed tenacity of that old comrade in arms, Maxime Weygand. He instantly dismissed the problem of Benito with the truly soldierly words: "My task is to round up the jackal nosing at the heels of the tiger of Europe and fawning on it for scraps of the kill." Concerning Weygand, he said nothing. He simply developed a feverish activity that transformed his little band of soldiers into a formidable, self-reliant army. He thought very little of the plans worked out between the allied General Staffs, according to which the French should supply the land forces for the African theater of war, and the English the naval support. He knew what sort of a customer was lording it in the Grand Sérail, Weygand's palatial headquarters in Beyreuth, Syria.

Since Wavell, for his part, is not "palace-minded"—to quote a word King George VI coined for himself—he settled down in a mansion right in the midst of Cairo's botanical gardens which already housed Lieutenant-General Henry Maitland Wilson, better known as "Jumbo," his second in command. Much to the disappointment of Egyptian gossip columnists, Lady Wavell and General Wilson's wife managed to run the joint household in perfect harmony. Wavell's children do not disturb the tranquillity. They are busy all day: Pamela, Wavell's eldest daughter, as a nurse; Felicity and Joan as their father's secretaries. The latter young lady, in particular, has taken very much after her father. The whole Army of the Nile calls her "Trooper Joan."

During the first months of his assignment the General was more often abroad than at headquarters. He flew all over Africa, the Near East, and the Levant, persuading those who seemed reluctant, enlisting such men as could be helpful, mobilizing the Empire's tremendous reserves in the colored world. His greatest success in this endeavour is the least conspicuous one. South Africa was torn and disunited when war broke out. General Hertzog, a veteran Boer leader, then

Dominion Prime Minister, refused to have his troops take an oath even to defend Africa. Their allegiance should belong only to "Africa south of the equator." The spiteful old man cared not at all for the Empire, from whose struggle for life the limited liability he suggested would have automatically excluded his forces. Contemporary history does not yet reveal whether this ruse sprang from his own mind or whether it had been planted there by Oswald Pirow, his Defense Minister, German-born and Nazi-inclined. Fortunately the great majority of the Dominion Parliament refused to follow such treacherous leadership. Hertzog was unseated. General Jan Christiaan Smuts replaced him, another veteran Boer fighter, but converted into a great British statesman; incidentally, a close friend of Winston Churchill's. Together with General Smuts, who pawed the ground like an old war horse in the expectation of another good fight, Wavell organized the co-operation of the South African Forces with his own Army of the Nile. The South Africans proved their mettle. They took the decisive part in routing the Italians in Abyssinia.

For General Wavell there was never a day of Sitzkrieg. He was aware of the moral dangers of a prolonged stalemate long before the French allies succumbed to them. "Bore wars," he explained, "sap an army's fighting spirit more thoroughly than the bloodiest battle." Untiringly he campaigned against apathy's insidious threat to his forces. "The British Empire will continue the struggle until victory has been won. Dictators fade away; the British Empire will never die!"

Suddenly it looked as if this prophecy was wrong. The Blitzkrieg struck at Norway and the Lowlands, and gave France the *coup de grâce*. Britain was alone. And General Wavell in his eastern corner, having lost his powerful ally, was terribly alone. It was the moment to do or die. Wavell did. He flew to London and persuaded the war cabinet to send him more men and matériel. With these, he declared, he would strike. At the head of the British war cabinet stands a man who does not need much persuasion to fling himself into a fight. However, he, too, had to listen to the voice of reason. How could England, anticipating the invasion at any moment, denude herself of men and matériel? If ever, this was the moment when the mother country had not a single gun to spare.

A decision on which the outcome of the war might well hinge had to be taken within a few hours. Churchill decided. Wavell flew back to Cairo. Men and matériel followed him. True, they came too little and too late. They had to be shipped all the way around the Cape, fifteen thousand miles of dangerous water. Not alone would men and matériel have been lost had they been intercepted by German submarines, but the plan of the African offensive would have been lost with them.

Months of terrible strain followed from September to the first days of December. Wavell used them to get his little army into shape. In his own words, the real crux of general-ship is administration. The matters of administration must be solved before the first bullets whistle. Not all the matters are to be solved simply by the process of reasoning. The mind of the general—to quote Wavell once more—is buried for days and weeks in the mud and sand of unreliable informa-tion and uncertain factors; plans may receive a fatal shock by any unsuspected move on the part of the enemy, an un-foreseen accident, or a treacherous turn in the weather.

War is a game, a very rough and dirty game. The man who plays it must have the robustness to stand the strain of re-sponsibility. Wavell proved that he has that robustness to a high degree. He would probably not admit that it is his character: he hates big words. He is too shy in his ways, and too sure of himself, to speak about his own courage and determination. He just admits as a rule that the ideal soldier must be something of a "poacher, a burglar, and a cat." Is Wavell a cynic?

Quite the contrary. The most impressive quality of this general is his deep understanding for the human element in war. The art with which he treats his subordinates is unrivalled. Sub-commanders have a perfectly free rein under him. He trusts that they will work as a team. Such commanders as he cannot trust, he gets rid of. He never tries, he insists, to do his own staff work, but he will just as little let the staff get between him and his troops. The staff receives unmistakable instructions and is left alone to work them out. The General does not belong to the desk, he belongs to his men. In his heterogeneous army Wavell has to cope with men of totally different sorts. He is fully aware that different nationalities demand different treatment. He does not court popularity with them. Their appreciation and respect are enough. But what he gets is their love.

The soldiers of the Army of the Nile must do this war's dirty work. Yet they would not swap their places for all the luxuries of the defunct Maginot Line. They love it when their general suddenly pops up in the advance line, when he picks up a handful of desert sand, lets it slide through his fingers, and says, with a thoughtful smile: "I really don't know why this sand reminds me of Australia. Is it a sign that the Australians should lead today's attack?"

The Australians cheer.

A young lieutenant from the Free French takes his heart in his hands, and shouts to the great little General: "Does the blue sky not remind Your Excellency of France?"

"All right," nods Wavell. "The French shall follow!"

And now the Free Frenchmen cheer. They rarely have a reason to do so.

Of course the disposition for the attack has long been made before General Wavell inspects his troops. But the touch of impromptu, he adds, gives his men an enthusiasm that compensates for their lack of numbers.

The brass-hats at home called him a lingerer, because he did not strike before he was ready—before the fateful 9th of December, 1940. There was even some talk in London of calling him back. When he had to relinquish Libya, to be ready in Greece, disgruntled politicians—true, only a handful of them—again urged his recall. But Winston Churchill stuck to him. However the tide of war turns, whether it mounts or recedes, Wavell's sentence stands; the sentence he said for England: "We can take the shock. We will come back. We always come back!" In this unbreakable conviction he assumed the supreme military command in India on July 1, 1941. Wavell is always a little ahead of the war. Again he will be fustest—though, unfortunately, hardly with the mostest men—if and when out of the battle for Europe emerges the titanic clash of continents.

PART FOUR

Eccentrics

A Canadian Yankee at King George's Court

LORD BEAVERBROOK

AT SCHOOL THEY CALLED HIM AN "IMP OF MISCHIEF." BUT
he was not a bad boy. His father, the Presbyterian
small-town minister William Aitken, educated his nine children in their duty to God and man, and to sell newspapers
at the age of six. Little Bill, the sixth child, did as he was
told. After school hours he did a thriving business distributing the local daily in Newcastle, New Brunswick, then a
community of 3,500 souls. Sometimes, older residents recall,
there was a little trouble over the change. Little Bill was
really not bad. He was just naughty. The world had driven
him into naughtiness. He was the tiniest shrimp ever to attend the Public Board School in Newcastle. Merciless, as
only children can be, his classmates made fun of his shortcoming. Their taunts would have broken another temperament. To him they were a spur that drove him on—and up.
In the end he arrived on top of the world.

Little Bill became William Maxwell Aitken, first Baron
Beaverbrook, of Beaverbrook, New Brunswick, and Cherkley,
Surrey. He made what is called an American career. He is
the only man in our generation who has made this American
career in England. He is a multi-millionaire, publisher of a

string of newspapers to which belongs the daily with the largest circulation in the world. His name is a household word throughout the British Empire, for many years both glorified and cursed. His race-horses, gay friends, and artistic tastes set the fashions for those who play at being the world's upper four hundred. His slogans were ruminated on by millions of little people. English farmers regard him as their redeemer; shopkeepers think of him as one of themselves, and a very fine chap into the bargain. Above all, as a member of the inner war cabinet he pulls England through this war. His job as Minister for Aircraft Production is to achieve aerial supremacy—victory, to put it in another word.

His daughter has married, and divorced, a British duke's son. Consulted or not, he has acted as counsellor to three kings. But the Beaver remains something of a stranger in the world he has conquered. He is well aware of it. The story of his singular success is an American dream that came true in England. His dynamic drive is of New World pattern. He has spent every free moment of his busy life, though such moments are few, on this side of the Atlantic. Once he crossed the ocean in his luxury yacht to spend a single night in New York. A British-American union, he recently stated, has always been the crowning aim of his life. Is he the personification of such a union? He has not the faintest English accent. He still speaks like the Canadian he is, that means like an American. He is a Yankee at King George's Court.

Lord Beaverbrook, the Beaver to some seventy million white inhabitants of the Commonwealth of British Nations, likes to recall the misery and privation of his early childhood. He is given to strong, sometimes histrionic, accents and to overdramatizing everything, including the story of his life, which is, even without exaggerations, dramatic

LORD BEAVERBROOK

enough. His eight brothers and sisters, who still lead quiet
lives in Canada, do not remember that their childhood was
as bad as that. True, sometimes it was hard for their reverend
father to make both ends meet and to feed eleven hungry
mouths on the small salary of a parish minister. But if a
mouth or two had to go unfed it was the father's and mother's
mouths. The children were reasonably well taken care of.
Big Bill as he was called on account of his midget size never
went very hungry.

He was born sixty-two years ago in the village of Vaughan,
in Northern Ontario, of Scottish stock. Undoubtedly much
of his combined shrewd worldliness and high-strung emo-
tionalism is the heritage of the Lowland Scot. His father
came from Bathgate, one of those minute towns which have
produced so many great men in so few square miles. The
Aitken family were always proud of their roots in Bathgate.
Why, the great Simpson, benefactor of mankind, the first
doctor to use chloroform, was the eighth son of a Bathgate
baker. At the age of four Big Bill decided to follow the
shining example and to become a medical man himself. But
at six began the struggle with orthography, and selling newspapers proved considerably more tempting than study. The
village bumpkin was not born for science. He was born to
outsmart the city slickers all his life. His scholarly record
is nothing much to boast of. On the contrary, Lord Beaverbrook boasts how poor this record was. He is proud of having won the race without an old school tie.

He does not disclose that he stuffed his quadrangular head
with the Bible throughout his youth. Nor does he reveal that
he read and studied the English poets of the eighteenth century. But he still speaks their diction. His sentences are clear
and direct. With the greatest ease his words build epigrams
and antitheses. He would never give away the sources of such

talent. It might mar his self-portrait of an upstart. But sometimes he amazes his listeners with his perfect command of the Scriptures. He knows the Samuels and the Kings by heart. He quoted them liberally during his years of political campaigning. Coming from such a worldly and often cynical speaker they never failed to impress his hearers. To this day he remains faithful to the hero of his youth, the Scottish Presbyterian preacher John Knox. He named the Lockheed monoplane, his favorite among his fleet of private airplanes, John Knox. On the lawn of his palatial country house at Cherkley stands a huge cross. In pre-blackout nights it used to be floodlit from dusk to dawn, a warning beacon to sinners. In a later stage of his career he was anathema to Tory leadership. How should he explain the difficult word *anathema* to the readers of his popular press? To simplify terms and matters he said: "They have cast me in the role of Ishmael." When he joined the inner cabinet he stated his personal war aims. He was fighting, he asserted, to save the teachings of the Sermon on the Mount. It is true that England fights for all the values of Christianity. Besides, the Beaver likes to use eternal values in his everyday arguments.

At eighteen, on quitting school, life began in a drugstore where he washed medicine bottles. He soon found that bottle- and dish-washing did not quite satisfy his ambitions. So he conducted a bowling alley. This enterprise was not successful. At twenty he was barely able to make a living. Undoubtedly, these early years of poverty have left a lasting mark on him. They explain both his lavish squandering of money and his grotesque parsimony. The multi-millionaire wears suits, mostly navy-blue, from the cheapest mass-production tailors. They crumple after the first hour of wear and tear. They cost fifty shillings. Once, at a distinguished party,

Lord Beaverbrook took off his coat to convince the company that his cuffs were held together by safety-pins, thus saving the expense of cuff-links. On the other hand the extravagant luxury in which he indulged until the outbreak of this war always benefited those around him. He raised an employee's salary from $10,000 a year to $50,000, simply because the man had given him a witty answer. The man, stunned, had tears in his eyes. But Beaverbrook, sentimental only when his feelings are not really affected, turned his back on him. "Goodbye to you!" he barked. That is his way of dismissing any visitor, Prime Minister or errand-boy.

In the beginning, his was the hard way. Broke after his adventure with the bowling alley, young Aitken went to Halifax, Nova Scotia, to the small-town boy the city of lights in the big world. He does not remember what he lived on at first. Probably it was selling a sewing machine now and then. He only remembers that he studied "a little law." He never took his degree. But he always avidly collected information, knowledge, sometimes wisdom, or, in his own language: news and facts. He was born for the city desk. But when he reached it, it was just an incident. Unless you believe that fortune has a way with her favorites. They fulfill their destiny as if by casual incidents.

In Halifax he first demonstrated his uncanny gift for winning friends and influencing people—the right people—that later made him the adviser, trustee, confidant of the great and near-great in his time and country. He struck up a friendship with Richard B. Bennett, then his teacher in law, soon a millionaire himself, later Prime Minister, and finally the grand old man of Canada. When Bennett retired from active politics he went to London. There he met Beaverbrook. As a result he stayed on in London. Today his office is next to the chief's in the Ministry for Aircraft Production.

The turn in life came when a Halifax investment banker, Mr. John P. Stairs, engaged the young hopeful as his secretary. The banker was impressed by the boy's facility, his unfaltering smile, his drive and push. He probably never knew that the young man crammed his nights with the study of figures, statistics, reports, books, documents, surveys. Beaverbrook is certainly not the intellectual type, but he is possessed by insatiable curiosity.

He rapidly demonstrated his gift for salesmanship, and his almost Yankee trading instinct. Mr. Stairs wanted to negotiate a merger with another Canadian bank. There were difficulties to be overcome that scared the oldest hands at the game. Bill overcame them. After he had successfully concluded the merger he had a free rein in Mr. Stairs's realm.

He was not contented with his free rein. The only thing he really wants in life is independence. He established himself as an "independent financial source" in Montreal and soon he put through some of the greatest industrial consolidations and reorganizations in the history of Canadian finance. However, he remained penny-wise. Selling insurance was a sideline not to be neglected. The insurance business had the added advantage of establishing contacts with the world outside of Canada. He frequently visited London, and more often Chicago and New York, selling insurance and also bonds. One result of his own antecedents and of his experience as an insurance-salesman is the fact that Lord Beaverbrook, to this day, carries neither life nor property insurance.

The first decade of the century was the heyday of capital expansion in the United States. The trees in Wall Street touched heaven. There was a good time to be had by all. Every newcomer was welcome. The young financier from

Montreal could not but challenge attention. He was the shrewdest pupil of the Street. Here he belonged. Beaverbrook has remained an admirer of American financial methods, as of all things American. But a little incident prevented him from settling down in the Street as had seemed pre-ordained. At home, in Canada, the rivalry among the thirteen major firms in the cement industry ran wild. It deteriorated into a throat-cutting competition. Beaverbrook returned to Montreal for a look-see. In due course he achieved what remains so far the biggest merger in Canadian industry. The thirteen rivals united. Cement was practically monopolized. And had the price per bag not risen from fifty cents to a dollar, he would have been considered a public benefactor throughout the Dominion. By now he was worth five million and was the luckiest fellow on earth since he had, in 1906, married the most beautiful girl in Canada—Gladys, the third daughter of the late Major-General Charles William Drury, of Halifax.

The Montreal press clamored that he was indulging in vicious monopolistic practices. That did not worry him. He had all he wanted, and, after his marriage, all that Canada could give him. There was nothing left except to become a country squire and spend the rest of his life (he was thirty-one) in peace. Off he went to England where nobody reads Montreal gazettes. And he swore he would never again touch a newspaper with a ten-foot pole.

It was meant to be a life-long vacation but it turned out to be the invasion of England, the first since William the Conqueror. The Beaver was too restless to abdicate. The high-geared dynamo inside him would not let him relax. The frail "little man"—as his friends call him with a touch of sober tenderness—was, and remains, in a state of constant eruption and explosion. He was not born to enjoy life as a

meek Colonial among condescending English gentlemen all
of whom he could outtalk, outwit, outsmart. In Canada he
had been a pusher. In England he felt when he first smelled
the rich English grass, this was not enough. England demanded a rebel. A country where the woods are parks and
above which the sun is too unobtrusive to be really hot even
in summer would thrill to a sharp, shrill voice. Well, Beaverbrook, then Max Aitken, had healthy lungs in his diminutive
body. He would be a Conservative rebel, having arrived as
a business-Tory, confirmed Imperialist and protectionist.
There was just one quality missing; he was not interesting
enough. So he decided to become interesting—and went eccentric. At the outset it was probably a matter of cold calculation. After thirty-odd years it has become second nature.
The phenomenon of Beaverbrook is his queer mixture of
eccentricity and calculation.

Immediately upon his arrival he visited Bonar Law. Pious
legends explain the intimacy that rapidly developed between
the two men by the fact that Bonar Law, like Beaverbrook,
was descended from a Presbyterian minister in New Brunswick. In truth, Beaverbrook had first met Bonar Law on one
of his early visits to London. At their first meeting he talked
into buying life-insurance the man whom he subsequently
helped to make Prime Minister. The common descent may
well have played a part in the sales talk.

Bonar Law received his friend and insurance-broker with
open arms. He took him to Tory headquarters. A General
Election was imminent and there was a constituency in
Northwest England which none of the old party horses
wanted to tackle. Ashton-under-Lyne was too close to Manchester, where a young Liberal cabinet minister exercised
uncanny influence with his slogan: "Manchester versus Birmingham!" meaning Free Trade versus Protectionism.

Bonar Law had himself to contest Northwest Manchester. It was a tough job. He felt rather relieved when his newly arrived friend promised to help him in his campaign. For himself, the young hopeful chose the hopeless fight for Ashton-under-Lyne.

The General Election was held twenty-one days after Beaverbrook's arrival in England. He had embarked upon an impossible task. He was unknown in Ashton-under-Lyne. He spoke with a strong American accent to Englishmen who are so easily bewildered about languages. He was a Presbyterian in an Episcopalian country. He stood for protectionism in a stronghold of Free Traders. Besides, his Liberal opponent, who had held the contested seat for a long time, was a popular local man.

The elections went as was expected. A landslide brought about an overwhelming Liberal victory. The Tories lost more than a hundred seats. They gained but one: Ashton-under-Lyne.

The votes were barely counted when the triumphant Liberal cabinet minister came from neighboring Manchester to congratulate the only man who had won for the Conservatives. Noted for his old-fashioned chivalry, the Liberal minister said with all the mature dignity of his thirty-six years: "I am so glad to see a new star in our skies!"

Big Bill was somewhat confused. There had been little hand-shaking after the murderous contests in the Canadian cement industry. And he was still a stranger in his new world. He did not know the faces among which he was now destined to live. "Who was that fellow?" he asked, surprised, when the well-wisher, always in a hurry, had left after uttering his polite congratulation.

"Winston Churchill!" he was told.

So began a remarkable association which has had its ups

and downs. For thirty years there was little love lost between Churchill and Beaverbrook, although each man showed some sort of predilection for the other's singular personality. But at the summit of his career, Churchill gave Beaverbrook one of the most responsible jobs, and certainly the most difficult, in his war cabinet. Churchill has many powerful and determined men around him, but only one to whom he attributes a share of his own quality—genius. That man is Beaverbrook.

Big Bill failed to impress Parliament. His appearance did not help him. He early became stocky, although he reduced again with incredible energy, as soon as he sensed the danger of becoming almost as wide as he was long. He succeeded in getting down to the hundred and forty-six pounds which he considers the correct weight for his size. His diet was the talk of London. His chef's duty was to prepare meals whose ingredients were so disguised that Beaverbrook could not guess what he was eating. If he did not know what he was eating, he argued, it did not taste so good and he did not eat too much. His drinking habits, incidentally, are equally temperate. Although champagne flows at his dinners, which are really General Staff conferences, whether Beaverbrook happens to be running a newspaper or an aerial war, the host seldom touches a drop. He does not exercise the same self-discipline in his bearing. His shoulders push forward. He seemed almost to crouch in his seat on the Conservative benches.

But his quadrangular head is impressive. The black, now distinctly greying, hair is thin and receding in front. At the back it grows down to his collar. His face is sallow, more square than round. It is lighted by a pair of gigantic cold blue-grey eyes. He knows how to use his eyes and he knows how to use his mask. His histrionic faculties are overdone,

but unexcelled. He can act intimate confidence, savage bullying, devastating gloom and deep piety with equal facility.
He exhausts his partners in conversation, but he has a
strange gift of re-charging their batteries. Invariably a talk
with Beaverbrook begins with his question "Well?" and
ends with his traditional "Goodbye to you!" In between he
tries to satisfy a devouring hunger for information. He talks
to few people but he listens to everyone who has something
vital or interesting to say.

His parliamentary speeches did not go well. A certain halt-
ingness developed which was hard to overcome. He did his
best to overcome it. He studied the art of speaking as he later
studied the art of writing—with a subdued fanaticism. Headlong he plunged into politics. He had the satisfaction of being knighted one year after he entered the House. Already,
in 1911, he was "Sir Max." As usual with him it was rapid
advancement. But the better he learned to understand politics, the more he was aware that leadership in the parliamentary system was not fashioned for him. He is a good loser.
The man behind the Prime Minister, he consoled himself, is
more important and lasts longer than the Prime Minister
himself. Already he had learned to despise the show of power.
To attain the substance of power he decided to make Bonar
Law, the Scottish ironmaster, Prime Minister.

Beaverbrook's country house in Cherkley, Leatherhead, at
the foot of the Surrey hills, at once became a center of lavish
entertaining. A host famous for his abundant hospitality, he
established connections with all and sundry. The worlds of
commerce and finance, politics, shipping, civil service, trade
and even the trades-unions, were nothing else to him but a
number of people whom he called by their first names—usually over the telephone. His telephonitis became an obses-

sion. Both in his country home and in palatial Stornoway House, his London residence, there are telephones in every room, even in the bathrooms. When he visited William Randolph Hearst, in 1922, on his ranch, Beaverbrook discovered that the garden is another possible place for a telephone. On his return he immediately furnished the park of Cherkley with the newest American device, garden-telephones.

Much to his regret, one neighbor alone kept aloof from the high-powered gaiety of Cherkley. Lloyd George, whose modest estate stands near by, had little use for a companionship that indiscriminately mixed duchesses and reporters. But Beaverbrook had to have Lloyd George, too. He went out of his way to court the Welsh wizard. Here is a little conversation piece which shows how Beaverbrook does his courting.

"I have two hundred and ninety pigs," Lloyd George once said, always proud of his achievements as a farmer.

"And I have seventy-three thousand hens!" Beaverbrook went him one better.

"You can't have as many hens as that!" smiled the suspicious Welshman.

"No, and you haven't as many pigs either!" retorted Beaverbrook. He is combative by instinct. He cannot help speaking the language of argumentative poker.

Their conversations, however, did not stop there. They were resumed during the first World War.

For Beaverbrook the war began with a bridge party. On the evening of August 3, 1914, he stepped into the Admiralty. Churchill was just playing a game of bridge to ease the tension while he awaited the relays of news. Immediately after the visitor a message appeared. Churchill tore a dispatch out of the box. "Germany has declared war on Russia!" he told his breathlessly listening friends. Up he jumped as if he would plunge headlong into the North Sea, swimming ahead of his navy. At the door he turned around for a moment: "Oh, yes, Max, will you play my hand?" The Beaver sighed as he picked up the cards. He had inherited a yarborough. There was trouble ahead.

Next morning he donned khaki. In 1915, he served as an "eyewitness with the Canadian Expeditionary Force." In 1916, he was Canadian Government representative at the front; in 1917, officer in charge of Canadian war records—throughout all these three years a glorified war correspondent.

The home front remained his main interest. Asquith, he clearly recognized, was not the man to win the war. Many other patriots saw the same sad spectacle. Winston Churchill left the Flanders trenches and in true cavalry style led a charge against the half-hearted and undecided government. Beaverbrook is no Hussar. Indeed, he did not ride a horse until late in life, and even then scarcely mastered the art of horsemanship. He prefers the airplane. It is faster. But in 1917, while Parliament was in a turmoil over the inefficient conduct of the war, he silently did the right thing. He invited his idol, Bonar Law, to meet his reticent neighbor, Lloyd George, at Cherkley. This time Lloyd George came. He sensed a coalition in the air. The immediate outcome of the conference at Cherkley was Lloyd George's willingness to join the Asquith cabinet as Minister for War. By thus joining him he gave Asquith the kiss of death. The War Ministry was the stepping stone from which Lloyd George could establish his own Liberal government with Conservative support. Asquith later called the whole business a "well organized, carefully engineered conspiracy." But England had a government that was able to, and indeed did, win the war.

Beaverbrook aspired to the Presidency of the Board of Trade in the new combination. But when Lloyd George formed his government, the Beaver was left out. Instead, he was rewarded with a peerage, choosing the name of a little village in New Brunswick, where as a boy he had fished. In addition, both Lloyd George and Bonar Law called on him formally to express their gratitude and appreciation. They had not dared to promote him to the rank of a cabinet member. In spite of his influence behind the scenes, he was not sufficiently popular. Nor was he a favorite with Parliament. Indeed, he dropped out of the House after representing Ashton-under-Lyne for half a dozen years. The peerage and promotion to the House of Lords offered a welcome excuse.

There remained no hard feelings. Beaverbrook seemed just a little sullen. He has a way of showing how he feels. Finally, in the last year of the war, Lloyd George decided to entrust the Beaver with the Ministry of Information, then regarded as a minor office. Beaverbrook accepted. He was a cabinet member and a peer after eight years in politics; not bad speed. But his slight resentment against Lloyd George persisted. Bonar Law's advice, he felt sure, had simply been overridden by the Welshman. He had no doubt of Bonar Law. To make him Prime Minister became more than ever Beaverbrook's supreme aim.

Again the American touch came out in the Beaver. He appealed to public opinion. He mobilized the man in the street. Firmly believing in publicity, he bought a paper with the single aim of boosting Bonar Law to Premiership. The aim was soon forgotten. The born journalist who had sworn never more to touch a newspaper with a ten-foot pole came helplessly under the spell of his own creation. The monster devoured Frankenstein.

In taking over the *Daily Express* Beaverbrook acquired a corpse. He had informed Northcliffe of his plan and the press lord had simply asked: "How much money have you?" Beaverbrook quoted his fortune. "You will lose every penny in Fleet Street," answered Northcliffe. That was all the encouragement the Beaver needed. Again, as so many times before, the ice-cold enthusiast had found the single task of his life.

The *Daily Express* was just emerging from bankruptcy. In spite of a circulation of 450,000, the paper had been losing 40,000 pounds a year. Beaverbrook bought both the good will and the deficit for 17,500 pounds. He was entirely confident that he could make a go of it. He trusted to his earlier newspaper experience. Hadn't he sold all those copies in Newcastle? True, until the acquisition of the *Daily Express* this had been his only venture in journalism. Yet he likes to boast: "I sold newspapers at six and I was selling them at sixty." It sounds like a lifetime of devotion. It is one of those half-truths that he enjoys. The press made him famous. But it had only passing importance in his life. He would probably have been equally great, if not quite so much publicized, as a showman, financial wizard or an evangelist.

In his first year as a publisher he lost a million dollars, in the second three hundred thousand, the third year he broke even and from then on the paper has been a gold mine, bringing in well over a million a year. Even now, when it has shrunk to six pages and advertisements are rationed owing to wartime restrictions, the *Daily Express* sells two and a half million copies every twenty-four hours. It has the largest distribution of any daily in the world; a phenomenal success in so short a time. There are various explanations, but the funadmental reason is this: Beaverbrook introduced the American press to the British public.

Of course, his uncanny instinct for business and showmanship helped him. So did his courage and his knack of picking the right people. He picked them where no other publisher would have thought of looking for his staff. And he stuck to them even when they failed. In such a case the job was not the right one. But the man, once the Beaver had chosen him, was all right. Lord Castlerosse, three hundred pounds of flesh and wit, is a typical example. The Beaver had met him soon after the war, in Paris. Huge—as Castlerosse is called by his friends—is the son of a fifth earl. He liked to poke fun at Beaverbrook's very recent baronetcy. The Beaver enjoyed the good-humored fun. He is responsive to ingratiating wit, perhaps because his own brand of humor is razor-sharp. When he embarked upon his venture with the *Daily Express,* he summoned Huge. "Is it true," he asked, "that you can never make both ends meet?" Lord Castlerosse is not the blushing type. Probably this was the first time that his rubicund cheeks had flushed dark red. Indeed, life is complicated if one must keep up an ancestral castle in Ireland while preserving one's fame for smoking the most extravagant cigars and drinking wines of almost medieval vintage. "All right," said Beaverbrook, a shrewd judge of men. He did not wait for an explicit answer. "You never knew how to deal with money. You are my man. I will make you business manager of my new paper."

The assignment was a ghastly flop. Lord Castlerosse, it appeared, had not inherited any considerable business instinct from the five earls. He was shifted to the editorial staff. But he could not write. His ever-flowing stream of gossip, inside information and anecdotes was not to be tamed in print. For two exhausting years Beaverbrook endeavoured to teach

Huge the art of writing. When he went to Fleet Street, true to type, he made a thorough study of this art. But like many a great editor he never developed into a great writer. He just knew the tricks. Lord Castlerosse, London believes, learned them from Beaverbrook. Today he is London's top-flight star-columnist. His Sunday column, the trade guesses, is worth half a million readers.

Beaverbrook picks his men wherever he find them. On a journey to Galt, Ontario, he was impressed by the porter in his hotel. He promised the boy a job in London. Sure enough, the porter came. Today he is the *Express's* general manager. His name is E. J. Robertson. When, on one occasion, Beaverbrook spoke in Manchester, the leftist *Manchester Guardian* attacked him in an ironic column. "A peddler of dreams," he was called. Who wrote this insult? Beaverbrook inquired. Then he licked his lips. Not bad . . . Peddler of dreams—a phrase that sticks. He immediately hired the author. So it was that Howard Spring, today a ranking English novelist of *My Son! My Son!* fame, joined the staff of the *Daily Express*.

Beaverbrook added the *Sunday Express* to his daily. With a lightning stroke he acquired the evening tabloid *Star* at the very moment two competitors were haggling over it. The editors of his newspapers are instructed to rib their publisher in print. It is the only way a newspaper publisher, to whom tradition and good taste forbid the use of his papers for personal showmanship, can keep in the public eye.

David Low, the world's leading cartoonist, whose drawings appear in Beaverbrook's *Star*, has the widest latitude in ribbing the boss. He arrived in London as a furious radical from Australia and found a comfortable niche in the "reactionary" penny press. He was not expected to compromise with his convictions. On the contrary, the English middle class is tickled to tears with Low's class-conscious cartoons. He is the creator of the immortal Colonel Blimp, England's most famous soldier since Wellington. In vitriolic cartoons Colonel Blimp, a fat fellow with a white walrus-moustache, always in mufti, frequently in a bathing suit, used to agree with "Lord Unbelievable." It proved that this did not disturb the boss. Soon, "Lord Unbelievable" turned outright into Lord Beaverbrook. His own paper poked fun at his world-embracing ideas. He had not much credit to lose with the intellectuals, on whom, as it is, a penny paper does not depend, but he became the hero of the funnies to the masses.

The masses of readers were attracted by Beaverbrook's presentation of what passes for the human side of life. In America this has long been taken for granted. In the London of the twenties it was strikingly new. Today it is food for the escapists. The *Daily Express* is read for its columns and news presentation, but largely also for its stories of Hollywood and American crime, whereas the headlines of all the other papers are stuffed with accounts of bombings, for which the London reader, indeed, need not look in his morning paper.

Finally, Lord Beaverbrook introduced peculiar methods of boosting circulation. It was almost too peculiar for the taste of Scotland Yard, and it was a good thing that it was called off before it had to be legally choked. The London popular press outbid one another in giving away premiums to subscribers. First, it was the Bible in a de luxe edition, then Charles Dickens's collected works, finally, life-insurance up to $50,000. These premiums cost the *Daily Express* $600,000 a year. But its competitor, the *Daily Mail,* lost two million a year at the same game and was soon ready for an agreement. In the course of events the *Express* had more than quintupled the original circulation which Beaverbrook had taken over. With two and a half million copies a day, it has outdistanced the *Mail's* circulation of less than two million. A few years later, shortly after the start of this war, Beaverbrook magnanimously handed over the Irish circulation to the *Mail*. It had become too difficult to dispatch the *Express* to its Irish readers. But this was no more than a belated, empty gesture. After the death of Lord Northcliffe, Beaverbrook was the undisputed lord of the press. Once more he was first past the post. Why gallop on?

Beaverbrook invested eight years of his life and a few million in either currency, sterling or dollar, in his newspaper ventures. The money brought handsome rewards. The years, however, were they not squandered? He began to wonder why he had ever embarked on this foolish adventure. From the very beginning he insisted that he had all the money he wanted. He had resigned all his directorships and business associations, by no means unprofitable ventures, to concentrate all his attention on Fleet Street. Did he really do it all for Bonar Law? True, Beaverbrook was largely instrumental in getting Britain's highest office for his friend. But he succeeded too late. Bonar Law was already doomed to die of cancer. He lasted four months in office. Only Beaverbrook was at his bedside when he died. And Beaverbrook will never forget how Bonar Law for the last time raised his lean body in the white shirt, looked into his friend's face, and murmured drily: "You are a curious fellow!"

Was this chap Howard Spring right? Had Beaverbrook been nothing more than a peddler of dreams? When he took command of the *Express* he moved his most important belongings into a small flat right above the city room in the old newspaper building in Shoe Lane. These most important belongings were: the Bible, the classics, a piano which he never touched, and a second pair of shoes. Both Cherkley and Stornoway House were forgotten. For weeks he did not leave Shoe Lane. When a friend asked him what his twenty servants in Cherkley could do all day long, he answered: "They are busy looking after one another." For himself the service of a single maid sufficed.

So enamoured was he of his paper. When he returned to the world after the exile in Shoe Lane, he carried nothing but the *Express* in his heart and mind. His innumerable personal and political connections had to serve as sources of information. He did not even forget his paper in the political activities into which he entered for the second time. Nor in his personal eccentricites, which increasingly dominated his behavior. He used to spend a month every winter in Miami. Instead of amusing himself in society he studied an assortment of American papers from cover to cover. He preferred lunch-wagons to night-clubs, and he surrounded himself with prize-fighters, gamblers, little artists, to hearken to the voice of the readers—the people. He loves the American people, with whom he does not feel solitary. To him there is no difference between England and America. He felt more at home at Hearst's ranch, which he visited in 1922, than at Windsor where he was also a frequent guest. Of course he talked shop with Hearst. How could he resist?

It was, he said, the proudest day of his life when the *Express* moved from its old quarters to the streamlined building with the famous black glass front, in Fleet Street. Here he would remain for life.

But one day he assembled his editorial staff in the big conference room of the new building. "I quit!" he barked. "My elder son takes over. Make a grand paper, boys!" The tear in his eye was certainly sincere. He pitied himself. Anyway, it was, by the same token, an impressive show. The iron man with the soft heart.

Since that day Beaverbrook has never again set his foot in the Express Building. His elder son did take over. But the Honorable Max Aitken seems not to have inherited his father's journalistic genius. He soon earned his laurels in another, loftier, field. The paper is run by an excellent, independent staff. Their only trouble is the telephone that rings incessantly. Day and night the retired publisher, fed up as he pretends to be with his old business, has information, hints, tips, scoops, for the boys.

The truth is that Beaverbrook was bored by his own success. He did not retire on account of fatigue. He was driven by his restless dynamism. Newspapers were not enough. For a short while he entered the field of higher literature. He wrote a few books, only one of which appealed to the public. Modestly, the author had named it *Success*. He was more fortunate in his contacts with other writers. In the middle twenties, an author could simply not omit Lord Beaverbrook in describing the London scene. His best known portrait is the character of Lord Copper in Evelyn Waugh's *Scoop*. He has also been portrayed by H. G. Wells and half a dozen minor literati. He took the novelist Arnold Bennett on a trip to Moscow, where he was despised as England's arch-reactionary. In return, he did not think that Moscow was a red hell. It was much worse. It was unexciting.

Since the loss of his wife, and the emancipation of his three children, to whom he is devoted, nothing could excite him very much. He tried riding but soon gave it up. He established a racing stable, but he did not really care which horse was faster, his or another man's. His American horse-sense never developed into British equestrian pride.

America was his last refuge. He bought an island in the West Indies. He could breathe more easily on this side, he said. He meant it both literally and figuratively. He suffered from asthma. Crossing the ocean on his luxury liner helped it, he believed. Flying was still better. Beaverbrook belongs among the pathfinders of British aviation. His own piloting was not impressive. But his understanding for the development in the air was. For years he bought the newest models of aircraft for his private fleet. For years he clamored for the development of civil aviation. Until the last moment he never expected a second war. But he did not mind saying that a trained reserve of civilian pilots would do no harm to the Empire, if the R.A.F., shamefully neglected since the end of the first war, should some day have to be rebuilt. Incidentally, he never pressed for this rebuilding. He was a fundamentally peaceful man. Perhaps he understood the blessing of peace so much the better since none was bestowed on him. Whether he sailed the seven seas or flew in the clouds above London, he was deeply entrenched in his business as usual. It was the most unusual business: collecting gadgets, torpedoing Prime Ministers, coups in the City, selling anything to anybody or purchasing art collections which soon were covered with dust. It was conferring, listening, talking and telephoning all the time, from some distant meridian in the Atlantic or from 10,000 feet above sea level.

Here was a man, possessed by the demon of work, who could not find a job of his size.

Of course he dabbled in politics. In America, he explained in his book *Success*, the best brains go into business, in England into politics. He never doubted the quality of his own brains. But they were American-made and somewhat wasted in England. In spite of his enormous influence and high connections, the political noise he made far outweighed his political importance. He was a strong patriot, if with a one-track mind. Since Rudyard Kipling, no one has boosted the Empire idea as powerfully. Combined with this idea of the prevalence of the Empire, which made him a staunch protectionist, the notion of Anglo-American union was foremost in his mind. To him the two countries were the sole carriers and defenders of white civilization. If they stood together, he did not care what happened to the rest of the world or how the other nations chose to arrange their affairs.

He fell out with his own party, the inner circle of which accused him of not "playing the team." Indeed, he did not play it. He almost split the party with his demands for Empire development as the Alpha and Omega of foreign policy, and for agricultural revival as the remedy for all economic evils. Baldwin felt tortured by the man who was now the "mole" to him, no longer the beaver. In anticipation of his expulsion, Beaverbrook quit the Conservative Party. He traveled throughout the country appealing patiently to the people. On many consecutive days he spoke four hours to crowds and meetings. Mostly he received a friendly welcome. Yet his effort to create an "Empire Party" failed.

Hitler's first appearance did not frighten him, since he was entirely uninterested in what happened on the dark continent of Europe. His attitude was downright isolationist. When Churchill uttered his first warnings, Beaverbrook grinned: "Churchill is a busted flush." He did not say so in public, but the words went quickly around and Churchill, of course, heard of them. The greatest orator in the English language was silent. Perhaps he pondered that he really might have remained a man of yesterday, a respected elder statesman without a following, had Hitler not forced him back into the arena. The only words with which Churchill subsequently took his revenge on Beaverbrook were those he used in welcoming him into his inner war cabinet as a "man whose genius rises in the darkest hour."

There were no longer many light hours left. Until the last moment Beaverbrook did not give up his most precious American heritage—his unbreakable optimism. Just before Munich, he ordered his paper, which he now ran by remote control, to carry the headline: "Britain will not be involved in a European war this year or next year either!" He argued that Hitler was not ready, France pacifist, England of course only interested in peace, and Italy "unable to withstand assault by a first-class military power longer than a month." His papers not only predicted, but promoted extreme appeasement. "We are not interested in rescuing Poland and Czechoslovakia from the gutter," Beaverbrook stated. And his *Daily Express,* discussing the growing horde of Jewish-German refugees in England, for the first time in the history of the London press, blew a few gentle tunes on the horn of anti-Semitism.

Beaverbrook was never a Hitlerite nor an anti-Semite nor anything of the kind. He could simply not always curtail his eccentricities. His instincts were infallible where money, power, push, were involved. His papers mixed the King's English with just the right amount of Cockney. Personally, he found the right word for every man. He had studied England as one studies microbes. But his instincts failed him when it was a matter of bearing, of unforced dignity, of having been bred by many generations living among cultivated green parks. So it could happen that Britain's queer peer stumbled, if only a few steps, into the embarrassing neighborhood of Hitler. He remained a trade genius from the New World, erring in the labyrinth of the Old World's politics.

Might he, a son of the American continent, better have devoted his "best brains" to business? Perhaps. Subsequently, however, it proved most fortunate for England that Beaverbrook made the wrong choice.

In October, 1939, a few weeks after the outbreak of the war, he visited America for the last time. There was no showmanship about his visit. He retired into his shell. He was a different man. He was unashamed of his peace forecasts which had miscarried. History was wrong, not he, he insisted. But the joke misfired. As he had reached his sixtieth year he began to understand that there must be something else in life, bigger than fun. He sounded out American aircraft manufacturers, not in any official capacity, just as a veteran flying fan. He is reported to have been a little highhanded. England would take care of her own production needs. Many such misapprehensions were exposed when the Blitzkrieg struck. In the hour of England's gravest trial, Churchill sent for Beaverbrook. "But I shall not take the Ministry of Information," the press lord protested. "The Aircraft Production, of course!" Churchill replied. He had known for many years to whom he would entrust a job that means business, when there was not a second to lose.

The first morning Beaverbrook assembled the chiefs of the airplane factories in his office, asking for the production figures for the next three months. "In three months," he answered on hearing their information, "we won't be here any more and nothing of this will be left." His hand waved toward the window, pointing out the Green Park and the heart of London. "I want more speed, gentlemen!"

Beaverbrook is always dangerous when he says gentlemen instead of boys. Indeed, a few days later, not many of the gentlemen were left. The honorable merchants who were still used to thinking in terms of profit and revenue were replaced by Beaverbrook's men thinking in terms of production, and production alone.

On his second day in office he had repeated the great coup that thirty years earlier had brought him a fortune in Canada. Again a gigantic merger was accomplished. Lord Nuffield consented to have his factories, every brick of which he had watched grow, joined with Vickers-Armstrong. Thus, the two giants of the aircraft and armament industry were united. Silently, Lord Nuffield bowed to necessity. He had given his all to the country. "The gratitude of the nation is due to Lord Nuffield," Beaverbrook commented tersely.

A three days' trip took him through all the plane factories in England. His luggage for this journey was a toothbrush, a second shirt, and an iron broom. Everywhere directors were superseded by men with practical experience of production. Many laborers were promoted to the rank of executives. "You have no longer any responsibilities toward the stockholders," Beaverbrook exhorted them: "your only responsibility is to the state." The state was Beaverbrook.

British labor roared its approbation of the man who had spent thirty years in building up his reputation as a red-baiter and pillar of capitalism. The seven-day week, in day and night shifts, he introduced in the plane factories was enthusiastically accepted by labor. Among the hundreds of thousands of men with calloused hands there was a single dissenter. His mates threw him out of the plant. A second time Beaverbrook evoked an enthusiastic response when he advised garage-hands, out of work on account of gasoline rationing, to apply for jobs in aircraft production.

He did not stop at regulating production and labor. He ended the constant re-designing of models, which necessarily slowed down the output. To increase their numbers, English fliers had sometimes to content themselves with yesterday's best. One of these young men is the Honorable Max Aitken, Beaverbrook's own elder son, an ace-pilot with a bag of twelve Jerries to his credit, so far. It is well known that the Beaver never goes to bed without making sure that his son has returned safely, to risk his life another day. All Beaverbrook's personal feelings undoubtedly belong to his children. But he does not weigh the safety of his son against the safety of England. There is no greater or smaller evil. There is only good or evil. He lives in a black and white world. He sees no lights or shades. A thing is right or wrong. An act is to be done or not done. The standardization of British aircraft had to be accomplished. The output had to be stepped up.

British planes were standardized, which, incidentally, did not affect their superior quality. By the end of 1940, Beaverbrook had trebled British aircraft production, despite the increased German bombings of factories.

Beaverbrook does not try to conceal the difficulties he is up against. Long newspaper experience has taught him the value of honest public relations, even in wartime. On the other hand, he is aware that the people sometimes need a shot in the arm. He publicly predicted that England's supply of American planes would amount to 3,000 a month in 1941. Mr. Knudsen had to correct him slightly. This goal, unfortunately, is still two years ahead. Like an incorrigible old poacher, Beaverbrook, although matured and reformed in many ways, cannot resist the temptation of an occasional stunt. His critics, at least, called it a stunt when he collected razor blades and aluminum saucepans for airplane production, or when he started to raise funds in every club and pub. The people, he retorted, want to have a hand in the war. Besides, his collections of money and material had covered the cost of all planes lost in the Blitzkrieg.

Next to Winston Churchill, no man has aroused so much antagonism and hostility in English politics as Beaverbrook. But again next to Churchill, no man has such a justifiable claim to having turned the tide after Dunkerque. Here, it is true, their similarity ends. Whereas Winston Churchill is the next thing to the British lion, Beaverbrook is more like a cat with nine lives. He has lived them all to the full. He was often wrong, but never beaten.

The war has done one thing for him. It has cured his asthma. Beaverbrook has not even time for coughing. Sixteen hours a day he sits in Stornoway House, transformed into an annex of his Ministry in the former Imperial Chemicals building. His office is large and comfortable, furnished with precious rugs and deep leather chairs. On his desk stand the inevitable six telephones. He uses them constantly, whether he has a scoop for his *Daily Express* or an irresistible urge to have a chat with New York or Washington.

In private conversation he is more reticent than he used to be. He still sees for or five people at once, but he lets his visitors do most of the talking. Six secretaries work in his anteroom. There is constant coming and going.

He does not conceal the fact that he enjoys American visitors the most. He was pally with Joe Kennedy, after they had agreed to disagree. He chaperoned Wendell Willkie and Harry Hopkins with equal hospitality. Political differences have lost their meaning for him. He regards them as a useless noise. Amidst the thunder of bombs, he has come to appreciate the blessing of silence.

He remained silent, even when, in the spring of 1941, a

reshuffle of the cabinet caused him to resign his post as Minister of Aircraft Production. Instead, he was promoted to the rank of Minister of State. Was it, indeed, a promotion? Or was it the beginning of a career's end, as some suggested? Beaverbrook's new position had no precedent in Britain's constitutional history. After a few weeks of wide-spread incertitude and popular guessing it developed into a new high honor and, by the same token, a heavy burden. The Beaver was never the man to stand in the twilight. The position he accepted on May 2, 1941, interpreted by some initiated as Vice-Premiership and by others as a glorified burial, lasted no longer than until June 29. At that day Skipper Churchill, under the impact of the terrific Soviet-German clash, called all hands on deck. Of course the Beaver had again to resume a place in the forefront. He took the responsibility for one of the most important jobs in the British war machine, in being appointed Minister of Supply. The man who in a short time had more than quadrupled Britain's plane output was obviously the right choice to become dictator in the vast realm of supply and production.

This promotion had a two-fold Beaverbrook touch. First, it was dramatic. With lightning speed the climax in the Beaver's career followed what had widely been regarded as a definite anti-climax. Second, it was paradox. No one was more firmly established or better known as an almost professional anti-Communist and red-baiter than this man, who, at the summit of his career, took charge of supplying the Bolshies with the tools of war: since this, one may presume, became one of the foremost tasks of the British Minister of Supply in the new English-Russian alignment.

Lord Beaverbrook is consistent in his inconsistencies. Like Churchill he derides the alleged logic that asks a statesman to remain the prisoner of his past. To him the true logic is adaptability. The methods change, provided the cause remains the same. Winston often explained that. The Beaver never bothered about explanations. Unlike Churchill he makes no claim to enter history. He "gives big," to put it in his favorite American slang; that is enough. He no longer expects recompense. But he would not object to being remembered, a few years hence, as His Majesty's most loyal and most successful subject from the other side.

Ambassador Most Extraordinary

SIR STAFFORD CRIPPS

IKE JACOB WRESTLING WITH THE ANGEL OF THE LORD, THE
Honorable Sir Richard Stafford Cripps was striving
with Stalin: "I will not let thee go, except thou bless me." In
this wrestling match the British ambassador had about the
same chance as the Biblical patriarch. A miracle had to come
to pass.

On the British side, the contact man is no ordinary go-
between. He is an ambassador most extraordinary such as
the world has never seen: an English diplomat in shirt-
sleeves. "When somebody calls me Your Excellency, I can't
help turning around to see if there's some Excellency behind
my back!" Thus Sir Stafford Cripps expresses the respect he
feels for his own high office. He wants to be a history-maker,
not a dignitary. Dignities, conventions and capital he regards
as his three arch-enemies. And yet he is His Majesty's Ambassador Plenipotentiary, the son of a British peer, and a
millionaire. Besides, he is what fiction toward the turn of the
century used to call the spleeny Englishman.

First and foremost he is his father's son. Charles Alfred
Cripps, first Baron Parmoor, of Frieth, was a pillar of throne
and altar. Duly educated at Winchester and New College,

275

Oxford, his Lordship does not forget in *Who's Who* to recall that he was first-class in Mathematics, History, General Law and British Civil Law. He became an Honorary Fellow of his old college, and a Fellow of St. John's College, also Oxford, into the bargain. It is impossible to list all his initials, the M.A.'s and P.C.'s, the K.C.'s and K.C.V.O.'s he collected. He was Vicar General of Canterbury, Chairman of the Canterbury House of Laymen, thrice appointed to the post of Attorney General to the Prince of Wales. He edited the *Laws of Church and Clergy*, and represented in turn three constituencies—the Stroud Division of Gloucestershire, the Stretford Division of Lancashire and the Wycombe Division of Buckinghamshire—in the House of Commons. Of course he was a true blue Tory member. But in the seventy-third year of his life, after a passing aberration into the Liberal camp, he cut loose entirely from tradition. His Lordship went over to the Reds becoming Lord President in the first two Labour governments, and proclaiming shorter working hours and wider human rights from the woolsack on which he was now enthroned as leader of the House of Lords. Polite society was outraged. "He got his seat from the Conservatives, his peerage from the Liberals, his office from Labour," commented the *Morning Post*, Colonel Blimp's own paper. His Lordship's three elder sons were inclined to look the other way in embarrassment. Only the fourth, the youngest, was delighted. He welcomed the prodigal father back into the poor man's house, patted him benevolently on the back when father and son rubbed shoulders in the MacDonald government. This fourth son is, of course, Sir Stafford Cripps.

Sir Stafford soon became the most unusual figure in contemporary British politics. There are stranger characters than one might believe in that nation of shopkeepers and cricket

SIR STAFFORD CRIPPS

players. Many fires are smouldering under the smooth surface. But Sir Stafford topped them all. He could not breathe in a stiff shirt, although he wears it as prescribed. So he revolted against England. He did not throw bombs, just firecrackers. His pyrotechnics spread no warmth. Sir Stafford himself froze. Around him was empty space. In vain he shouted for an echo. Into a decade of political activities he crammed more hatred and contempt for the powers that be than the average revolutionary gets off his chest in a lifetime. This lasted until Hitler came and made him think.

In fact, Sir Stafford has been thinking all his life. He is credited with the most brilliant brain at the bar of London. Some time ago, a junior cabinet member decided to close the case with a shoulder-shrugging "Sir Stafford is a damned humbug!" But a wise elder statesman of Tory persuasion retorted: "I don't agree. Can't you enjoy an intellectual treat?"

"He lives in the intellectual stratosphere," Ernest Bevin said of Cripps, indulgently, and somewhat condescendingly. Bevin cares for higher wages and shorter hours for his men. His feet are firmly planted on this earth. The general judgment of British Labour was expressed by a Trades Union veteran. "With Cripps," he said, "you stand shivering on the frozen plains swept by the icy blasts of cold logic."

Sir Stafford's first obsession was chemistry, a science delightfully bloodless and solitary. His research work at Cambridge attracted the attention of no less a savant than Sir William Ramsay. "Keep at it," Sir William counseled the young scientist. "You will become a pride of British science." The danger of ever becoming a pride of British science induced Cripps to relinquish his work immediately. He switched to law. He first specialized in Church law, revising his father's standard work *Laws of the Church and Clergy* into a red-hot *Cripps on Law and Clergy.* English country parsons never ask for the tome in their book shops without adding: "The old edition, of course!" In 1913, Cripps was called to the bar and a year later, on the outbreak of the first World War, he had already become famous as a defender of poor persons who had suffered occupational accidents.

He went through the first war behind the front. He was a conscientious objector and a radical pacifist. At the outset of the first war he was with the British Red Cross in France. Then his conscience allowed him to become assistant superintendent of His Majesty's Factory Queens Ferry, a government-owned ammunition plant. He did not object to furnishing the tools as long as others were doing the job. His son, incidentally, later followed in his footsteps. A year ago the young man was relieved of military service under arms and assigned to work in the fields, with the wise provision that on at least two days a week he must not merely supervise but physically share in the work.

By the end of the first war Cripps had washed his hands of bourgeois society. British socialism had no more radical champion. With perhaps one exception. Sir Oswald Mosley, now leader of the British Fascists—though momentarily prevented, in Brixton Reformatory, from carrying on his duties as Hitler's Gauleiter in England—was equally blood-red during his socialist years. This turncoat has always been held up to Sir Stafford, and that by the Labour leaders themselves. On October 5, 1937, at a Labour Party demonstration in Bournemouth he made the statement: "Lord Cecil, Winston Churchill and the Archbishop of Canterbury are the most bitter opponents of the working class you can find in England!" Thereupon a simple Lancashire miner got up to look long and earnestly into Sir Stafford's face, then cleared his throat and said: "Sir Stafford is a rich man. He has got some

rich pals around him and they are the biggest danger to the
Labour Party in this country. You will find this chap and
Mosley together before very long." Bournemouth expressed
the Party's distrust of Sir Stafford by a nine-tenths majority.

All his life Sir Stafford has been in the minority, always a
dissenter. He has contradicted all and sundry—himself most
of all. Despite his vociferous socialism he succeeded in becoming one of the busiest and highest-paid barristers in England. His advice was sought after particularly where knowledge of technical details was essential. True, he was out to
upset the entire existing system of law, which he calls "the
iniquities of a wicked and wasteful system." But while it
prevails he interprets it faithfully at astronomical fees. He
has an uncanny knowledge of law and unprecedented talent
in pleading. A clause is more exciting to him than a romance.
He actually licks his lips in discussing complicated points.
He makes legal problems come alive.

He was soon able to choose his clients from the ranks of
big industry. Among them in particular were a number of
American concerns with business interests in England. His
yearly income from his legal practice is estimated at $100,000
—a considerably larger sum in the island kingdom than in
this country. No red-hot hatred of the capitalistic system
could prevent him from profitably investing his income. He
has an interest in a number of commercial enterprises; among
other things he owns one of the country's largest stone-
quarries. He is a country squire who lives very comfortably
in a charming manor house, Goodfellows, Filkins, Ciren-
cester. Incidentally, he is happily married and the father of a
large family.

Now the spectacle of a rich corporation lawyer with leftist
leanings in his spare time is neither particularly common nor
particularly attractive. Sir Stafford Cripps has provoked op-

position all over England; indeed he has courted it. But even his most violent adversaries have never called him dishonorable. They have simply become reconciled to the phenomenon of his double life. The gentlemen of the upper class merely shrug their shoulders. There are many eccentric outsiders in their ranks. Why shouldn't Sir Stafford make millions if he has what it takes? And why should he not try to cut down the tree whose fruits give him more than a mouthful? That is his private affair.

To Labour, his own group, however, Sir Stafford has for many years been not a private affair but a danger to the Party. Since his entry into politics he has antagonized every comrade and felt himself alienated by most. His debut was unorthodox as his entire life has been. MacDonald made him his Solicitor General before he had a seat in the House. In January, 1931, a safe Labour seat fell vacant in East Bristol and Cripps was elected by a big majority. Right from the beginning of his experience of the House of Commons he sat on the Front Bench. He did not serve any parliamentary apprenticeship, he never learned the temper of the House. Perhaps that lack of parliamentary grooming—in addition to his intellectual haughtiness—explains his cold detachment among the M.P.'s.

His efforts to appear as a popular figure backfired. He overdid his metamorphosis into a proletarian. Even his outward appearance underwent a visible change. His face, once round and rotund as a country squire's face should be, became lean and ascetic. He insisted that he was on a vegetarian diet without analyzing the question of whether border-line cases like lobster and caviar belong to a vegetarian's forbidden fruit. His high forehead towered above an ever thinner, shrinking face. His rimless spectacles covered a pair of dark eyes, illuminated by cold flames. His prominent, pugnacious nose contrasted with tight, close lips that could spill torrents of abuse when they opened.

He was not so tough in taking the punishment he courted. Once Winston Churchill condemned his "loathsome speaking." Churchill was a rather solitary man at that time, but this indictment on his part evoked terrific applause. From the press gallery one could distinctly see how Sir Stafford crumbled under the hammer blows that fell upon him. He could not conceal the pain he felt. His legs writhed as though he was near agony. His mouth was open as if in physical pain.

Is he a coward? On the contrary. For many years Cripps has been one of the most aggressive British politicians. But he is a deeply sensitive man. His position was honest—but absurd. He felt it. When he called his party friends by their Christian names "Jim . . . Charlie . . . Herbert" the Labour people around him smiled cynically. They resented the benevolent condescension of a man who stands so high above them in family, fortune and intellect. Their smiles turned to grins when his suddenly melancholic voice deplored the miseries of the working class. Among themselves they called their millionaire-comrade Jeremiah, Job or Cassandra.

Labour believed in his honesty, but less in his usefulness. From his first day in politics he got the party into trouble. As MacDonald's Solicitor General he was teamed with Sir William Jowitt, then Attorney General, another top-flight lawyer. Sir William was a handsome, courteous, cultured man; MacDonald had "converted" him from the Liberals in 1929. He and Sir Stafford made a formidable pair of law officers. But Cripps missed no opportunity to steal a march on Jowitt. When the Trades Unions Bill was introduced Jowitt endeavoured to explain it harmlessly. Cripps, on the other hand, excelled once more as a fire-eater. He advocated the bill because it was dangerous. To a House in which the governing Labour Party only had a minority, he recommended the bill as making possible a general strike. Socialism, he declared, exists only "to completely destroy" the capitaLIstic system. This time the "li" sounded like spitting. He must have gone to great pains to use the vulgar split infinitive. But he forced his tongue into vulgarity. It was his gauche way of courting popularity.

The Trades Unions Bill contributed much to the undoing of Labour. At the next General Election Sir William Jowitt, who had represented Preston first for the Liberals and then for Labour, no longer dared to contest his old constituency. Instead he stood for the Combined English Universities, whose electorate votes by mail. Sir Stafford was more courageous. He again contested Bristol. But while he had previously been elected by a crushing majority, this time he escaped defeat only by a few dozen votes.

Did he mellow? No! As Labour went into opposition, Sir Stafford decided to establish himself as their dynamo. His speeches became so violent that they were physically odious to hundreds of members on the benches opposite with whom he was naturally allied by his station in life, his fortune and his education. Still, the gentlemen opposite, although they avoided him personally, respected his integrity and felt the intellectual impact he made.

Labour could not affect a similar detachment. The British Labour Party depends basically on the semi-conservative Trades Unions, which will have nothing to do with Socialism, and have no liking at all for radical intellectuals. They stand for the little man of England, who wants a higher standard of living, but no upset of the social order. This "complacency" is what Sir Stafford Cripps has always reproached his party with. Their leaders, he has been saying for years, are too feeble. One after another, he objects, has succumbed to the glamour of the British tradition. In the second place, as he has been shouting during years of agitating, the Labour Party makes another mistake. It wants to "play the game." It believes in parliamentary rules and peaceful progress, whereas big business and the landed gentry will use any means in their resolute determination to retain power. They would even sabotage a Labour majority, he has warned, through financial panic, the civil service, the courts and the armed forces. As soon, therefore, as Labour receives power by parliamentary means it must establish its dictatorship in order to prevent sabotage.

This program brought Sir Stafford Cripps next door to Bolshevism. The country was in an uproar, and nowhere was the opposition so violent as in his own ranks. Sir Stafford made the situation worse by saying: "If Labour comes into power, we shall encounter difficulties at Buckingham Palace." Now the Englishman, no matter of what party, will not tolerate having the Crown brought into political debate. Sir Stafford excused himself at once, saying that by the term Buckingham Palace he had not meant the wearer of the crown, but of course only the court clique. But already he stood condemned in the House and before the public.

His speech, it was generally assumed, cost Labour a million votes. Was Sir Stafford cursed with blindness not to see it? It was impossible. His party friends began to look for a motive behind his scheming. And suddenly the motive was found. Sir Stafford Cripps, they believed, wanted to damage his own party. He despised his moderate colleagues and was afraid that they would blunder and wreck the entire labor movement if they came to power in their immature state. Better to let the Conservatives rule a few more years and give Labour time to grow up politically. That is why he deliberately marred his own party's chances. It was, of course, never established whether this was really his conception, but everyone felt that such plotting was just like him.

Needing a change of air, Sir Stafford came to America. He has many good friends in New York—particularly around Union Square. In March, 1934, he took part in a "trial at Town Hall," wherein some local Reds and Pinks "sentenced" the then Austrian Chancellor Dr. Dollfuss for putting down the socialist risings of February, 1934. Calling on President Roosevelt, he expressed his opinion of him in the words: "No man has made a more heroic attempt to save capitalism than President Roosevelt." Of course he considered this heroic attempt futile. In order to assure social progress, he believed, Roosevelt would be forced to give up capitalism. "The only way to obtain planned economy is to get rid of private ownership," as he put it at the Canadian Club in Toronto on April 10, 1934.

The following winter, however, returning from a trip half around the world, Sir Stafford disagreed with the world as well. England was still the best place after all, he realized. "It is better to have a constitutional monarchy," he declared in February, 1935, to the astonishment of his friends, "than to have a Hitler or a Mussolini. It is also better than to have a President of the French Republic or a Roosevelt who is a political boss and is intended to be a political boss who has more power than his ministers, because they are personally appointed by him. And it is better than Stalin."

This was the first time that the high-born semi-Bolshevik ventured to criticize Stalin. Perhaps it was only a slip of the tongue. Sir Stafford Cripps has always been a persistent advocate of the Russian orientation in British foreign policy. As long as Russia was not a member of the League of Nations, he sharply attacked that institution. It had become use-

less for peace and socialism, he declared. But as soon as the
U.S.S.R. went to Geneva he demanded a more vigorous policy, particularly against Japan—Russia just then was involved
in an acute conflict with the yellow empire—and active par-
ticipation in the Spanish Civil War. When no Russian interests were at stake he was still not particularly enthusiastic
about Geneva. He had serious difficulties with his own Labour Party when it supported the League of Nations sanctions against Italy.

From this time, apparently, dates also Sir Stafford Cripps's
fanatical opposition to Mr. Neville Chamberlain. The object
of his constant attacks was the fundamental anti-Bolshevik
attitude of the merchant of Birmingham, rather than his
yielding disposition toward the dictators. "If we continue
raising ill-feeling among the Russians, we shall seriously
jeopardize all our future relations with her," he was proph-
esying two years before the Moscow-Nazi pact.

At that time, it is reported, Stalin first began to take a
personal interest in Sir Stafford. The great man in the Kremlin seems to have indulgently overlooked the quip that the
English king would be better than Stalin. After all, every
Englishman, even an arch-radical, somehow succumbs to the
glamour of the Crown. For the first time a visit to Moscow
by Sir Stafford began to be talked of. But it was postponed
to a later, a historic moment.

Once more Sir Stafford dragged the Crown into the debate, this time to defend the King. Along with Winston
Churchill, an unusual neighbor, he was the only man who
upheld Edward's right to the choice of his heart. "The King
is old enough to know his own mind," he declared, "and it
is his marriage, not one of a robot, we are discussing. I cannot help feeling that if the lady in question had been a member of the English aristocracy, under precisely similar cir-

cumstances, a quite different position would have been come to by the Government."

At about the same time, indeed, in May, 1936, he declared, as if to eat his own words, "The belief in the divine right of kings has long ago passed away." And he demanded the "demolition of this false façade with all its tawdry and out-of-date ornaments. Look at America," he went on. "Every man there is equal to the President. Yet he honors him, and there are no two million dollars a year to pay for the civil list."

However, Geoffrey Lloyd, member for Colchester, proved by statistics that from 1868 to 1932 every presidential election year in America had depressed business by four per cent. This represents a total sum far higher than what Britain pays for her kings and queens, princes and dukes.

Sir Stafford remained incorrigible. A few months later, on May 10, 1937, he called the Coronation "bunkum and bunting, a show simply run as a political stunt by the Conservative Party."

He was now definitely the black sheep of England.

To Sir Stafford the fighter this was but one more reason for carrying the attack forward. In his private creation, the Socialist League, he gathered together three thousand intellectuals, dark-glowing pinks, who urged the Party to form a united front with the Communists. He forged a far more important weapon, the "Left Book Clubs," where a hundred thousand fellow-travelers met. The Party could no longer idly watch these goings-on. British Labour would never unite with the Communists, who had practically no following among the English people. The trades union leaders, members today of the War Cabinet—Major Attlee, Morrison, Bevin and Greenwood—were furious. On January 28, 1937, the Socialist League was "disaffiliated" from the Party; on

March 24, Sir Stafford Cripps was given an ultimatum ordering him to break off his flirtation with the Communists within two months. On January 25, 1939, he was expelled from the Party's national executive committee "for disobedience in persistently advocating the popular front" by 18 votes to 1, the 1 being red-headed Ellen Wilkinson, M.P. By roughly 2,000,000 votes against 400,000 the Party congress at Southport confirmed this ouster on May 29, 1939. "The Party has blown its brains out!" Sir Stafford said with a modest sigh.

He carried on his one-man fight in the House of Commons. He was Mr. Neville Chamberlain's sharpest critic. As in the tussle over the abdication he found himself side by side with Winston Churchill, of all people. Pitilessly he assaulted the Tories, and above all the policy of Lady Astor's Cliveden Set. "The noble lady and her set are not exactly popular with the people of this country," he declared in the House.

Lady Astor, who has always denied the existence of any secret group at her castle of Cliveden, interrupted him: "What set?"

"I withdraw the word set and apologize, and I substitute the word gang!" Sir Stafford replied chivalrously.

With the war already in progress he had still not made his peace with his own countrymen. At an election meeting in East Bristol, his constituency, he declared: "We have two enemies in this war, the Fascists abroad and the Fascist-minded at home, and we must fight each with equal determination. It is big business that is running this war."

The "proletarian war" in China, he said, concerned him much more deeply. And in the darkest hour of his own country he left England to study war conditions in China, via India. Deserter! his countrymen shouted after him. There is reason to believe that this act of apparent desertion was actually the beginning of his conversion. Sir Stafford would rather have bitten off his tongue than join in *God Save the King*. But in the end he understood that Hitler was the worst of all evils. Perhaps a man in his fifty-first year, which Sir Stafford had then attained, is no longer satisfied with being the stormy petrel of the Kingdom and the black sheep of society. There is something particular about erring Englishmen—sooner or later they find home.

The mystery of Cripps's journey to China has yet to be resolved. His utterances there were contradictory, as usual. "Great Britain has made a profound mistake in not allying herself with Russia," he declared in Shanghai. "Had she done it, there would never have been a war." In the same breath, however, he described Russia's assault upon Finland as "a stupid mistake." With a vigor that no one would have suspected of the professional pacifist, Sir Stafford went on to say that England could well afford a showdown in the East; she would not lose Hongkong.

At Urumchi, capital of the province of Sinkiang, where no non-Russian white man has been allowed for years, he took lunch with certain mysterious gentlemen who were later identified as Soviet agents. Not all his time has been accounted for, but he met Chiang Kai-shek in Chungking. When he turned up in Urumchi again at the beginning of March, 1940, after four weeks of China, he admitted that he had meanwhile taken a short plane excursion to Moscow, to see, quite privately, officials of the Soviet government. He went home by way of America. In New York he appeared cheerful and in high spirits. According to his account Russia was not an aggressor at all, despite the Finnish blunder. She would push forward in the Balkans only if the Soviet Union found herself forced to "meet" Germany.

Arrived at home, he presented a more cautious report of his Asiatic journey—the first public speech in which he did not attack the government. Indeed he had very quietly made peace with Churchill. He set out once more, this time to take charge of the British mission in Moscow. He did not even have time to pack his trunks. Mussolini was already threatening Italy's entry into the war, and the shortest way from England to Russia at that time was by way of Italy.

Sir Stafford got through Italy by a hair before the Duce delivered his celebrated "stab in the back." He took a plane from Athens. Fifteen hundred feet above Sofia the craft flew into a storm. Lightning struck straight through the machine. Incredibly, there was no accident. At Odessa the French ambassador, Eric Labonne, joined him. Meanwhile Signor Augusto Rosso, Mussolini's ambassador, roared past the two allied diplomats. It was a matter of honor for the Fascists to arrive in Moscow before their competitors.

Sir Stafford Cripps arrived in Moscow at 12:30 P.M. on June 12, 1940, accompanied by Mr. D. N. Wilson, his private secretary, and Mr. Lascelles, the Embassy Attaché. He was received at the airport by Vladimir Barkoff, Chief of Protocol of the Russian Foreign Office, wearing morning coat and high hat. The tovarisch was visibly surprised to see His Britannic Majesty's ambassador descend from the plane hatless and in an ordinary flannel suit. This was the first misunderstanding that disturbed the modestly initiated Russian-English reunion. A number of similar incidents followed. They all sprang from the same source: His Majesty's ambassador was not ceremonious enough for the Russian comrades. Nowhere are the niceties of diplomatic etiquette so important as in the fatherland of proletarians. The new masters want to be constantly assured that the old ones take them at full value.

And Sir Stafford had appeared in a grey flannel suit! Why, doesn't a British ambassador *sleep* in evening dress? Besides, he did not look in the least like a well-pressed diplomat. On the contrary, Sir Stafford is inclined to be short and, since he no longer harangues the House, he can grow stocky again. His manner is anything but Olympian. He is constantly on the move. Instead of the monocle that Moscow had a right to expect, he wears oversized spectacles. His high forehead, prominent nose and razor-sharp, ironic lips make him look like a homemade Bolshevist intellectual—certainly not a cavalier from the royal court.

He was not even introduced by the court. In the rush of Sir Stafford's precipitate departure his King had no time personally to sign his credentials. The Narkomindyel—the People's Commissariat for Foreign Affairs of the U.S.S.R.— were sorry. According to a protocol of the year 1756 a royal ambassador might not pay his official respects until he was able to present an introduction signed by the hand of his sovereign.

Accordingly Sir Stafford had to let his call upon Comrade Kalinin, President of the Soviet Union, wait. But the very day after his arrival he had his first interview with Foreign Minister Molotoff. The gentlemen talked "cordially" for an hour—entirely about the trade treaty that they then hoped to conclude. The following day Comrade Molotoff left his calling card with a note of congratulation at the British Embassy. It was the official birthday of the King. This was the first time that it had been properly recognized by Soviet diplomacy.

The autographed credentials finally arrived, two weeks late. On June 28, 1940, Sir Stafford presented them to the President of the Soviet Union, Comrade Mikhail Kalinin. Now at last he was officially welcomed. There is always considerable uneasiness in the Narkomindyel when the President is receiving a foreign diplomat. The old comrade is rather garrulous, and more than once his audiences have led to painful leakages. They usually last ten minutes. Sir Stafford, however, was detained for three-quarters of an hour by the old gentleman.

Count Friedrich von der Schulenburg, the German ambassador in Moscow, an old Russian hand—he remembers the Kremlin from the days of the Tsars, and knows that nothing but the color has changed—offered a high reward, as is his custom, for a secret report of the interview. This time he was able to save his money. The report was in all the papers the next morning. Sir Stafford himself had authorized it. He had talked with the President about Russian flowers and Russian handicrafts. Thus in his first release the amateur ambassador showed the subtlety of his diplomacy. Flowers and handicrafts are, of course, the only things you can buy without any difficulty in Moscow.

Sir Stafford's conversations with Molotoff were resumed sooner than was agreeable to the eternally vigilant Schulenburg. Sometimes Comrade Anastasius I. Mikoyan, Commissioner for Foreign Trade, took part. Then it might be about the publicly announced, if never concluded, trade treaty. But more often it was Vice-Commissioner of the Foreign Office S. A. Lozovsky who assisted his boss when the British ambassador called. Of course Comrade Lozovsky was a vigorous proponent of the Nazi orientation, and owed his career to the Pact of Moscow. But, as Schulenburg knows, you can never be too careful with the Russian allies.

Moscow diplomacy goes on in dark-rooms—a regular atmosphere of conspiracy. Only Stalin held aloof from the plot. He received no one. Saw no one. Talked only to his three or four most intimate associates. Even Count Schulenburg had to content himself with the attentive amiability of Molotoff.

But one day the British Broadcast allowed itself an indiscretion—no doubt carefully prepared. Stalin had spent three hours "a few weeks previously" with the British ambassador. That was all; not a word more.

The mystery of those three hours long occupied the minds of the diplomatic world. Both sides were silent as the grave.

Sir Stafford Cripps once outshouted Parliament. Now he outsilenced Stalin. His silence lasted, almost to the day, throughout a year. On June 11, 1941, twenty-four hours before the first anniversary of his arrival in Moscow, he suddenly returned to London. His mission, it was obvious, had ended in complete failure. All sorts of rumors popped up upon his spectacular return. The initiated said that Sir Stafford, according to his own complaint, had never again, since his first official visit, been received by Molotov. The august *Times* of London, every line of which breathes official air, went as far as to suggest that Sir Stafford's brilliant gifts should no longer be wasted in distant Moscow; they could be used at home to better purpose. The ambassador himself was credited with having expressed the wish again to take his seat in the House of Commons. He still believed, rumor had it, that Soviet Russia would ultimately have to switch to the Allied side, but not before Germany had suffered serious military reverses; in a year, perhaps, or in two. For the time being, the breach between the British Empire and the Soviet Union seemed beyond repair.

History will reveal in due time whether such rumors were founded on fact, or whether they were just features of a diplomatic drive. It is not unlikely at all that Sir Stafford, probably the one Western diplomat with the deepest knowledge and understanding of the Russian enigma, saw that the time had come to apply a little pressure from the British side. He will certainly never claim to have brought about the Anglo-Russian co-operation in arms—not a downright alliance—which, with logical necessity, followed Hitler's rapacious attack on Russia. But it is more probable than not that Sir Stafford's timing was excellent and that he knew exactly when to bluff.

Fundamentally, it was not a bluff to him. Throughout his political career his supreme aim was to bring the British Empire and the Soviet Union in line. Permeated by almost communist ideology, he was in England a pillar of a creed dangerously resembling Soviet philosophy. But when the time for action came, he acted as a British patriot in Russia; sixteen eventful days after his departure he was back in Moscow. The change might not be easily visible on the surface. Yet it is the decisive change in Sir Stafford Cripps's political life. He has an uncanny hand in the war. But peace is bestowed on him.

PART FIVE

Symbol

The Life of King George VI

THEY HAVE TURNED THE ROSE BEDS AT WINDSOR CASTLE INTO vegetable gardens. The squire's lady, although a Scotswoman, no longer goes grouse-shooting in the season; she practises sharpshooting instead, for the invasion is looming and every British housewife will help to defend her home. She is no longer married to a symbol. The symbol at her side has become human. Her husband, George VI, King of Great Britain and Ireland and of the British Dominions Beyond the Seas, Defender of the Faith, Emperor of India, is today a very plain Englishman. Dodging bombs—and courting them sometimes—eating à la ration card, working twenty hours a day, he remains Defender of the Faith; more so, perhaps, than his ancestors and predecessors in a thousand years of British monarchy. The King inspires the nation that Winston Churchill leads.

Outside Great Britain the King's share in the conduct of the war goes almost unnoticed. He is grateful for being overlooked. Never has a more unassuming man occupied the throne. Never has modesty to the degree of self-effacement been more humbly and hence more gloriously embodied. He has changed his name, the date of his birthday, almost his identity to serve his country. Yet the example he gives,

297

the style he sets, the courage and creed he spells, affect every man within the United Kingdom.

The war has transformed King and nation alike. No longer are the English people the sleepwalkers, easy-going, satisfied, and, above all, a little self-satisfied that they were for twenty years. No longer is the monarchy a pleasant, glamorous institution, with a faint touch of nostalgia. There will be no Royal Courts for the duration. American debutantes must wait a while to visit England and for a further opportunity to curtsy before their tired, smiling Majesties. Since another generation is growing up in this country, too, perhaps the next batch of American visitors will prefer to see the new social centers, the housing projects that are replacing the slums. If they ask for the chief architect of this new England, they will hear many names—but not one. The King's large share in the rebuilding of the realm remains hidden. He is not only the noblest of reformed Englishmen, but, by the same token, himself a great reformer. Only insiders, however, know it, and they hesitate to speak of it. It has been a surprising transformation. Born for a life of privacy, almost of seclusion, the King assumed leadership in the gravest crisis in modern history. A fragile, ailing boy, inhibited, with an impediment in his speech, grew up to become the hardest-working ruler Great Britain has ever had, and, next to Churchill, certainly the busiest man in England. The heir to ancient tradition has become a pathfinder into the future; everything revolutionary in England, from mechanized warfare to the abolition of the class system, is intimately connected with his personal endeavors.

His life is a triumph of will power over handicaps, physical and otherwise. Such a case, if rare, is not unique. President Roosevelt, psychologists are agreed, also derives much

KING GEORGE VI

of his spiritual power from the conquest of his own body. The typically English quality of George VI's transformation, however, is that it has left no outwardly visible mark.

Millions of his subjects see him, thousands of them every day, since the King has left his ivory tower. They see a young man, looking as many Englishmen do, much younger than his age, slender but well built, with an unforced smile on his rectangular, bony face. His fine, brown hair is carefully brushed. His eyebrows are just thick enough to reveal energy. Nose and mouth are of orderly proportions. Everything is orderly in this clean-shaven face. The expression is patient, kind-hearted, a little curious, and very innocent. The vessel does not know that it is endowed with grace.

"Georgie's first feeling was regret that this dear child should be born on such a sad day." Queen Victoria wrote this line in her Journal on December 14, 1895. The King's life began in melancholy. He was born on the thirty-fourth anniversary of Prince Albert's death, a "terrible anniversary" to the aging Victoria. Two days afterward, however, she noted "with the greatest pleasure that Georgie intended the baby to have the name of Albert."

As a second son he was permitted to grow up quietly, without official interference, undisturbed by the efforts to groom a coming sovereign which weighed so heavily on his elder brother's brilliant and erratic youth. Albert's childhood was spent at White Lodge, Richmond Park, a comfortable, rather modest country house, in which the then Duke of York's family lived a peaceful, patriarchal life. The atmosphere was permeated with the father's stern, Christian morals. To the Duke of York, later George V, the Ten Commandments established the laws of everyday life. The rules for bringing up and educating the children were rigid. To remain inconspicuous was one of the chief maxims. When the quarterly *Horoscope* celebrated Prince Albert's seventh birthday with the prediction, "This boy will be extraordinarily lucky . . . His planet, Jupiter, will raise him to a higher sphere than that to which he was born," his father shook his head. To him there was no higher sphere than royal humbleness in a country house.

A similar prediction followed a few years later during Prince Albert's term at Osborne, where he received his first naval education. Court gossips liked to compare the two royal Princes, usually favoring Edward, "the sardine." But one evening an officer stood up for the junior Prince, who was entrusted to his care, and said: "The younger will outstrip the elder." Not until 1937 was this forecast vindicated.

In January, 1911, Prince Albert went to Dartmouth to finish his training as a sailor. He had just emerged from a grave attack of influenza that had turned to pneumonia, the first of the illnesses with which he had to wrestle throughout his entire youth and young manhood. His courage in combating sickness amazed those about him. The quiet strength, with which he later rebuilt his health and ordered his life, developed early. Despite his tender constitution—or probably because he had to conquer it—he became a fearless horseman and an excellent swimmer.

After two years at Dartmouth his naval education was complete. Early in January, 1913, he joined the *Cumberland,* a cruiser of 9,000 tons, carrying sixty cadets. On January 18, in the early afternoon, the ship left Devonport for the West Indies.

Prince Albert experienced his first adventure. It is sweeter to recall adventures than to endure them. Life aboard the *Cumberland* was not easy. In the first days of the cruise it rained incessantly. "All cadets miserably ill," the log-book notes. A few days later it stated briefly: "Raining hard, cadets still ill." At Teneriffe the sun broke through the clouds. The sons of John Bull gradually realized that they had been baptized with salt water. "Cadets now beginning to enjoy life." They enjoyed it primarily by making the life of their royal comrade thoroughly miserable.

Being born a prince of royal blood, far from proving an advantage, is a considerable handicap to a midshipman in the Royal Navy. "Middies" are no respecters of persons who do not rank above them in the service. George V, the father of the present King, had already had a hard time going through the navy mill and its merciless ragging. In his personal memoir, published by John Gore, the late Sovereign recalled: "It never did me any good to be a Prince, I can tell you, and many was the time I wished I hadn't been. The other boys made a point of taking it out on us on the grounds that they'd never be able to do it later on."

Like father, like son. Prince Albert was made to fight bigger boys, run their errands, and lend them his scanty pocket-money. Good-humoredly he took the hard knocks that came his way. He did not dream of trying to hide behind his rank. He had never been pampered at home, and the grim realities of life in the rough sea-school, he understood, were a necessary part of the training that turns out future leaders. Indeed, he enjoyed being treated as a cadet and nothing more. He was weighed down rather than exultant on account of his high estate. Sometimes it hurt. But it was always a delight to be permitted anonymity. The stern rules of educating a British Prince and Albert's own escapism were harmoniously mingled.

The graver was the test when, for the first time, he was forced to step into the limelight. The *Cumberland* anchored at Kingston, Jamaica. The ship arrived in time for the open-

ing of a new wing of the Yacht Club, which had been cere-
moniously dedicated by King George V when he himself was
a sailor. Naturally his son was expected to follow suit. Prince
Albert rehearsed his speech, his first public utterance, carefully. Today the King's voice, as millions of radio listeners
know, sounds warm, pleasant, self-assured. There is nothing
to remind one of the ordeal of his debut in public. He was
aware and afraid of his own shyness. His stammer was hard
to overcome. Yet he overcame it—almost. Unfortunately the
hall was crowded with Jamaica belles. These colored ladies
are among His Majesty's most loyal subjects. To them any
member of the Royal House is a dream prince. If you but
touch his suit it will bring good luck, the faithfulness of
your prospective husband will be assured, and little black
babies will never catch the whooping-cough. While Prince
Albert was praising the Atlantic as a bridge not a gap between the far-flung islands of the Empire, he overheard a
whisper: "Say, have you touched the Prince?" "Yes!" came
the answer. "Three times! And I'll try it once more!" This
was the signal for the royal speaker to end his peroration
abruptly. With a jerk of his head toward the audience he
abandoned the Atlantic.

The journey continued to Canada. Prince Albert was
swamped with ceremonies and speeches. The Canadians did
not hide their eagerness to be on good terms with the King's
second son. True to its French tradition, the City of Quebec
gave a ball in honor of His Royal Highness. Young ladies
thronged about him. Every waltz was a torture. To his tutor,
it seemed, every waltz was a delight. The otherwise stern
gentleman danced with such recklessness that he lost two
buttons from his trousers. "I must hold my garments with
both hands," he confessed to the Prince. "It's awful. Please
don't tell anyone."

Now Prince Albert had a topic to amuse his dancing partners. Of course he told the dreadful secret to everyone. The gaiety of the ballroom rose to pandemonium. Toward dawn the Prince left, reluctantly.

The next day he went Salmon fishing in the Dartmouth River but only landed kelp. However on his second day's fishing he got five splendid fish. Life began to look considerably brighter. Thus far he had not been spoiled by the pleasures of life. Now a silly joke with the girls and a good catch with the rod made up for many privations. The visit across the sea taught him that things have a lighter side as well. He heartily enjoyed Canada. In the years that followed there grew out of a young man's innocent and modest pleasure a deep understanding of British life overseas. The Dominions reciprocated the good feeling. They have never looked to any King in Buckingham Palace with more pride of possession than in their regard for George VI.

On his return from Canada Prince Albert was a grown man. He spent the summer with his parents at Balmoral, mingling freely with the Scottish people and losing something of his feeling of isolation. He learned the directness of Scottish speech; occasionally he even dared to give his dry humor free rein. Frequent contacts with the tenant farmers became an important part of the education of the Prince. He shelved his princely title, incidentally, when he was gazetted a midshipmen aboard H.M.S. *Collingwood*. The appointment came in September. He immediately joined his ship at the naval base of Rosyth in the Firth of Forth. He reported as "Mr. Johnstone." Yet, as the *Collingwood* cruised the Mediterranean the rumor persisted that there was a Royal Highness aboard. While she lay at anchor at Toulon, a French family insisted upon being presented to the Prince.

The Commander shrugged his shoulders. What Prince, if you please? The French allies persevered in their demand. Finally the Captain assigned Mr. Johnstone to show the importunate family all over the ship so that they might see for themselves that they were the victims of an illusion. Mr. Johnstone discharged his task with the greatest tact.

At the outbreak of the first war Prince Albert was most anxious to do his bit. He was up against a mighty power in England—tradition. Since William IV, who had been a midshipman at the relief of Gibraltar in 1780, British princes had not been allowed to risk their lives in naval battles. Besides, there was little hope that Albert's health could stand the rigors of active service. His doctors and the Court officials protested his appointment with equal stubbornness. But the First Lord of the Admiralty overrode the protests. Neither doctors nor Court officials stood a chance against Winston Churchill. After summoning Prince Albert to the Operations Division of the Admiralty—"where I am sentenced to desk-work," as the Prince put it—the First Lord allowed him to rejoin his ship and return to Scapa Flow. For nine months Albert served aboard the *Collingwood*. Then a new attack of his ailment, a painful stomach disease, forced him back to the shore. Again he sat at a desk in the Admiralty, this time close to the First Lord. He gained considerable insight into the complicated mechanism of naval strategy. He learned to admire Winston Churchill. Both lessons proved their value at a later, historic date.

When Winston Churchill left the Admiralty after the tragedy of the Dardanelles, Prince Albert, too, grew restless. But he had to control his impatience until May, 1916. Then only was his health sufficiently restored to permit him to go to sea again. It was the last moment. At the end of May the battle of Jutland was fought. H.M.S. *Collingwood* sailed in

the First Battle Squadron. Prince Albert was at his station
as the second officer in command of A-Turret. The *Collingwood* fired eighty-odd rounds at enemy ships. Five hundred
yards away the *Marlborough* was hit by a torpedo. Another
torpedo approached the *Collingwood's* starboard side. The
Commander was able to avoid it. "The worst part of all was
the night afterwards!" Prince Albert recalled. His ship
steamed in darkness, ready to resume the fight at dawn. But
when dawn came nothing was visible of the enemy forces but
a "bloody Zeppelin." The *Collingwood's* A-Turret fired two
shots at the monster of the skies. But the monster escaped to
report the ship's position to the German fleet. However,
Jerry showed no further inclination for a fight and the *Collingwood* steamed undisturbed into the harbor at Scapa
Flow.

A new attack of illness beset Prince Albert. A time of terrible strain followed, a duel between a weak physique and
an indomitable will-power. Despite his critical state he
worked under the Commander-in-Chief in Portsmouth. After
a few months, still an ailing man, he obtained his reappoint-
ment to service in the naval front-line. He joined H.M.S.
Malaya. But at the close of 1917, a terrible attack of gastric
pain again disabled him. Now only an operation could bring
relief. The medical men warned of the seriousness of the
operation. The Prince, they feared, could not survive it. No
heroic words of Prince Albert's are reported. He simply decided to gamble for life. The operation proved a blessing.
The gastric pains were ended for good. Prince Albert's health
was restored. It was a miracle—the miracle of spiritual
strength.

After his baptism of fire at the battle of Jutland and his
wide experience with the navy, Prince Albert, much to his

own surprise, was something of a national hero. The innovation of flying began to capture the nation's imagination. King George V could personally never quite reconcile himself to this innovation. But he understood that a new world was about to be discovered and he felt the necessity of having one of his sons identified with the air effort. He assigned Prince Albert to the task. So it happened that the present King is the first sovereign to hold a qualified air pilot's license. Again Winston Churchill proved instrumental. Two years before the first war the then First Lord, together with his inseparable friend Sir Archibald Sinclair, now British Air Secretary and Chief of the R.A.F., instituted the Royal Naval Air Service, after his predecessor at the Admiralty had refused to buy the Wright brothers' invention. In April, 1918, this service was transformed into the Royal Air Force of second war glory. Prince Albert went to Cranwell to join the new service. He remained there until the end of the war, collaborating in the mushroom growth of the Air Force during the last months of fighting, and becoming increasingly mechanically minded.

His superiors, however, declined the responsibility of allowing the Prince to take to the air himself. Only after the war, in April, 1919, did his training begin, forty-five minutes a day. Wing-Commander Coryton, his instructor, attested that his royal pupil was able "by instinct to use eyes, hands and brain in unison," and that he was amazingly quick in learning to land, the most difficult part of a pilot's training. The air had a marvellous effect on the Prince. Suddenly his stammer disappeared. Now he was sure of himself.

The navy and the new air force were but the initial training. A young man's education has to be continued at Oxford or Cambridge. His elder brother had been at Oxford before the war, so Albert, by King George's wish, was sent to Cambridge.

In the spring of 1919, in his twenty-fourth year, Prince Albert began the life of an undergraduate. It was the regular University life, with the only difference that he lived in a house and not in rooms in college. Other exceptions in his favor were not made. Once he was seen smoking in the street while wearing his academic gown. He was fined in the usual way. "Come with me, sir, to the Proctor!" said the voice of authority. In vain Prince Albert endeavoured to explain to the Proctor that he was only smoking because he was so excited by a marvellous speech of Mr. Winston Churchill's which he had just heard at the Union Society. "It was the most expensive cigarette I ever smoked," the King remembers his adventure, "valued by the authorities at six shillings and eightpence."

The main reason for sending Prince Albert to Cambridge was to give him an education in civil government. Another reason may have been his father's desire to see him thaw, and gradually lose the rest of his painful shyness. Prince Albert could completely forget it at work, but it recurred when he was what is misleadingly called at ease. The decision to allow his second son the freedom of an ordinary undergraduate probably did not come easily to King George V, a conventional man with strict ideas of royal privileges and duties. But it proved a most fortunate decision. Riding on his bicycle to and from the lectures, mingling with the stream of undergraduates, lounging with his books, Prince Albert's tension relaxed. His talent for hiding his achievements— today, still the King's fundamental quality—was as highly developed as ever. He did not excel as a scholar. But no one could apply to him the phrase that the President of Magdalen College, Oxford, had used in speaking of his brilliant elder brother: "Bookish he is not!"

To tell the truth, civil government was not his only love. Up in the Scottish Highlands, in ancient Glamis Castle, near Forfar, twelve miles from the sea, lived a distant cousin. The Lady Elizabeth Angela Marguerite Bowes-Lyon, youngest of the ten children of the Earl and Countess of Strathmore and Kinghorn, one of the highest ranking families of Scotland, was born on August 4, 1900. She was five years younger than Prince Albert. Five years make little difference in a relation that dates back to Robert II of Scotland, who ascended the throne in 1370, and whom both the Royal Family of England and the Lyons of Glamis count among their ancestors.

"Lizzie," as the Lady Elizabeth, not entirely to her relish, was affectionately called, was a mischievous child, inseparable from her brother David, now Mr. Bowes-Lyon, Press Officer in the Ministry of Information. The pleasures of her childhood were manifold. She used to climb on to the roof of the castle and pour water on arriving guests. She scared the visitors to the ghost-ridden castle with unaccountable devices such as secret staircases, trap-doors and supernatural flashes of pale light. Occasionally the guests found ghostlike dummies in their beds: the children had put them there. Sometimes Lizzie showed sightseers over Glamis Castle; on these occasions she did not refuse a modest tip, given and accepted in equal innocence.

Her youth was quiet and untroubled. She early acquired that harmonious balance that has distinguished her as Queen. By nature she belongs in a peaceful, unproblematic world. When fate destined it otherwise, she accepted what must have seemed to her a difficult task with courage, devotion, and a quick sense of humor.

Her old-fashioned charm endeared her to Queen Mary, who used to spend much of every summer at the Royal Castle at Balmoral, thirty miles from Glamis. When the Princess Royal was married, in 1922, Lady Elizabeth was a bridesmaid. This honor was tantamount to inclusion in the list of "eligibles," the list of girls from which the Prince of Wales might make his marital choice. A year previously a fortune-teller had predicted that Lizzie would become a great Queen and the mother of another Queen. In ghost-ridden Scottish castles fortune-tellers are listened to credulously. Their words are gospel truth. Glamis was ready to receive the Prince of Wales.

Instead, Albert came, and he was a frequent visitor. The story goes that he and Lizzie had built a solid friendship at the tender age of thirteen and eight, respectively. Fourteen years later they again made friends. At first, Lady Elizabeth was somewhat suspicious. She feared that "Bertie"—Albert—had "been sent" by his mother. How was he to convince her to the contrary? One day, while both were riding in the park at Glamis, Prince Albert mustered all his courage. This was a more dangerous moment than even the battle of Jutland, or the first flying lessons in the suicide-machines which, at that time, passed for airplanes. It took tremendous courage to risk the question. He opened his mouth . . . In that very moment his long forgotten stammer again overcame him. The embarrassment lasted for a single heartbeat. Then Prince Albert tore a leaf from his note-book. His flying fingers scribbled a few words. With a desperate gesture he handed the scrap to her. Elizabeth nodded. The horses neighed. The trees of Glamis Park were hidden behind a screen of smiles and tears. His Majesty the King consented "with the greatest of pleasure." Queen Mary added: "Thank God, she is not one of those modern girls."

On January 14, 1923, the Court Circular published this paragraph:

> It is with the greatest pleasure that the King and Queen announce the betrothal of their beloved son, the Duke of York, to the Lady Elizabeth Bowes-Lyon, daughter of the Earl and Countess of Strathmore, to which the King has gladly given his consent.

The wedding took place in Westminster Abbey, where there had been no royal marriages for five and a half centuries. This glamorous scene was chosen—instead of one of the smaller royal chapels—to give the people in the Dominions, to whom Westminster Abbey means so much, a better chance to picture the marriage ceremony. It was the Duke of York's personal wish to have the Britishers overseas share in his happiness.

The Duke of York was married on April 26, 1923. All England rejoiced that he was taking a woman "so truly British to the core." The sudden outburst of popularity that surrounded him was almost astonishing. Was he no longer Prince Cinderella? The *Times* of London alone could not refrain from pointing to the modest state of the Duke of York in comparison with his "brilliant elder brother." "There is but one wedding to which the people look forward with still deeper interest," the Old Thunderer stated. But the *Times,* later to become the mouthpiece of appeasement, was not always right in its predictions. When the "one wedding" came to pass, the people turned away. At least in England no one disturbed the privacy in which the brilliant elder brother made Mrs. Wallis Simpson his wife. Queen Elizabeth, it is reported, expressed her sisterly feeling in speaking of "that woman."

As anxiously as her husband, the Duchess of York tried to guard her domestic life from the limelight. The newly wedded pair spent their honeymoon in the house of Mrs. Ronald Greville in the Surrey Hills. Then they retreated to White Lodge, to privacy again. There the Duke dug in the rose garden; already in his Cambridge days he had been a keen gardener. The Duchess enjoyed good talk, music and literature. Her reading tastes are conservative, with Hardy, Kipling and Conrad among her favorites. She has even done a little writing herself. Her first essay, written in her early childhood, began with the words: "Some governesses are nice, others are not." Although the truth of this statement is un-challengeable, the essay did not meet with family approval, and Elizabeth soon left the art of writing to others.

On their return to London the couple took a modest house at 145 Piccadilly. They preferred to spend their evenings at home and not in patronizing night clubs and the then popu-lar bottle-parties. The smart set regarded them as a hope-lessly dull pair. The people, however, liked them. Queen Mary shared the approval of the simple folk. She took her daughter-in-law very close to her heart, taught her to dress in a completely unglamorous, but becoming and dignified fashion, and educated her carefully in the exercise of her social and public functions, as if she had a premonition of things to come.

Soon after the marriage the Duke of York took his bride to visit Cambridge, where in the previous year he had ac-cepted the honorary degree of Doctor of Law. He walked with her over the old scenes just as Queen Victoria and her Prince Consort had done seventy-five years earlier. The young couple basked in the mellow sun of tradition. The Duke, although still in his twenties, appeared somewhat archaic to most observers. Few could pierce his smooth, ami-able surface.

At heart he was a restless seeker for the new, concerned with grave problems, very much a product of his age. This, he understood, was an industrial and social age. "That country," he expressed it, "will be the richest in this century which nourishes the greatest number of happy people." To help in the task of nourishing the people was a greater privilege for royalty, new style, than to attend Court banquets and State dinners. Perhaps this conviction grew in him because he did not care for Court banquets and State dinners, anyway. He did care very much, however, for the welfare of the people.

The merit of having mobilized the Duke of York's social conscience goes to a man who was a benefactor of thousands, but remained practically unknown to the world. The Reverend Robert Hyde had worked for fifteen years among the poor people of Hoxton, a slum district in London's East End. During the first war he joined the Ministry of Munitions, working under Winston Churchill, and dealing with social conditions in armament factories. After the war Hyde laid out the scheme for creating the Industrial Welfare Society, to raise the living standards of industrial workers. To promote his work he wanted the inspiration of Royal patronage. He succeeded in bringing his cause to the personal attention of George V. The King called his second son to a conference in Buckingham Palace. The Duke of York listened. Then he rose from his armchair, walked to the window, looked out on the teeming London streets, turned around and said: "I will do it. But I don't want any of that damned red carpet!"

He had taken a heavy burden on his slender shoulders. In the four years before the war no more than twenty factories had been visited by the King or one of his sons. Now the Duke of York assumed the responsibility for inspecting plants all over Great Britain. Dutifully he carried out eight hundred engagements. There was no fuss and only a minimum of ceremony about these visits, which acquainted the Duke with the actual conditions under which the laboring people lived and worked. Usually the manager of a factory was informed that His Royal Highness would arrive the next morning. The workers were not to be notified in advance. The Duke wanted to see them as they were, not wearing their Sunday best, or what Queen Victoria once called "Sunday faces."

Cheerfully the British workers welcomed their visitor. They have always been aware that a Prince belongs to no class. The Royal Family of England, indeed, gave abundant proof from the very beginning of the industrial age that the King is in truth the toilers' King as well. Queen Victoria, writing to Lord Beaconsfield, deplored the "English zest for growing rich," and as far back as 1849, the Prince Consort called "the unequal division of property and the dangers of poverty England's principal evil." In establishing close personal relations with the laboring masses the Duke of York was following a noble family tradition. He did, unwittingly, even more. He became the workers' trustee. Chains of confidence, stronger than steel, bound Britain's poorest sons to their King when the grave test came. One bulwark which Nazi bombs have failed to destroy is the people's monarchy.

The Industrial Welfare Society, sponsored by the Duke of York, embraced a wide field of activities. For many years it spread the principles which were finally embodied in the Factories Act of 1937, England's social magna carta. The Industrial Welfare Society's legitimate offspring is the Miners' Welfare Fund, which has considerably bettered living conditions in the mining districts. The Duke took a personal interest in every stage of its organization. He was particularly interested in the miners' living conditions, which, at that time, were bad. He visited the "red soil" of Wales. To be sure, the Welsh miners did not conceal their color in front of the Duke. Mr. Frank Hodges, Secretary of the Miners' Federation, received him wearing a red tie and with a red carnation in his buttonhole. In some of the cottages which the Royal visitor passed on his tour the housewives, to demonstrate their political convictions, had hung bright red petticoats on the clotheslines.

The Duke of York smiled. He visited the cottages, talked to the housewives, inspected their gardens, and modestly offered an expert gardener's advice on the best way of cultivating Brussels sprouts. Rapidly the flaming red petticoats disappeared. The red carnation in Mr. Hodge's buttonhole faded surprisingly quickly. He threw it away. The red tie remained to embarrass him. He had to continue wearing the symbol of revolution since there was no other tie at hand. But he offered a very English revolutionary's excuse: "Blimey, I can't run around in front of a duke without a tie!"

Closely connected with the work in the Industrial Welfare Society was another social enterprise—the Duke of York's Camp. The aim of this camp was to nip class consciousness in the bud. It brought together boys from public schools— a misleading term, since England's famous public schools, Eton and Harrow and the others, were the haunts of privileged youth—and errand boys, young workers and farm hands for a summer holiday. The camp, true to English custom, really began with a football match, or rather with two matches. A team of boys from the Briton Ferry Steel Works, in Wales, was brought to London to play soccer against teams from the Ordnance College and Westminster School. The Duke of York attended both the matches; at one he kicked off the ball.

The ball rolled a long way. It was not the last time that

factory boys and Etonians were to play the game together.
The Duke was determined to establish a camp. Each year
four hundred boys, two hundred from the factories, two hundred from the public schools, should be his personal guests
for a week. The first group received His Royal Highness's
personal invitation. From every corner of Great Britain they
came to New Romney, in Kent. The Duke presided at the
lunch table. Jubilantly, they chose him as their "Great
Chief," and he, in turn, made them leaders in new camps.
Since then about eight thousand boys have been the guests
of the Duke, first at New Romney, and later at Southwold
Common. According to this pattern, hundreds of camps were
established, not only all over England, but in the Dominions
as well. The movement encompassed the youth of the whole
nation. To many R.A.F. flyers whose holidays were spent in
these camps, the King is still, above all, their Great Chief.
In 1937, incidentally, ten German boys were invited to join
the camp in the park at Chatsworth. They returned to Nazi-
land singing England's praises. Recently a Goering air pirate
was shot down after having tried in vain to blow up Chatsworth Castle. He had been singled out for this particular
raid, he explained, because he knew that part of England so
well. Had he not had the time of his life in the camp at
Chatsworth?

The Duke of York's Camp was first copied in Australia.
Lord Somers established a similar institution "down under."
The youth of the most youthful Dominion responded joyfully. When the Duke and Duchess of York traveled to Australia and New Zealand, in 1927, they were enthusiastically
welcomed. Auckland, where the New Zealanders pride themselves on being "more English than the English," ran riot
with delight. Their journey over the wide spaces of Australia
was a continuous holiday for the whole continent. The trip

assumed a more serious aspect when the Duke took part in the celebration of Anzac Day. Thirteen years later this solemn celebration was not forgotten. When a new generation of Anzacs boarded their ships to prove their gallantry in the sun-baked deserts of Africa, and in the snow-covered Greek mountains, the soldiers waved pictures instead of flags. Their families had carefully kept the photographs of the Duke of York, who is now their King.

The personal relation between the King and the Dominions is becoming more and more the true basis of the Commonwealth of British Nations. Politically, the Dominions have achieved full independence. Economically they belong to various "living spaces," socially each member works out its own pattern. As the old ties loosen, the allegiance to the Crown remains as the one bond that holds them together and to the mother country. George VI reaps the harvest he sowed as Duke of York by visiting the Dominions and proving to them his interest and by identifying himself with them. His relationship with the countries of the Empire is unique, as is his hold over the imagination and affections of the people overseas. General Smuts, war-premier of South Africa, expressed it in the words: "Here for the first time we have a King of kingdoms spread over the whole globe. A new chapter has been written in the constitutional development of mankind. In a deeper sense than ever before, the King and Queen have now become ours. . . ."

In May, 1935, London celebrated the glorious pageant of King George V's Silver Jubilee. The Empire was elated. The days were great. A greater future seemed assured. The old King alone, close observers noticed, did not join in the universal happiness. He felt that his world was vanishing. The insecurity of things to come depressed him. His span of life lasted but another eight months. His closing weeks were spent in undisturbed domesticity, at Sandringham.

His eldest son came and went, to "quit altogether public affairs," before he had acquired the habit of calling himself Edward VIII. On December 11, 1936, the day of abdication, the British Crown was in the gravest crisis of her history. In the midst of the turmoil and general upheaval a slow, quiet voice said: "I am willing to accept the throne."

Undoubtedly, it was a sacrifice. Only a strong sense of duty could force it upon a Prince whose deepest longing, despite his constant readiness to help where help was wanted, had always been the peace and sanctity of private life. The task of a constitutional king in the twentieth century is neither easy nor enviable. Monarchs have lost most of their privileges, and have kept only their obligations. Statesmen and generals are able to satisfy whatever ambitions they may nourish. The King cannot have ambitions of a mundane kind. His influence is strictly limited, yet his responsibility covers the whole life of the nation. He belongs to all, but nothing belongs to him. If circumstances warrant it, he is deprived of the individual's most elementary rights. When the Duke of York ascended the throne, he had to change his name from Albert to George, which, it was felt, sounded better. His birthday, in fact on December 14, was henceforth celebrated in June at the peak of the London season. Probably even the process of easing up, of adjusting himself to the world—in its initial stage a slow and often painful process—was interrupted as the young man rose, silently, dutifully, to become a symbol. He was well aware of the fateful change. On the morning of his Coronation he said: "I stand on the threshold of a new life."

Five million Londoners jammed the streets to watch the Royal procession leaving Buckingham Palace for Westminster

Abbey. The cavalcade that passed was to them more than a glorious show. Their tension proved that the abdication crisis had deeply shaken the English people. Now they could breathe once more.

Their confidence was rewarded. When the King opened Parliament for the first time, in October, 1937, his address was brief as far as matters of high politics were concerned. But in a calm, well-modulated voice he spoke at length about his government's social plans. Slum clearance, improvement of agricultural housing, State medical care for the young after leaving school, meals for boys and girls attending instructional centers, and the lowering of the pension age for blind persons were introduced—nothing very glamorous, but all of them measures inspired by a young, progressive King.

With King George VI and Queen Elizabeth in the Palace, English people felt that the immaculate state of monarchy was to survive. A new sense of security spread over the Island —a delusive sense, in view of the catastrophe that was closing in on Europe. Still, it was a feeling of relief. With the exception of one very solitary man, who, John Bull reborn, today embodies them all, nobody cared very much about Hitler's armament, the frighteningly increased danger from the air, and the breakdown of international law and morale. Appeasement had its gayer aspects, too. Again it was a joy to be alive in England. At the top, at least, Great Britain was safe.

George VI is a King after his people's heart. The English don't want a witty king, nor an interesting or forceful one. They rejoice in seeing a family man in Buckingham Palace. They like to share in his domestic happiness to such a degree, incidentally, that George VI once said: "My chief claim to

fame seems to be that I am the father of Princess Elizabeth."
When they come home, put on their slippers and listen to
the radio, they like to fancy that the King does the same. Of
course their allegiance goes deeper, and is more serious. To
many Englishmen the institution of kingship is a condition
of their own well-being, an almost physical necessity. The
times when Charles II "dispensed healing influences" by the
touch of his hand are gone. Yet the present King had a similar experience. As Duke of York, visiting the boys' camp at
Southwold, he was frequently surrounded by East Anglians—
the most superstitious of his subjects—who pressed forward
to touch him in the hope of being cured of sickness. More
rational people trust in him because he satisfies to perfection
the modern conception of monarchy. They do not regard
him as a picturesque survival, but as an impartial authority,
above classes, parties, interests, having access to all shades of
opinion, the judge of politicians and the exalted servant in
government of the people.

Whatever the reasons for their loyalty and allegiance may
be, the English reserve the right to control their sovereign's
private life. King George VI and Queen Elizabeth met the
test from the very outset. For a short time Queen-Mother
Mary groomed her daughter-in-law in her new duties. It was
widely remarked that Queen Elizabeth had acquired the old
lady's characteristic hand wave on public appearances. Then
the Queen-Mother retired that she might not herself attract
too much popularity away from the ruling Queen. She left
Lady Helen Graham, daughter of the Duke of Montrose, to
guide Elizabeth through the problems of the first years of
her reign. The problem of dress was a serious one. The English expect their Queen to dress conservatively. They even
entertain definite ideas about how a Queen should look.
Queen Elizabeth, who is only five feet and two inches tall,

went on a diet in the first year of her reign. She lost fourteen pounds. But the diet had to be abandoned when a female reader wrote to a newspaper: "We want to think of our Queen as a mother. None of us would like to hear that our mothers were losing weight." On the other hand, all the writers of letters to the editor approved of Their Majesties' missing the opening of the opera season at Covent Garden, since they preferred instead, on that evening, to see "Me and My Gal," the popular musical show that gave the world the Lambeth Walk. With this theatrical choice, George and Elizabeth proved once more than they really belong to the people.

Their Majesties visited France in the spring of 1938, for their first state visit. The Entente Cordiale was loudly acclaimed. The President of the French Republic, M. Lebrun, gave a state dinner, at which the toasts outdid one another in assurances of unending solidarity with Great Britain, and of unbreakable alliance with her King. For her visit to Paris, the Queen had escaped from the rigid rules that governed her dress at home. Norman Hartnell, who revolutionized English dress-designing, created dreams in silk, lace and tulle for her. The oldest Parisian boulevardiers fell under her spell. Maréchal Pétain, then aged eighty-two, and still going strong, placed his right hand on his left breast, and swore everlasting fidelity.

Their next journey, in 1939, took the King and Queen to Canada and the United States. The Royal visit has not been forgotten in this country. Its success echoed across the ocean. The English people were delighted that their sovereigns had gone over so well with the Americans. On their return warm waves of proud affection for George and Elizabeth swept the British Isles. The skies were blue and bright.

Then, on September 3, 1939, at six o'clock in the evening,

the British Empire, America and the world, heard the King's voice broadcasting from Buckingham Palace: "In this grave hour, perhaps the most fateful in our history, I send to every household of my peoples, both at home and overseas, this message, spoken with the same depth of feeling for each one of you, as if I were able to cross your threshold and speak to you myself . . . The people of the world would be kept in bondage of fear, and all hopes of settled peace and of the security of justice and liberty among nations would be ended, if we gave in. This is the ultimate issue that confronts us. For the sake of all that we ourselves hold dear, and for the world's order and peace, it is unthinkable that we should refuse to meet the challenge."

The first forty-four years of King George VI's life were, despite their color and weight, their sadness and success, simply a preparation. The man he is emerged when the bugles sounded. But the preparation, it appeared, had been by no means accidental. As if preordained, his service at the battle of Jutland, his association with the R.A.F., his social studies, his preoccupation with the working classes, the youth of the nation, the British peoples overseas, seemed to have followed a straight line of inner necessity. George VI was not born to the throne. But he is of the stuff of kings.

Figuratively and literally the lights in Buckingham Palace faded. The blackout regulations apply to England's first family as rigidly as the rationing regulations and all the other stipulations for the war-conduct of British citizens. Since the beginning of hostilities the King has not worn civilian dress. He feels a soldier first. In the uniform of a Grand Admiral he visited the Home Fleet from October 6 to 8, 1939. A crowd of old comrades from his own naval days surrounded him. The King expressed the wish to inspect the merchant

navy as well. That was an innovation. Dreadnoughts, cruisers
and destroyers had frequently paraded before crowned heads.
Old freighters, however, trawlers and tankers, fishing-smacks
and the tramps of the seas, were for the first time in their
battered lives honored with Royal attention. They steamed
slowly ahead, as veterans march on parade. Yet these very
freighters and tramps keep the sea-lanes open and the British
Isles alive. King George knew that theirs would be the heaviest burden and the most dangerous job of the war. In a message he issued on his return to London, he expressed his
confidence in the English merchant marine.

His next inspection, on November 2, 1939, took him to
R.A.F. stations in the North and Midlands. Again the King
was among old comrades. Almost without ceremony he decorated five men in the hangar of an aerodrome. They were
those pilots who first bombed the German port of Cuxhaven
early in the war, and the first boys to fly over Berlin and
Potsdam. One of them, a South African, had sunk a German
U-boat in the North Sea. The King talked to the men who
fly blind for ten hours under arctic conditions, to the first
reconnaissance pilots who had crossed the skies over distant
Southern Germany, and to those who escort Atlantic convoys.

In the first days of December, 1939, the King visited the
British Expeditionary Force in France. Again, as on his previous trip to France a year before, M. Lebrun, President of
the French Republic, tendered the exalted visitor a state
dinner. Again champagne flowed—the King, however, excused himself for not drinking—and French speeches over-
flowed with assurances of eternal blood brotherhood. After
dinner, it is true, M. Lebrun showed little inclination to
accompany his guest to the front-line. It was raining hard
and Monsieur le Président might easily have taken cold.
This was, to quote Winston Churchill, "indeed a very dan-

gerous war." Accompanied by his brother, the Duke of
Gloucester, and by Lord Gort, then Chief of the Imperial
General Staff, George VI motored to the front. Everywhere
French soldiers cheered him. He had to get out of his car to
tramp through a muddy field to the gun pits of a concealed
English 25-pounder battery, which was his first stop. The
gunners at first could not believe that the King had come out
so far to chat with them. When they recognized him beyond
doubt, they gave him a rousing cheer. Lunch was taken in a
little village inn. Assisted by the guards, the *patronne* herself served the chicken pie and cheese. When a plum pudding followed, the King begged the *patronne* to be excused.
Plum pudding at lunch would make him sleepy in the afternoon. "My husband never gets sleepy from a bit of plum
pudding," she retorted, her pride as *cuisinière* obviously
hurt. But the King, she explained later, had such a friendly,
apologetic smile that she could not feel cross with him.
"Enfin, my husband is not a king," she admitted.

The Royal family spent Christmas Day "somewhere in the
country." It was an intimate family gathering. The Duke
and Duchess of Kent, with their children, Prince Edward
and Princess Alexandra, were the only guests. In view of the
difficult times, presents were neither given nor received. The
King made only one exception. He received a huge bunch
of red and white roses, his favorite flower. On Christmas,
1939, one could still accept those roses with a smile. They
came from the city of Coventry.

As long as the war did not rise to its full fury, the life of
the Royal family, on the surface, continued undisturbed.
Queen Elizabeth spent much of her time running the household, which had become a more difficult task since more
than half the members of the staff were with the fighting
services. The meals, always simple, were further restricted.

When the Court is at Buckingham Palace, London's North Kensington "control" deals with the Royal household's ration cards as with those of Mr. Jones and Mrs. Smith. When the King is traveling he uses the same ration cards that are provided for commercial travelers. The coupons are removed by the various tradesmen and sent in the normal way to the food offices in the districts concerned.

The King's personal contacts show distinctly his social inclination. In one of the most informal gatherings ever held in the inner quadrangle of Buckingham Palace, Mr. George Gibson, Chairman of the General Council of the Trades-Union Congress, presented the King with a specially struck gold badge. "If Your Majesty ever feels disposed to visit the Congress," he said, "this will be your Open Sesame." The Queen examined the badge closely. "Where shall it be worn?" she asked. "On the left side!" Mr. Gibson said, indicating the ribbons on the King's breast. George VI fixed the badge where it belonged. The Trades-Union emblem looked highly respectable on the uniform of an Admiral of the Fleet the King was wearing.

On March 21, 1940, the King and Queen stood with eighty-eight aged men and women in the shadows of Westminster Abbey, distributing Maundy money, a symbol of the monarch's humility before God. The ceremony dates back six hundred years. It follows a rite that began when Jesus washed the feet of His disciples. The King, in his turn, no longer washes the feet of the poor old people—the last Christian ruler to do so was the Emperor of Austria. The British monarch instead hands out tiny red and white purses, each containing forty-four pennies. For the last two hundred years these funds were given out by proxy, usually by the Archbishop of Canterbury. In 1932, King George V set a present-day example in personally observing the Maundy Thursday custom. On the first Maundy Thursday in this war, his son, George VI, followed suit. He has decided to carry on the custom during his reign.

Such little incidents reveal the King's deep religious feeling. The Queen shares this feeling. Not a single Sunday goes by that the Royal Family does not go either to the Palace Church or to the chapel wherever they are in residence. Each of the Royal castles or palaces, of course, has its chapel. Lately the sovereigns have made a point of attending church with the people or the local garrison. From time to time they have been to St. Paul's Cathedral or to Westminster Abbey, more often still to the Guard's Chapel right across the square, where they occupy the Royal pew at the front.

Today St. Paul's, the Abbey, the Guard's Chapel are abodes of destruction. Bomber Goering has done his best to spoil the King's prayers and to make them a little more difficult. He has only aroused the prayers of all Christianity that the Lord may destroy the destroyers.

Early in May, 1940, George VI suggested that all over the world the last Sunday of that month should be kept as a day of national prayer for a "just, lasting, honorable peace." Hitler countered with the Blitzkrieg. The arch-pagan, of course, mistook the King's religious faith for a sign of political weakening. Besides, Herr Hitler is in the habit of hitting, and hitting hard, those who lift their hands in prayer.

Goering outdid his Führer. He encouraged his ace-pilots to try for the King's life. He had a personal reason. Claiming to be a scion of the Plantagenets, he aspires to the British throne—where Hitler would be delighted to see him, in order to have his pushing lieutenant and possible competitor at a safe distance. Obediently, German flyers engaged in a man hunt against the King. Buckingham Palace, St. James's Palace, even Royal Lodge at Windsor, miles away from any military objective, were repeatedly bombed.

Simultaneously German science was commanded to prove Goering's descent directly from Henry II (1154-1188), who is remembered for having instigated the murder of Thomas à Becket, Archbishop of Canterbury, in 1170. Even in choosing his so-called ancestor Goering remained true to type. Of course authentic history long ago established the fact that the Plantagenets became extinct in 1449.

George VI laughed heartily when he heard the story. Someone in his circle—a high-ranking personality whose identity it is not permitted to reveal—commented: "Herr Goering definitely underrates his pedigree. He is clearly a descendant of the Neanderthal Man, and brings his manners and his morals with him."

It is easier to laugh off aspirations than bombs. At the height of the aerial Blitzkrieg, on September 13, 1940, Buckingham Palace was subjected to merciless, rapacious bombing. The German bombs backfired. As one man the British people rallied around their King. "We are all in it together!" the Cockneys said, and, more than ever, their King belonged to them.

That nothing happened to him, King George believes he owes to a dispensation of Providence. In fact he stood with his Queen at one of the Palace windows and watched the bombs dropping while explosions rocked the building to its foundations. A minute later both were downstairs in the Palace shelters, inquiring whether anyone had been hurt. Another fifteen minutes later, both King and Queen hurried to visit the bombed areas in London's East End, the poorest and, at the outset of the German air attack, most heavily pounded slums.

The passers-by on the streets forgot the dangers when they saw the King's maroon-colored, high-bodied, old-fashioned limousine racing along. It did not proceed in the usual Royal cavalcade, which has been abandoned for the duration. Beside the driver—William Hawes, Corporal of Horse—only one man protects the sovereign, Chief Inspector Henry Cameron, of Scotland Yard, and, incidentally, the best pistol shot in England. When His Majesty inspects battered parts of London or other cities and towns, Herbert Morrison, Home Secretary and Minister for Home Security, once a rabid socialist, later the political ruler of London, widely known as the King of the Cockneys, usually sits at his left. Perfect harmony reigns between the King and the King of the Cockneys. The King likes Mr. Morrison's sharp wit and his tight-lipped, but so much the more fanatic, devotion to England. The King of the Cockneys, in turn, regrets that George VI holds an exalted job. Enviously the man who runs the City Council sighed: "What an excellent Alderman of London the King would make!"

While the aerial assault on London lasted, George VI visited the battered East End every night. The battle of Jutland made the old navy man immune to danger. He is entirely undisturbed by the dropping bombs and their infernal shrieking. Physical danger only stimulates him. Speaking to the people in the crowds that throng about him cheering, he is ready with practical ideas and suggestions. The words come easily to him. He is quick to answer remarks he overhears. Sometimes he gets back a reply that leaves him silent. In shattered Bristol he remarked: "They have made a terrible mess of your city!" Thereupon an air-raid warden, a grey-haired man with his right arm in a sling and a bandage about his head, said: "It only increases our determination in the cause!" To this there was no answer.

Frequently the King walks through wrecked streets and ruined quarters, well knowing that there are still unexploded bombs about. In these circumstances he leaves the Queen behind. He also forbids his entourage to accompany him. Harold Campbell, the King's equerry, and a rebel by instinct, doesn't care much what His Majesty forbids him. But he keeps at a respectful distance, a few steps behind. And so the King goes alone, with quick, sure strides and head erect, as if he wanted to cut through all the misery that surrounds him and challenge the danger in exposing himself to it. It is the same man who, years ago, staged a precipitate retreat before the giggling colored belles of the West Indies—in both his shyness and his heroism an Englishman, indeed.

The personal conduct of the King in this war is in itself a grave setback to aggression. The King does not quit. Nazi propaganda understood that if the British people's morale was to be broken this living stumbling-block must be removed. One day in June the B.B.C. announced that the bandits—R.A.F. slang for the German raiders—had attacked Royal Lodge, Windsor. No one's morale was shattered, but all the windows were. The next day clubfoot Goebbels himself took the air. He had an important announcement to make. The King of England had decided to send the two Princesses to Canada.

Queen Elizabeth herself answered in public. "The Princesses will leave the country when I leave, and I will leave when the children's father leaves, and their father will not leave this country under any circumstances." It was then, incidentally, that the Queen and her two sisters-in-law, the Duchesses of Kent and Gloucester, began to practise sharp-shooting.

The King simply overlooked the incident. The King's standard flies above Buckingham Palace; George VI carries on. In the first four hundred days of the war he fulfilled well over a thousand public engagements. On at least half of them he was accompanied by the Queen. Places near London the sovereigns visit by car. For longer journeys they have recently accepted the gift of a new Royal train from the four major railway companies in England. This train replaces the museum piece built forty years ago for Edward VII, with its heavy décor and old-fashioned appointments. The new train is a definite contribution to the conduct of the war. It offers a traveling dormitory and study for the hardest-working man in the Kingdom.

The Royal train is of all-steel construction, but not equipped with armor plating such as is favored by Hitler and Mussolini. There are no bodyguards and no secret service men among its crew. To dodge the German raiders, however, only the vaguest information about the Royal train's time-table is published. Three or four times a week the people read: "The King and Queen inspected an industrial plant in the North of England yesterday, and have now returned to Buckingham Palace." Each day there is an inspection or an official visit—to Canadian encampments, to the aerodromes where Polish fliers are trained; to the Dutch contingent at their bases, the Fleet Air Arm, units of the Royal Navy, factories, and particularly to damaged areas.

While aboard his train the King works incessantly. Telephone and wireless are installed in his study, features taken from the famous American Presidential train. The train is always in communication with Buckingham Palace and Whitehall. There is a waiting room for cabinet ministers. George VI grants most of his audiences while speeding through the country. He has been working at this terrific pressure from the first day of the war. Yet in all his life he has never been so perfectly in trim. Has this man ever been a weakling, an ailing youngster, suffering what seemed an incurable disease? The four Royal physicians—Lord Horder, Lord Dawson of Penn, Sir John Weir and Sir Maurice Cassidy—shrug their shoulders. They don't know much about their patient's state of health. In fact they have no patient. They are never called to Buckingham Palace. It is the first time within memory that there has been no resident medical man.

Relaxation is rare. Ceremonies are practically non-existent. The Royal Garden Party used to mark the end and climax of the London season. There was no Garden Party this year. Instead, the King visited an ammunition factory. He chatted with the workers in their greasy overalls against a background of pounding machines, screaming drills, glaring furnaces. On August 3, the Queen's birthday, all ceremonies were eliminated. On this occasion it was the Queen who gave presents instead of receiving them. Queen Elizabeth is Colonel-in-Chief of the Highlanders, a Toronto Scottish regiment, of the Canadian Army overseas. She sent her men a hundred and forty two-pound puddings, made after a recipe from an old family cookbook. The Master of the Household, Sir Hill Child, was hard put to it to find the necessary ingredients. As a rule he is not too much worried about feeding his sovereigns. They don't mind the meat shortage. It affects them less than many of their subjects. They are quite content with a curry or an omelette.

Another birthday present the Queen gave was the furniture from sixty rooms at Windsor Castle, which went to refurnish bombed homes in London's East End. Every suite was complete with wardrobe, chairs, bed, linen, a carpet and rugs. There were many fine pieces used by Queen Victoria. Such gowns, incidentally, as the Queen can spare, arrive regularly at the Central Depot of the Women's Voluntary Service. Young mothers of about the same figure as the Queen wear them without knowing the name of the donor. Otherwise they might well save them as souvenirs, which the Queen, herself an eminently practical woman with a shrewd sense for value, would certainly consider a "waste."

Although his official birthday is in June, George VI privately observes the real day, December 14. His last birthday, his forty-fifth, he spent working on the "King's Fund—1940." This fund is heir to one established by King George V in the last war. It was nursed into existence by Sir Adair Hore, a veteran benefactor and philanthropist, who is in charge of the new fund as well. The Fund distributes grants to disabled soldiers, sailors and fliers, their widows and orphans, and to civilian fighters who "are engaged in this war on their own doorsteps." Sir Adair sits in his Westminster office and ponders how to take care of the forty grants that come in every week. The fund gives "occasional help in directions quite outside the scope of the State scheme of compensation." Its help is essentially practical. The King himself sees to it that disabled officers and men may receive money for clothing, especially if it is to help them to obtain employment, or traveling expenses and equipment—tools, perhaps—for the same purpose. The grants allow moving costs for home and family, if they are "bombed out" of their houses, furniture where it is needed, loans for business purposes; medical and surgical requirements—such as artificial limbs—requiring funds over and above the State insurance.

The trouble is that the available money cannot meet all the needs. There are no appeals to the public, which the King believes is already overburdened with social obligations. However, after having devoted almost all his birthday to his favorite welfare work, the King modestly concluded that he had done a good day's job. In the evening he saw

"The Great Dictator" in his private cinema, and laughed throughout the show.

On Christmas, ten days later, the customary cards to the Forces were omitted. This was partly to avoid placing an extra burden on the postoffices and partly because the King of England, too, must curtail expenditures. Only two hundred personal friends received photographs of the Royal couple. The picture showed them standing in front of the Belgian Suite in Buckingham Palace which Jerry's raiders had destroyed in September, and smiling—not into the camera alone.

In his Christmas broadcast, the King said: "Our feet are planted on the way to victory." And to the Lord Mayor of London, Sir George Wilkinson, George VI sent this message: "The City of London has shown the world that the terror of women and children and the destruction of their homes will never break the spirit of a stout-hearted people, but only strengthen their will to win through to better days."

The first Sunday investiture was held on January 26, 1941. It set the key for the new year. The King decorated eighteen officers and men of the R.A.F. Coastal Command for "deeds of gallantry in the face of the enemy." Simultaneously he assumed the Honorary Colonelcy of the Newfoundland Heavy Regiment, Royal Artillery, which was raised only last spring, to honor Great Britain's oldest colony.

In the last days of January he was visiting the service men's clubs for Australian, Canadian, Dutch, Czech and Polish soldiers, when an air-raid warning sounded. Unperturbed, George VI continued his inspection. As the first bombs dropped, he shook hands with a demolition worker on duty. Again it was an innovation, since the protocol forbids the King to shake hands with his subjects. The demolition

worker, of course, was ignorant of the niceties of the protocol. Yet he felt embarrassed. He apologized for the state of
his calloused hands.

A string of bombs exploded in the vicinity. Yet the King
did not seek shelter. An old fishwoman came out of a near-by
house. In the midst of the heaviest raid she planted herself
in the street, and ecstatically she whispered, " 'e is with us!
'e is with us!"

A similar scene took place in Southampton. The King inspected the badly damaged harbor and engaged the long-
shoremen in conversation. He asked to the point: Have you
plenty of tools? Is the mobile canteen feeding you all right?
How is the drinking water? He continued his questions as
the German bombers reappeared. The crowds broke ranks;
they overwhelmed the police cordon and engulfed their sovereign. In his presence, and physically near him, they felt
safe.

Inspecting the overage American destroyers in Portsmouth, the King asked the officers and men about the performance of the ships. "The only pity is that we have not
got more of them," a rating observed. Two admirals, standing near by, were visibly embarrassed. But the King nodded,
"I agree with you!"

He is a great admirer of things and men American. He
receives every official or semi-official American guest with
ready hospitality. Wendell Willkie made a strong impression
on him. Mr. Willkie, in turn, back in America, spoke about
"the simple, unpretentious, earnest-minded King" without
forgetting to mention the "gracious, charming Queen." "I
wanted to pay her a sort of jocular compliment," he recalls,
"and, without referring to the person, I said to her, 'You are
doing a better job on me than you did on another person.'
She looked at me steadily and simply, and without pretense

of play or attempt at stage-acting, she said: 'Well, Mr. Will-kie, it wasn't because I didn't try on him.' "

Such is Mr. Willkie's recollection of a conversation about ex-Ambassador Kennedy, a little talk that certainly resounds to both Willkie's credit and the Queen's. Whether Her Majesty actually used the expression "I tried on him," and whether she might not have been a trifle astonished to hear that she was "doing a job" on someone, remains anybody's guess.

When Mr. J. G. Winant, the new United States Ambassador, arrived in England, King George VI made history— at least history of ceremonies—in personally going to the station and greeting the American envoy. The Royal couple had tea with Mr. Winant before the latter had presented his credentials. It was the first time that a British monarch has accorded such a welcome to a new ambassador.

No other man on earth is subject to so many rules, restrictions and regulations as the King of Great Britain. No previous King has broken so many precedents, and yet remained so true to type. It has been said that George VI's life demonstrates how a symbol becomes human. Indeed, the King, like any other creature, cannot escape his fate. Where he is most deeply human, he is most deeply symbolic—the symbol of England's miraculous transformation.

INDEX

Addison, Dr., 106
Aitken, Max, 271
Aitken, William, 245
Alexander, Albert Victor, 184-197; as
First Lord of the Admiralty, 184-
188; his responsibilities, 186; early
life, 188; as Baptist lay-preacher,
189; elected to Parliament in 1922,
190; served as First Lord of Ad-
miralty in 1929, 191; reform of
Dartmouth Training College, 192;
cruiser building program, 192; return to Admiralty in World War
II, 195
Allenby, General, 232-235
Amery, Leopold, 75
Aosta, Duke of, 234
Asquith, Herbert, 23, 91, 94
Astor, Lady, 287
Attlee, Clement, 140, 151, 168-183,
204; characteristics of, 168-170, 175,
176; early life, 170-171; service in
World War I, 172; elected to Parliament in 1922, 173; as Under
Secretary in the War Ministry,
173; hopelessly a gentleman, 175;
as Postmaster General in 1929, 177;
as Leader of the Opposition in
1935, 178; his hobbies, 179; demanded aid for Finland, 181; at-
tacked Chamberlain gov't, 181; as
Lord Privy Seal, 182

Bagnold, Major, 226
Baldwin, Earl, 25-28, 34-36, 53, 54,
59, 62, 65-67, 76, 107, 112, 132, 168,
173, 179
Baldwin, Lady, 21, 51
Balfour, Captain, 83

Beaverbrook, Lord, 131, 141, 153, 190,
195, 245-274; characteristics of, 245,
246, 254; birth and early life, 247-
250; gift for salesmanship, 250;
marriage, 251; his invasion of England, 251; election to Parliament,
253; his abundant hospitality, 255;
service in World War I, 257; as
Minister of Information, 258; his
newspaper successes, 259-265; interest in aviation, 266; his unbreakable optimism, 268; as Minister for Aircraft Production, 269;
comparison to Churchill, 272; as
Minister of State, 273; as Minister
of Supply, 273
Beaverbrook, Lady, 251
Beckett, Beatrice, see Eden, Mrs. Anthony
Begbie, Harold, 26
Benes, Dr., 56
Bennett, Arnold, 265
Bennett, Richard B., 249
Bevin, Ernest, 121-143, 149, 170, 177,
277; characteristics of, 121-123;
birth and early life, 123; as a professional union-man, 125; recognized as Britain's Labour Tsar,
126; opposition to Churchill in
1926, 129; help in reorganizing the
Daily Mail, 131; contempt for
the "intellectuals," 131; warning
against Naziism, 133; as Minister
for Labour, 135; his working day,
136, 137; aid in speeding up production, 138; his colorful language,
139; his absolute control over
civilian jobs, 140
Bevin, Mrs. Ernest, 125

335